THE EARLY HISTORY

OF THE

ANCIENT NEAR EAST

9000–2000 B.C.

THE EARLY HISTORY
OF THE
ANCIENT NEAR EAST
9000–2000 B.C.

HANS J. NISSEN

Translation by Elizabeth Lutzeier, with Kenneth J. Northcott

The University of Chicago Press
Chicago and London

The University of Chicago Press, Chicago 60637
The University of Chicago Press, Ltd., London
© 1988 by The University of Chicago
All rights reserved. Published 1988
Paperback edition 1990
Printed in the United States of America

05 04 03 02 01 00 99 98 97 96   5 6 7 8 9

Translation with new material of *Grundzüge einer
Geschichte der Frühzeit des Vorderen Orients*, copyright
1983, Wissenschaftliche Buchgesellschaft, Darmstadt

Translation by Elizabeth Lutzeier, with Kenneth J. Northcott

Library of Congress Cataloging-in-Publication Data

Nissen, Hans Jörg.
    The early history of the ancient Near East,
9000–2000 B.C.

    Translation of: Grundzüge einer Geschichte der
Frühzeit des Vorderen Orients.
    1. Middle East—History—To 622. I. Title.
DS62.2.N5713   1988   939.4   87-25530
ISBN: 0-226-58656-1 (cloth); 0-226-58658-8 (paper)

⊚ The paper used in this publication meets the minimum
requirements of the American National Standard for Information
Sciences—Permanence of Paper for Printed Library Materials,
ANSI Z39.48–1984.

This book is printed on acid-free paper.

Contents

List of Figures

List of Figures

Preface to the English Edition

In this English translation of the original German edition of my *Grundzüge einer Geschichte der Frühzeit des Vorderen Orients*, substantial changes have been incorporated. Due to strict space limitations and the impossibility of including photographs, parts of the German version were substantially abridged and the illustrations could not meet the quality intended. I was happy to be able to restore and, at the same time, to revise the text. Also, the bibliography could extensively be enlarged to include more technical titles but still be important for a general presentation. Last but not least, I was grateful for the opportunity to increase the number of illustrations, most of which serve their purpose better in the form of photographs than in line drawings.

Reviewers of the German edition have voiced some criticism: archaeologists would have appreciated the discussion of more archaeological details, and philologists would have preferred a larger presentation of the vast written record of Early Mesopotamia. But as the German title implied, this book was intended to be the outline of "a" history—of several possible ones—with a particular general view in mind. Again, it is true that aspects of religion are not treated with the same weight they enjoyed in the life of the ancient inhabitants of Babylonia. But more than twenty years after A. L. Oppenheim's statement in his *Ancient Mesopotamia* that "a Mesopotamian religion cannot and should not be written" I still see his arguments fully justified: the difficulties result from the "nature of the available evidence, and the problem of comprehension across the barriers of conceptual conditioning."

This having been said regarding the "historical" periods, it applies even more to the earlier periods. Yet, future research still may give us better insights.

A word should be said about the geographical terms used here, as they may differ from what the reader is used to. In order to avoid ethnic designations for areas and periods that we have no certain information about, like "Sumer" or "Akkad," I prefer using more neutral terms as they were coined in the Hellenistic period. Thus I am using the terms "Babylonia" designating the plains between modern Baghdad and the head of the Gulf, and "Susiana" for the plains of modern Khuzestan. "Mesopotamia" stands more or less for the territory of modern Iraq, of which "Northern Mesopotamia" means the area north of Baghdad, whereas "Southern Mesopotamia" refers to the same territory as Babylonia.

I should like to express my thanks to those who helped me in the process of producing this book in English: to those who instigated the idea, to the translators, to those who provided the photographs, and, particularly, to the people at the University of Chicago Press.

Preface to the German Edition

Few other disciplines in the humanities have increased their share of public goodwill in recent years as much as archaeology, whether concerned with the relics of the past at home, in the countries of classical antiquity, or in more exotic lands. Opportunities available to the modern tourist have caused distances to shrink and have made travel to distant lands almost routine for an ever-increasing number of people. At the same time, our uncertainty about many aspects of our own history has led to greater interest in the history of older, more self-contained periods, and especially in the history of problem solving. And with this increase in interest, there has also been an increase in the legitimate demand of the public to be informed in a comprehensive, but generally comprehensible, manner about the history of countries and periods that do not lie within our normal field of vision. The various branches of archaeology are in different states of readiness to meet this demand.

Even today, our knowledge about the ancient Near East is at the stage where new research is more likely to bring to light new problems than to help complete the picture. The early history of the region is heterogeneous, and there is an imbalance in the evidence that has been handed down to us. Despite all the gaps in our knowledge, however, we must not abandon our attempt to draw a larger, more coherent, picture of the whole, an endeavor that not only helps us formulate new research projects but also illustrates the current state of research into the ancient Near East to the public.

Apart from attempting such a summary, it has also been my concern to emphasize a historical view of developments. For periods before the discovery of writing, the usual generalized presentation of the archaeological finds has had to be sacrificed to this goal. Such broad documentation seems dispensable because it may be found in a great number of readily available handbooks and individual accounts, which have been listed here in the bibliography.

There is naturally often a yawning gap between different interpretations of historical contexts, and it is hardly necessary for me to stress that the responsibility for this account rests solely with me. I do not even seek to impute a share of this responsibility to others by naming the many colleagues with whom, over the years, I have been able to discuss individual problems. However, I do wish to express my gratitude to my students at both the Oriental Institute of the University of Chicago and the Freie Universität, Berlin, who were prepared to follow my example in assuming that nothing is ever certain, and who were never satisfied with the information I gave them.

Sources and Problems

The historian of the early periods of the ancient Near East faces many problems. The geographical terms "the Near East" and "Asia Minor" provide only a rough indication of the area whose early cultural development is to be traced. It is perhaps better to define the region as an area distinguished from the outside world by a multiplicity of internal ties, or as a fluctuating sphere of interactions.

This densely woven network of developments was seldom limited to what we commonly refer to as the Near East. Parts of the area, such as Palestine and Syria, at times had close contact with Egypt, which was very important for development on both sides. And we do not count Egypt as belonging to the Near East in the narrowest sense of the term. Similarly, parts of what is now Turkey were for most of their history oriented more toward the West and the Aegean, and the Iranian plateau kept up a rather more regular exchange with its neighbors to the East than with the other parts of the Near East. This situation is underlined by recent attempts to treat most of present-day Iran, Afghanistan, and the western part of present-day Pakistan as a single area, connected in many different ways and fairly autonomous in its significance for the development of early civilizations.

However, any account that included both internal entanglements and connections with the outside world would not only go far beyond the confines of the present discussion, but would also make too many demands upon the information provided by our sources. Though we know of contacts outside the narrow, limited area of the Near East, or must at least postulate such cases, it is only rarely that a comprehensive picture emerges. Even more rarely are we able to follow such contacts over any significant period of time.

We shall see in what follows that the demand for a balanced presentation taking equal account of all the contributions to cultural development cannot be satisfied even for the actual Near Eastern area. The available material is distributed far too unevenly over the region and over different periods of time. There is also the fact that the epoch we are dealing with embraces preliterate, paraliterate, and literate periods. Again and again, we run the risk of overestimating the importance of regions or periods about which we quite fortuitously possess a great deal of information, and of underestimating that of other regions or periods of which we—equally fortuitously—know little or nothing. Thus, for example, early interest in the ancient history of Mesopotamia (Abraham's biblical homeland being "Ur of the Chaldees"), especially after the written tradition had become known, produced an imbalance in the information about this region: for far too long, it allowed Mesopotamia, and more especially the southern part of Babylonia, to appear to be the natural center of the ancient Near East. One aim of this work is to distribute the emphasis more evenly and, wherever possible, to define the parts played respectively by all the regions of the Near East in building up its ancient civilization.

However, it is not the intention of the present work to propagate the other extreme—frequently defended in recent years—that maintains that all developments in every region were equally important, as though they all played an equal part in the development of Near Eastern civilization, whose great achievement must be seen as the creation and further development of universally valid forms of political organization that had an influence far beyond the chronological and geographical boundaries of the ancient Near East.

In the course of history, all the regions of the Near East were more or less involved in this process, but some areas certainly progressed more consistently and energetically than others. This work will show that the role of trailblazer in the most momentus phase of development—from city to regional state—fell to Babylonia. To deny this would be to deny the driving impulse behind, and the special peculiarities of, ancient Near Eastern history. A relatively large amount of space is thus devoted to discussion of what happened in Babylonia.

The more ambitious aim of including areas outside the Near East could not be tackled in this book, but should be kept in mind. Although complete in itself, the following survey should be seen as the preliminary work for a more comprehensive synoptic presentation.

By choosing to discuss both the preliterate and literate periods, the author has complicated things still further. This is a consequence of the concept underlying this work, which highlights historical development, and especially the development and changes in early forms of political organization in the ancient Near East. This development can in no way be said to start with the beginning of writing. It was not even particularly influenced by it.

The Near East is exceptionally suited to the documentation of all stages from the earliest human settlements up to the emergence and evolution of regional states. The invention of writing in Babylonia around 3100 B.C. was only one of many significant innovations in this early period. It is thus impossible to assign it the value given to it, for example, in the concept of a differentiation between "prehistorical" and "historical" phases of human development, depending on whether written sources of information are available or not, as if one could only speak of history when written evidence existed.

Unfortunately, this concept, which was held to be valid for a long time, and led to an overestimation of the importance of written sources, also led to a development under which works like the present one still have to suffer. Because the philological disciplines claimed to be able to make universal pronouncements about the state, the community, the economy, religion, and "daily life" based on written texts, archaeologists hardly ever felt it necessary to deal with any fields apart from those manifestly allotted to them, above all art and architecture. Any archaeology of the "historical" periods was therefore in a position to exclude whole areas of research dealing with ancient civilizations. However, for the branches of archaeology concerned with civilizations without writing and those that existed before writing was invented, it was a totally different story. They naturally had to investigate all aspects of the civilization in question, including, for example, society and the economy.

This different type of approach has, in fact, had some effect on the treatment of the ancient civilizations of the Near East. Although, as noted, the invention of writing did not mark any particularly significant historical turning-point, it subsequently acquired importance owing to the division of academic study of the ancient Near East into two spheres. Thus, for example, we know much more about basic nutrition and the domestic flora and fauna of the early period than we do about those of the "historical" period, because remains of animals and plants have been found and analyzed in excavations of "prehistoric" settlements, which is hardly ever true of excavations of "historical" settlements. In the latter case it was assumed that the relevant information could be recovered from an analysis of the texts, by asking the right questions. This can hardly be expected, however, since a selection process was already in operation in choosing what was considered worthy of being written down, and we have no way of knowing what the criteria of selection were.

Archaeology should therefore make use of the methods valid for research into earlier, preliterate periods even when it is concerned with "historical" periods. A barrier seems to have been reached when, parallel to its responsibilities for the preliterate period, archaeology is also expected to pronounce on the economic, social, and political context of the "historical" period. This seems to belong so clearly to the realm of textual interpretation that any of the, admittedly rough, statements and estimates an archaeologist can make appear superfluous. However, though this is fundamentally true, it does not hold good for the early literate period in Mesopotamia, because here we have only comparatively few historically useful texts at our disposal. In addition, these early texts were obviously not written to inform people in later ages about circumstances at that time. In fact, their usual aim was not to describe things exactly as they happened, but to describe them in such a way as to make them fit in with a specific view, follow a particular trend, or legitimate a certain course. Hence it seems possible, not only that the rougher outlines sketched by archaeological surveys have at times been more objective than the literary evidence, but that in many cases archaeology can contribute information in areas where texts have nothing to add to our knowledge—for example, we need only mention the important issues, discussed later in more detail, of the origins of settlements and settlement systems, the changes that took place in them, and almost all contacts between different settlements that fell short of hostilities. If one disregards economic texts, it was mostly wars and conquests that motivated men to write about relationships between settlements, not the normal relationships whose description would give an account of the actual development of those settlements.

Since they have hardly ever been manipulated, archaeological sources are usually more dependable than literary ones, but they are difficult to use. Hence, even the construction of a firm foundation for all further investigations, dating, or the confirmation of chronological contemporaneity or noncontemporaneity, causes considerable problems, especially when we take into account the role played by chance in the way evidence has been handed down to us.

The difficulties standing in the way of arriving at an absolute chronology—that is, fixing the exact chronological distance between any event and our era—are self-evident in the case of a period about which we have no historical documentation. On the other hand, techniques such as the so-called carbon 14 method have not yet achieved a degree of dependability and accuracy that would allow us to use their results without some reservations. However, in spite of these reservations, a chronological framework based partly on carbon 14 dating, which has been accepted by many researchers as a working hypothesis, has been used here, inasmuch as our historical imagination is incapable of managing without the aid of *some* reference to dates. In using this chronology I am not making a judgment as to whether the system is

Figure 1. Chronological chart.

	Western and Northern Neighbors			Babylonia	Eastern Neighbors		
	Domestication of plants and animals	Çayönü/ Jericho/ Çatal Hüyük	Prepottery Neolithic		Prepottery Neolithic		Domestication of plants and animals
7000	Permanent settlements in favorable locations	Umm Dabaghiyah				T. Sarab/ T. Guran	Permanent settlements in favorable locations
6500						Ganj Dareh/ Q. Jarmo Q. Rostam	
6000	Settlements in dry-farming areas; far-reaching trade	Hassuna	Pottery Neolithic Kolkolithic		Pottery Neolithic Kolkolithic		Settlements in dry-farming areas; far-reaching trade
5500							Local centers
5000	Local centers	Halaf			Susiana sequence		
4500				Ubaid			
4000		Northern Ubaid			"Susa A"		Regional centers
3500				Early Uruk — Isolated settlements			
3000	Early Bronze Age			Late Uruk Jamdet Hasr — Regional centers; Early dynastic I; II City states; III Regional states	"Susa D"		
2500	Regional centers	Tell Chuera Ebla		Akkad			
2000	Regional states			Ur III Old Babylonian			Regional states
1500							

Figure 1. Chronological chart. Author's original.

right or wrong. It simply makes it easier for those interested in the history of Mesopotamia to communicate, as well as making it easier to use other literature (see fig. 1).

However, as a rule, absolute dates—that is, dates giving the exact length of time up to the present day—will be used as little as possible. Instead, reference will be made to the relative chronologies developed for the individual regions of the ancient Near East. In these chronologies, observations that an event happened before or after another event and of the chronological contemporaneity of different finds and events are combined into groups or systems even if the intervals of time or the distance in time from our own era cannot normally be exactly defined.

These relative chronological systems are based on stratigraphy and typology. The principle of stratigraphy is based on the hypothesis that, where excavations of an undisturbed site are concerned, the very top layers and the things found there are generally more recent than the objects buried beneath them. This is most obviously true for sites where a house has been built on the remains of an older house, but of course it is also true of layers of rubble, whose position one on top of the other shows how the layers were piled up one after the other on the site under consideration. The chronological sequence of the different constructions, or at least the point in time at which the objects under discussion landed upon the site, can be clearly established, both for the houses and for the objects found in them or in the layers of rubble.

Beside this assured method of establishing differences in age, we have to set the typological method, which it is true cannot do without borrowing the results of stratigraphy: still in essence it bases its theories upon different observations. The basic principle underlying typology is that the causes of the changes that take place in everything subject to molding or shaping by man lie in changes in raw materials, technology, functions, taste, or artistic expression.

Series of such changed forms in a given category can be arranged so that their individual members can be closely related in time to neighboring ones, as either precursors or further developments of the latter. In determining the chronological direction of such a group, we are dependent on those cases in which it can be proved without doubt that the form of one link in the chain would be inconceivable without a prototype in the shape of another link or in which one form is a vestige of a previous one. The more nearly perfect form or prototype is then quite obviously older, and hence only the direction of the series derived from these observations can correspond to reality.

One additional, more frequently used, way of fixing the chronological alignment of a typological series is possible when two or more individual links in such a chain are found in some stratigraphic context. The study of objects in terms of stylistic evolution, a method borrowed from art history, can also be counted among the typological methods. This particular method attempts to find clues to a "before" and "after" from the decoration of the objects themselves, and from this it attempts to abstract criteria for the general thrust of development.

Our relative chronological systems are accordingly based, directly or indirectly, on stratigraphical sequences discovered during excavations. This explains why the names of excavation sites are often used as the accepted terms for the periods referred to in such relative chronological systems. Such terms, which do not entail value judgments, have not been used consistently, however, and as one approaches "historical" periods, for which, it is assumed, "historical" terminology should be adopted, they gradually give way to less value-free terminology.

Thus, for example, the periods from which the names of rulers and their dynasties are known to us are called after particular dynasties, although these were not the only dynasties that existed at that time, and possibly were not even the more important. An "Early Dynastic" period was *designated* as preceding these well-known periods, although there is absolutely no reason to suppose that there were no dynasties prior to it.

Periods that were not clearly understood were promptly defined as transitional periods. In one particular case, in order to name a period, the name of a ruler was used, even though in the meantime it has been shown that he was not even alive during the period named after him.

In addition to this vagueness about names, archaeological contexts only infrequently permit a clear demarcation between one period and the next. Drawing such dividing lines is thus very much a matter of the judgment of the individual scholar, depending on which criteria are used in each individual situation. It is therefore clear that it is not possible to have one universally valid chronological scheme, but only systems that fit specific criteria in given situations and show certain inadequacies in others.

The view that it is not one of the least of the aims of a relative chronological system to serve as a general foundation for the understanding of as many interested people as possible led, in the end, to the setting up of a hybrid system that took individual names for particular periods from different systems and put them together in new and different ways. Here, too, the subjectivity involved in the selection process cannot be overlooked. However, in spite of its inconsistencies and vulnerability to criticism, this combined system is generally accepted, and it is therefore used here. It would have been nice to have developed a chronological system of my own that would have been better adapted to the particular direction pursued in this work, the development of forms of political organization as an aspect of historical development. Nonetheless, I resisted this temptation in order to guarantee the comparability of scientific results.

In this book, the role of the natural environment and the changes that took place in it during the initial growth and subsequent development of the early civilizations of the Near East will be emphasized more strongly than usual. In contrast to mere assumptions made about these influences in earlier times, new research has provided enough evidence for us to make direct connections between changes in the environment and the growth of these civilizations without falling into the dangerous proximity of ecological determinism.

Unfortunately, the evidence we have for the chronological and geographical area we know as the Near East is very unevenly distributed. In addition to the difficulty of, for example, gaining evidence about the climate in antiquity, there is the fact that hardly any research has yet been carried out into the ecological microstructures of the Near East. Results that hold true for one part of the Near East may not be accepted for the whole area and can therefore only be applied with reservations to other parts or to the whole region. Nevertheless, for at least part of the area—Babylonia and western Iran—these findings are just sufficient to permit us occasionally to use ecological conditions to explain cultural phenomena.

This work is, of course, in no position to offer a history of the rulers, the dynasties, or the centers of power in the early preliterate periods. On the other hand, the author does not wish to restrict himself to an account of the sequence and possible relationships between different archaeological sites and the things found there. Without making the mistake of using situations known to us from a later time to project back to earlier ones, we shall try to elicit, from the materials available for the early periods themselves, some statements about economic and social structures. From the position and type of settlements, and the spatial relationships between them, one can, for example, make statements about the individual settlement systems of one particular region or period, which can then provide points of departure for statements about the size and centrality of the organizational structures that existed there. In this case, we make use of the basic theories and methods developed by settlement geography.

The basic patterns, founded on the opposition between centralization and decentralization, which view the growth of centrality as the visible expression of hierarchical subordination, and see the degree of centrality as a measure of the organizational stage of development of a settlement system, fit in very nicely with our aims and resources.

The different sizes of the settlements and their positions in relation to one another are one measure of hierarchical subordination. Here, one assumes that, as a rule, places in which "central functions" can be found—that is, institutions that existed to serve a larger area than their now home settlements, such as central administration, centralized cult establishments, and so forth—would be bigger than the settlements they catered to and that these larger places could be reached equally well from all the outlying settlements. Hence they represent, more or less, the geographical center of such a group of settlements.

The basic facts necessary to describe these ancient settlement systems, such as the location and size of the settlements, and the chronology of their existence, are all archaeologically tangible. The necessary proviso is that the settlement systems of the ancient Near East conformed to the same laws as do the systems we find in the modern world, on the basis of which the methods of settlement geography were developed.

This conformity has been demonstrated by so many examples that we can definitely assume we are treading on firm ground. It must, however, be mentioned that not all systems of relationships between settlements can be understood in this way. For example, if the central place differed only qualitatively and not quantitatively from the other places, the distinguishing mark of greater size would be missing.

However, with this process it cannot be stressed often enough that success depends not only on whether such methods are transferable but also on the dependability of the archaeological information used. In concrete terms, this means that success depends on how far it is possible to judge the period of a settlement and the size of the place in question from surface finds. The process needs no justification when we are dealing with an appraisal of the last phase of the settlement, because by definition these remains will be lying undisturbed on the surface, but clearly problems arise in connection with more ancient settlement phases, whose remains will, as a rule, be covered up by the remains of one or several more recent phases.

However, experience has shown that, as a rule, signs of all the different settlement phases will be present on the surface. The deeper the level in question, the fewer remains there will be on the surface, of course, but in every period the construction of wells or shafts exhumed much material from older layers. Great care must be taken in any appraisal of these more ancient finds, especially in assessing the size of the settlements during such phases. This means that any figures that refer to the size of a settlement or the length of time it was settled must, as a rule, be understood as minimum statements.

Here we must also mention one further point. The terms *village, city,* and *state,* which are normally used in the archaeological literature, are so changeable that one would really prefer to do without them. Their definition becomes easier if we follow the example of settlement researchers, who assess the importance of a settlement by its relationship to its (settled) surroundings. The main terms that must then be used are *center* and *surroundings,* which together form a compact system, insofar as both parts of a settlement system are permanently dependent on each other.

The people living in the surrounding area are dependent on the "central functions" in the center, such as, for example, temples, warehouses, and the administration or social leadership. On the other hand, the center requires compensation for its services in the shape of tribute or taxes paid by the inhabitants of the surrounding area. Such interdependence between the inhabitants of a central settlement and those in the surrounding area first becomes comprehensible to the archaeologist, however, when the people living in the surrounding area have also organized themselves into settlements. The place where the central functions are carried on for settlements of this sort is on a higher organizational level precisely because of its centralized functions and may thus be called the center of the settlement system. Since this mutual relationship provides us with a lowest common denominator, we may define this place as a "center of the first order" and call the system a simple, or two-tier, settlement system (cf. fig. 11).

Such a system works only if the settlements are close enough together to make continuous exchange possible. Hence there are optimal limits. On the one hand, there are maximal limits, determined by transportation between the center and the remotest dependent settlement, and, on the other, minimal limits, determined by the area required for the central functions to have sufficient clients to employ them to capacity.

If this system is located in a larger, cohesive geographical area in which there are no physical barriers, it is theoretically possible to extend the system. This expansion will, however, be frustrated if the maximum size, as determined by the maximum transport radius, is ever exceeded. Hence we must assume that expansion will take place in a manner that takes this limitation into account. Instead of a mere spatial expansion of the simple settlement system, a further system will grow up in the available open space, and the two systems will become immediate neighbors. What happened at the lowest stage therefore repeats itself once individual settlements are established in geographical locations such that it is possible for them to coexist as direct neighbors on the same level.

This process is of great significance because, just as subordination causes a network of mutual interdependence to grow up among settlements capable of moving away from each other, possibly with the establishment of one settlement as a center, the close proximity of two simple settlement systems will lead to a situation where the centers of the two systems of the first order come into competition with each other. Because of this, new ranking orders are established, which finally end up with the creation of a higher-ranking center. From several systems of the first order, a system of the second order is thus created by close physical proximity in a larger unified area (fig. 11c).

At this point it must particularly be noted that in this development there is clearly a direct relationship between the size of the area to be settled and the level of organizational settlement. If, for example, a simple system grows up on a plain that it exactly occupies, no expansion—and hence no higher stage of development—is possible.

This is only possible when larger plains offering space for several parallel simple systems are settled. Incidentally, when suitable areas are available, this process can be repeated several times, resulting in systems of the third or fourth order. We shall see that all these levels can be shown to have existed in the ancient Near East.

Although it would doubtless be in the interest of accurate definition to speak exclusively of the "center" and the "surrounding area," the following common terms are also used in this book for the sake of clarity: *village* (the lowest level of organization), *town* (a middle-level settlement), *city* (the level or organization below that of the state), and (*regional*) *state* (the unit of organization at the highest level). *Local center* defines the center of a simple settlement system, *regional center* the focal point of a larger unit. Any further differentiation will be found to arise naturally out of the respective contexts.

We ascribe such a high value to the reconstruction of settlement systems because they represent the comprehensive framework around which the social and economic aspects of an important part of any civilization are systematically interwoven. Knowledge about the growth and functioning of settlements, gained by the study of how an area was settled and of the settlement systems and the changes that took place in them, makes it possible for us to gain insight into the opportunities in any particular period for finding suitable forms of organization for the prevailing socioeconomic needs and ideals.

Obviously, this is all that we can know. Our efforts hardly ever allow us to press ahead and find out all the details of this complex network, details such as the actual ways in which the inhabitants of a settlement lived and worked. Further work is needed to find out more about this.

In fact there is a whole series of other possibilities for research open to us, since we can definitely assume that changes in archaeological material are reflections of changes in the community at that period. However, in our efforts to establish connections between archaeologically tangible changes and changes in the community, we soon come up against enormous problems, because the scope of our interpretation is often far too great. Even where possibilities exist for narrowing the field, we must still bear in mind that there are great differences in the certainty with which we can designate the causal connection. In this process we have to treat the connection between the appearance of an object, and/or its material, and the technology needed to produce that object, as it appears to us, as the relatively most certain criterion. However, because particular technologies imply specific social preconditions or general patterns of society, or can only be produced under particular forms of economic organization, it is possible, to a limited degree, to draw from such artifacts certain conclusions as to the social conditions under which they were produced. The list of types of finds available for this kind of evaluation can be extended by examples from architecture, or by archaeological connections by which, for example, we can recognize sequences of operations.

It is quite clear that we can never hope to get anywhere near to completely filling in the picture of all the conditions within the community, or the changes that took place in them, especially as it is not possible to turn the above sentence around: in no way do all the changes in society translate into processes that can be grasped by the archaeologist. The effect of this systematic error of interpretation is increased by the fact that the sort of observations thought necessary by today's standards were hardly ever carried out during excavations in former times. This book will, however, demonstrate that in spite of all the limitations I have mentioned, there are enough points of reference to justify an attempt at an overall view, precisely from the aspect of the reconstruction of economic and social conditions and the changes that took place in them.

It is in keeping with the total concept of this book that the method of interpretation does not change with the first appearance of the names of rulers or dynasties. On the contrary, from the moment when it first appears, information from written sources will be regarded as an obvious and very welcome complement to results achieved in other ways. Methods used in the earlier period can still give results for the time for which written evidence is available.

Here we should point out the difficulties one is confronted with when one decides to include written sources as evidence. The written tradition from Babylonia is dominated by two languages, Sumerian and Akkadian. Although they belong to totally different language groups—and are therefore easy to differentiate and to recognize—they were written with the same system of writing.

Sumerian is an agglutinative language that so far still cannot be linked to any other language in the world. Apart from Eblaitic (see chap. 5), Akkadian is the oldest of the great family of Semitic languages to be fixed by writing. Akkadian, with its various dialects and linguistic stages, was the main language of Babylonian civilization up to and including the late period. It was recognized fairly early on that in the later period Sumerian was only used in cult literature and had already died out as a living language.

As progress was made in research into more ancient periods, it became clear that Sumerian was spoken in lower Mesopotamia at a time when Akkadian speakers had not yet settled there, or at least had not yet begun to express themselves in writing, and that there must have been a period when both languages were spoken. In this context, it seemed as though the texts of the Early Dynastic III period were in Sumerian, the ones of the Akkad Dynasty were in Akkadian, and the ones of the following period, that of the Third Dynasty of Ur, were again—for the last time—composed in Sumerian.

Hence, though there were local differences, Sumerian was recognized to be the language of the early period until the end of the Early Dynastic period; it was replaced by Akkadian at the time of the Akkad Dynasty, but used again as the general language of (written) communication among its successors, the rulers of the Third Dynasty of Ur. The Early Dynastic III and Akkad phases were the first ones in which the potential of writing to reproduce complex relations in language was fully exploited—at a time, moreover, when Babylonian civilization already had a long blooming behind it. This distinction calls for an explanation, since writing had, of course, already appeared at the end of the fourth millennium B.C.—that is, about six hundred years before the period we have just referred to.

Writing was developed at the end of the fourth millennium B.C. by a mixed language group in which Sumerian was apparently the main component. For centuries, writing was hardly ever used except for recording economic procedures, until it was finally used to make short votive inscriptions. It was only in the middle of the third millennium B.C. that, owing to changes in the system of writing, writing evolved into an instrument that made possible the reproduction of complicated texts, as we shall see in chapter 5.

Because language in all its details was first fixed in writing at this point in time, this is the earliest stage from which it is possible for us to carry out linguistic research. These earliest detailed texts can still not be understood in every part, and the sometimes clumsy way in which, for example, grammatical categories were reproduced has sometimes produced the feeling that the preceding period as a whole indeed was but an early stage in the development of higher civilization.

However, this book will in any case show that this phase in the development of writing can already be regarded in many respects as a later period in the development of complicated higher forms of organization. For a period that, regarded from the overall historical point of view, demonstrates complexity—as the result of many centuries of political, economic, and social development—we find ourselves confronted with the most primitive difficulties in vocabulary and grammar. Nonetheless, even these considerations hardly justify changing the whole method of presentation when the first historically interpretable texts make their appearance.

Chronologically, this book follows the development of Mesopotamian civilization from the beginnings of the original settlements down to the establishment of fixed forms of supra-local regulated coexistence which is first evident in the states of the Akkad Dynasty and the Third Dynasty of Ur. Expressed in figures, this covers the period from approximately 9000 to approximately 2000 B.C.

The date 2000 B.C. is, of course, not a historical caesura. It merely signifies the end of a long span of time that, in spite of many diversions and occasional periods of regression, saw steady progress toward more complex organizational structures. At the same time, it signifies the beginning of a phase of consolidating what had been achieved, especially a refining of administrative structures. A new dimension was only reached more than a thousand years later with the formation of empires.

The Time of Settlement
(ca. 9000–6000 B.C.)

Just as in other parts of the world, traces of human existence are known to us in this region from as early as the Palaeolithic period. Habitation layers and the remains of skeletons from the Neanderthal (i.e., Mousterian or Middle Palaeolithic) period have been found in different areas of the Near East in caves, for example, at Shanidar in Iraq, in northeastern Iran, and on Mount Carmel in Palestine (fig. 2).

In such caves deposits from different cultures can frequently be separated out into a great number of different levels of usage, each of which bears witness to a different period of human occupation. However, these periods are distributed over thousands of years, embracing the Neanderthal period, for example, and we have no means of specifying the total length of time, or the periods of time that elapsed between each phase of occupation.

Judging by the material that has been found, there can be no doubt that the caves were only in use during particular seasons of the year. Although it is true that early humans seem often to have returned to such places, since caves undoubtedly offered welcome protection from the elements, there is no evidence to prove that this took place regularly every year. It is probable that during his or her lifetime a person would seldom have returned to such a place for a second time, and certainly not more often than two or three times.

Basic subsistence was provided by hunting, fishing, or gathering plants and fruit to eat. We are not in a position to say anything about the respective size of the groups of early settlers. Sites on open ground, which must have served as campsites during the warmer seasons, have not yet been found, although they, too, can definitely be expected in the Near East, as they have been found to have existed at this time in Europe, where research has been much more intensive.

Unfortunately, as it happens, the few places where remains from the Palaeolithic period have been found in the Near East were discovered by chance. Even small areas have hardly ever been systematically investigated for remains from this period. No far-reaching conclusions should therefore be drawn from the fact that so far all our finds came from caves located on the middle slopes of the different mountain ranges of the Near East.

This picture changes with the beginning of the Neolithic period. In addition to deposits indicating short stays with long intervals of time in between, just like those of the previous period, we now come across traces of human existence that, even if they do not point to a stay

Figure 2. Entrance and cross section of the cave of Shanidar (Iraq). From R. Solecki, *Shanidar: The First Flower People* (New York, 1971), pl. 8 and fig. 1.

lasting a whole year, at least suggest a very extended period of residence in the area. Statements about the position of the settlements and camp-sites for this period can now be made with a good deal more certainty because the number of places found is much greater. They are usually far apart from one another, and are situated for the most part in more or less strongly differentiated terrain, chiefly in mountainous regions

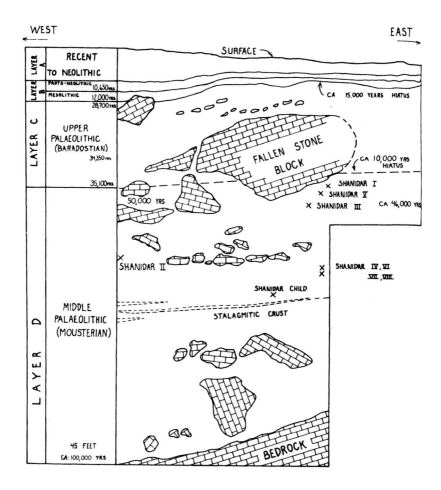

and never on the great alluvial plains the Near East possesses in southern Iraq (ancient Babylonia) and Khuzistan (ancient Susiana).

Perhaps this phenomenon can be explained by the assumption
that the site for a settlement—whether permanent or temporary—was
not chosen at random, but that consideration was also given—or perhaps this was the prime consideration—to whether the environment
would afford people good opportunities to utilize it. The optimal situation would have been felt to have been afforded by places where
varied sustenance was available close to the campsite in sufficient quantity for as long, and as regularly, as possible.

Nature provides such sites in only limited numbers, and because
there is a varying supply of plants and animals that can be used as
nourishment depending on the season, we may rule out the possibility
that situations existed where a constant supply of food would have
been available for the whole year. This made it all the more necessary
for man to settle down in places whose external conditions—even if
only temporarily—came as near as possible to those considered desirable. Even if it were not available over the whole year, the food supply
should at least be available for as long as possible. If not available in
every conceivable form, there should at least be sufficient variety. And

Figure 3. Neolithic sites in the Near East. After J. Mellaart, *The Neolithic of the Near East* (New York, 1975), map 1.

even if the food could not only be gathered right next to the settlement site, it should at least be within easy reach.

Sites that fulfill all these conditions are actually not so rare in the Near East. They can be found wherever small-scale ecotopes lie very close to each other, and where, in addition, there is optimal access to animals and plants that can be used for subsistence. The difference between ecological units is, as a rule, shown in the differences between land formations, the types of wild animals inhabiting an area, and the types of plants that grow there, with their varying times of ripening.

A camp that sprang up on the borderline between such ecological units would have made it possible to use all the resources the different areas had to offer, either simultaneously or consecutively. The distances to be covered could be minimized, while at the same time maximizing the variety of food and the length of time that the food supply was available.

Sites in which as many small ecological units as possible lie close to one another tend to go hand in hand with differences in relief and/or differences in the composition of the soil. For this reason, they are more likely to be found on a terrain that is externally strongly differentiated—that is, above all, in hilly or mountainous terrain. It is surely no accident that traces of early permanent or temporary human settlements in the Near East are found almost exclusively in areas with differentiated structures in the landscape, and there at sites from which there is the easiest possible access to as many different ecological units as possible (fig. 4).

However, for the earliest phase, during which guaranteeing subsistence consisted almost exclusively in gathering what food there was to be had—that is, through hunting, fishing, and gathering plants and fruit—these considerations must remain hypothetical because, as already mentioned, such sites are not known to us in sufficient numbers.

Nonetheless, a detailed investigation of the region around the Kamarband cave in the mountain region southeast of the Caspian Sea has revealed that this cave was in a situation that was nearly optimal, at the focal point of an area with substantially varied food yields. The site, halfway up mountains rising relatively steeply from the coastal plain, allowed the inhabitants freely to exploit animals and plants from the coastal plain, from the slopes of the mountains, and from the higher mountainous regions, as well as from the high plateaus.

For the period of permanent settlements that was now beginning, the examples are once again more numerous. The principle described above can here be recognized with even greater reliability. Thus, for

19

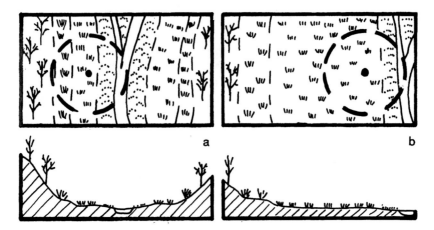

Figure 4. Catchment area (large circle) around a campsite, projected onto (a) a narrow mountain valley, and (b) a larger river plain. Author's original.

example, the little settlement of Qalʾe Rostam from the pottery Neolithic period lay at the edge of a small plain surrounded by high mountains in the Zagros range, providing easy access both to the bodies of water and marshy areas in the middle of this undrained plain and to the gently rising verges and scree slopes at the foot of the mountains, which—on account of their good natural drainage—were, and still are, the natural habitat of many plants. There was also easy access to the different mountain levels, which are home to a variety of wild animals.

As already mentioned, our knowledge of the phase covering the beginnings of permanent settlements and of the production of food is so much better because we know of hundreds of sites in the Near East from this period. By "phase covering the beginnings of permanent settlements," we understand the long period during which the first attempts to obtain plant and animal food by cultivation and animal husbandry led to a diminution in the proportion of food acquired by hunting, fishing, and gathering. However, such sustenance still remained the main source of food for a very long time because food production practices were still too unreliable.

The beginnings of food production are hard to pinpoint. People certainly had some knowledge of the basic principles of the development and growth of plants by the Palaeolithic age. We may surely continue to picture early humans carelessly dropping grains or berries they had gathered, failing to pick them all up again, and then after a while noticing that new plants were shooting out of the earth at the very place where they had dropped them.

It is, however, a mistake to believe that such observations marked the beginning of plant cultivation, which was linked not only to what people knew about plants but also to their needs. It is precisely here that the problem arises, because it is hardly possible to discover why there was a need for plant cultivation, let alone to fix the exact point in time when it first occurred. Perhaps we should seek the reason for this purposeful cultivation of plants, and the time frame in which it began, in the constant endeavor of early humans—who, as noted, chose their settlement sites with such great care—to extend their stay beyond the maximum length of time permitted by the ripening period of the plants that occurred naturally near their campsites.

It is clear, from the fact that evidence of both phenomena appears at about the same time that there was a direct connection between the beginnings of permanent settlements and the production of food. However, this connection does not go so far as to imply that no permanent settlement would have been possible without food production. We have too much evidence showing that subsistence could provide more than the mere satisfaction of everyday needs. In fact, it also offered possibilities of piling up supplies without which a whole year's stay on one site would have been impossible.

In remote areas of the Near East it is, for example, still possible to harvest crops of wild grain even today, and 2 to 2.5 liters of grain can be gathered per man per hour. Improved storage techniques were, however, even more crucial than the creation of grain reserves, and we may assume that it was progress in this technology that made more extensive cultivation a sensible proposition.

Whereas simple pits dug into the ground, such as have been found in several prepottery settlements, indicate the beginnings of stationary storage, arrangements more suited to the purpose very soon began to be made. One of the most important aims, protection of the grain from small rodents, was achieved by plastering these pits with a solid layer of clay, occasionally hardened by firing. Optimal protection was provided by keeping food, and above all grains, in large fired vessels, which in the Neolithic settlement of Hajji Firuz in northwestern Iran, for example, were half buried in the floors of special storerooms (fig. 5). Round or square storage containers, or small storerooms constructed on the spot out of clay, have been found either inside houses or in courtyards, but also outside.

However, before the cultivation of plants, and more especially of grains, could become the main source of plant food, it was necessary to make changes in two respects. For one thing, the uncultivated forms of edible grains have two unwelcome properties, which though they

21

promote natural reproduction, and are the results of natural selection, proved an obstacle to their use by human beings. The stem of the ear of barley on which the grains hang grows in such a way that it very easily breaks apart after the grains have ripened, thus allowing them to fall to the ground separately. This was obviously highly inconvenient for the process of gathering. Even the slightest shaking causes the ear of barley to disintegrate, so that some of the yield was, at least at first, very easily lost. The second drawback was that the individual grains are coated with hard husks, necessary to protect the grains from pre-

Figure 5. Storage jars at Hajji Firuz (Iran). From M. M. Voigt, *Hajji Firuz Tepe, Iran: The Neolithic Settlement* (1983), pl. 22. Courtesy, University Museum, University of Pennsylvania.

mature germination if they fall onto the ground, so that early humans had to devise elaborate procedures to separate the grains from the husks.

It was only after a long time that improvements in both these respects facilitated optimal use of these grains by people. Only through long-term selection could mutants that had a firm stem and a husk that was easily removed be made into the main cultivated species. At first, this selection obviously did not take place consciously, but occurred quite naturally, although now the main aim was definitely better exploitation by man, as opposed to nature's main aim of creating optimum conditions for reproduction. Because, for example, the percentage of ears of barley with a firm stem that actually fell into the hands of the harvesters was greater than the percentage of such plants in the whole crop, grain from such ears was, as time went on, present as an ever-growing percentage of the seed corn set aside from the grain that had been harvested.

However, we cannot rule out the possibility that, at a later point in this development, these connections were recognized, and that after this the seed corn began to be sorted out more purposefully, especially since seed corn had in any case to be treated differently from other grain earmarked for storage. A longer period of storage was only possible if the grain's capacity to germinate was restricted—that is, if the sort of change was brought about that was naturally not desirable for seed corn.

It happened—once again probably only after a long time—that one single measure could deal with two of the above mentioned difficulties. The husks could most easily be removed if the grain was first roasted, after which the husks came away relatively easily during pounding or grinding. But roasting also had the effect of limiting or destroying the grain's capacity to germinate, so that the grain could be stored for much longer. Our findings do, in fact, show that this process—roasting the grain—was the norm.

Again, in the case of the second aspect—the technique of cultivation—we are faced with a less than ideal point of departure. Apart from the great uncertainty about whether enough rain would fall, if it fell at all, there was a whole series of reasons for failures—sowing at the wrong time, wrong choice of soil type, the wrong quantity of seed—that could only be ironed out by long years of experience and tradition.

How long this process of evolution lasted is not clear. At some time, however, the point was obviously reached where techniques of cultivation and the types of grain available had reached a high level of dependability as far as production levels and ways of exploiting the grain were concerned. Nevertheless, for climatic reasons the cultivation of plants remained on the whole a rather precarious business and was therefore inadequate as the sole source of basic subsistence. All the known settlements from this period were in areas where, nowadays at least, it is highly likely that enough rain will fall every year to guarantee the growth of plants, but even in these regions dry years cannot entirely be ruled out. The uncertainties governing the procurement of food through plant cultivation alone had to be taken into account. Hence, during the whole time in which the processes described above were taking place, but also even after there had been a certain amount of consolidation, the various forms of food gathering had to be continued. It was only when opportunities for gathering food continued to exist and to be exploited that it was possible to compensate for the unavoidable mistakes made during plant cultivation. The other branch of food production, animal husbandry, was also in no position to provide any security and was even more subject to failure than plant cultivation.

Maintaining herds of wild animals may well have been practised very early on. The fact that among the bones found during excavations of the prepottery Neolithic period there are cases of definite concentration as regards the sex and age of the slaughtered animals of a particular type indicates that early humans had the sort of exact control of the animals' age and sex that it is impossible for hunters to have. After these early examples of keeping herds of wild animals, it probably took a much longer time to arrive at some sort of planned breeding that aimed at more strongly reproducing characteristics of the animals useful to people.

An example is the development of the wool sheep, which differs in one important aspect from the wild sheep, namely in the type of coat. The wild sheep has a coat like a goat's, made up chiefly of long hairs, between which a light, woolly undercoat can be found. There are two different types of hair root that are responsible for this. Under normal conditions there are more roots for long hair, so that a thick coat of hair prevents the further development of the lighter covering of wool. But there is also a variant in which the relationship of the two different hair roots is reversed, enabling a thick pile of wool to develop unhindered by the hair. After a long interval, planned breeding of this variant finally produced the prototype of our present-day wool sheep.

Keeping herds of animals that will reproduce while they are in captivity requires great experience if the herd is to develop uniformly once the animals taken for human consumption have been removed, since a complex balance must be maintained between the sexes and age groups in any herd. There was also a great danger of things going wrong on another level. Apparently, the process of domestication led to animals becoming less resistant, and, to make matters worse, when they were being cared for by man in a herd, it was possible for more animals to live together in the open country than ever before. Epidemics could therefore spread much more quickly among the animals and have much more serious consequences, so that long years of work could be wiped out in a very short space of time. This must have had a critical impact on people who would have depended on animal husbandry as their only means of livelihood.

For a very long period of time, therefore, it was essential to have multiple means of ensuring subsistence, and this brought in its train a mixed economy in which the shares of food production—whether by cultivation or animal husbandry—and of the procurement of food through

Figure 6. Wild sheep (*Ovis ammon anatolica*). Photographed in 1983 near Konya, Turkey. Photo by S. M. Tarhan. Courtesy, Dr. G. Heidemann, Institut für Haustier-kunde, Universität Kiel.

25

hunting and gathering could shift according to the external circumstances prevailing. If worse came to worse, they could always go back to hunting, fishing, or gathering.

However, this did mean that in spite of the new ways of securing an existence through food production, humans were still tied to those camp or settlement sites from which food gathering could be carried out with as few problems as possible. In this phase, too, where man gradually began to free himself from total dependence on nature, sites located in highly differentiated terrain, from which as many ecological units as possible could be reached, were therefore much preferred, as the material we have found shows.

One of the best-known prepottery settlements, Beidha, situated southeast of the Dead Sea in Jordan, is to be found in just such a differentiated landscape (fig. 7a). Between a ridge of hills that ends in the Arabian Desert and the line of fault in the Wadi Araba, there is a high plateau about four to six kilometers wide, which is intersected by channels and wadis. The prepottery settlement lay in the center of this segmented area and therefore had easy access to the different animals and plants of this plateau, as well as to the higher mountain ridges to the east, and to the land of the rift valley of Wadi Araba, almost a thousand meters lower down to the west.

The part of the settlement that has been excavated shows the remains of buildings whose walls were built of layers of thin stone slabs plastered in white, on which it was still possible to discern some traces of a decoration made up of red bands. In addition to a building of relatively generous size, there were a series of units, all of the same type, consisting of an irregular-shaped long room with chambers on both sides (fig. 7b). The remains of grain and implements for processing grain—such as grinding stones or pestles—reveal the great part played by food production, while the remains of other plants and the bones of hunted animals bear witness to the fact that subsistence was secured by hunting and gathering.

The settlement of Çayönü, near Diyarbakir in southeastern Turkey, belongs on the same chronological horizon. It is situated on the high bank of a tributary of the Tigris. The river terrace is only a few kilometers wide until the slopes of the foothills of the Taurus are reached. The site is especially interesting insofar as the animal bones found in the different levels of this settlement allow us to perceive a demonstrable shift in the main emphasis from the use of wild animals to the use of domesticated ones. For the time being, developments as far as plants were concerned remain less clear. In addition to the gathering of a great number of plants, emmer and one-grained spelt do seem to

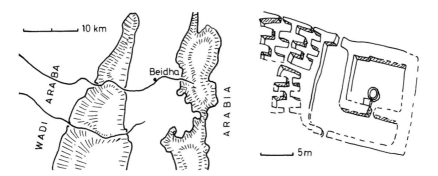

Figure 7. Surroundings and plan of the Neolithic settlement of Beidha (Jordan). After D. Kirkbride, "Five Seasons at Beidha," *Palest. Explor. Quarterly* (1966), figs. 2 and 21.

have been cultivated there, whereas barley, which is indigenous to this area, is inexplicably missing in both its wild and cultivated forms.

The phenomenon of permanent settlements without pottery was originally encountered for the first time during the excavations of the small settlement of Qalʾat Jarmo, where, beneath five layers that contained a limited amount of simple pottery, a series of eleven layers was found that contained no pottery, in spite of indisputable evidence pointing to the existence of a permanent settlement and to a high percentage of produced food. As far as can be seen, this settlement does belong to a rather more highly developed phase than the places already mentioned, because the proportion of animal and plant food produced was very high as opposed to what was gathered. This site, too, situated on a sloping bank above an eastern tributary of the Tigris on the roughly segmented high plateau of Chemchemal in the Zagros Mountains, has access to a richly differentiated hinterland.

The appearance of the first pottery does not seem to have been accompanied by changes in architecture, means of subsistence, or the other areas for which we have finds. What was said above about the relative importance of the first appearance of writing as a pseudoindicator for a division into "prehistoric" and "historic" phases of the history of mankind holds good as well, if in a different way, for the introduction of pottery vessels.

Although these vessels have great significance for us today because we try to use them as points of reference for the reconstruction of earlier developments, and pottery is used to a large extent to provide us with chronological subdivisions, they must in no way be taken to be an indicator of far-reaching fundamental changes. The form of pot-

27

tery vessels developed, on the one hand, from a long tradition of the production of containers of every sort and, on the other hand, from experience in working with clay as a medium that could be shaped and moulded. It probably also developed out of many different attempts to create durable, fireproof, transportable containers.

Even if it is true that this innovation also brought with it changes in (household) economy (for example, by making available cooking and storage vessels), the overestimation of the importance of the appearance of pottery rests more on the fact that this event has had a decisive influence on our chances of gaining access to the civilization of these early periods of time, a fact that emerges from a short comparison with the way we use another type of find.

Before the emergence of pottery, stone implements are almost the only excavated objects from which we can draw conclusions about the civilizations that produced them. The ways in which stone can be worked are, however, limited. With the available techniques, which depend very much on the extent to which the different types of stone can be split, any individual shaping is as good as ruled out, so that the type of chipped stone tools manufactured seems to be largely independent of external influences. Any changes that occurred on the basis of changes in technique and use seem to have taken a long time to come about. The potential for refining our classification and assessment of those periods from which we have scarcely any other findings but stone implements is correspondingly small, and we are limited in our interpretation of these finds. We are seldom able to make anything more than very general statements, restricted to technical differences.

In contrast to stone, clay is a material that permits countless variations and ways of shaping. In addition, it can be transformed into a hard, very resistant material through firing. Through special preparation of the clay, and also through the use of different types of additives, the material can be endowed with all the properties necessary for each individual process, and we can also, within certain limits, exert some influence on the color of the end product. Moreover, the possibilities for molding and shaping clay are almost unlimited, as are the opportunities for decoration through engraving, cutting, and/or the use of colored slip or painting.

In the category of painting alone there are countless ways in which a work can be individualized, through the use of different types of paints or different styles of painting and patterns. Because the abundance of possibilities for shaping pottery is so varied—ranging from the insignificant to the comprehensive—and because they rely so little upon a preformulation by external pressures, ceramics belong to the most "sensitive" of the genres of human products. They are sensitive because tendencies to individualization, to fashionable and artistic structuring, can establish themselves visibly in pottery more rapidly than in other genres.

This breadth of opportunity for forming and molding clay is accompanied by what is, on the average, a rather short "life span" for objects made out of clay, when measured, for example, against those made out of stone or, later, out of metal. The fact that they were comparatively more fragile, coupled with the cheaper and simpler production of pottery vessels, considerably increased the number of vessels produced, and therefore the numbers available at any one period, so that finally not only did the "generations" follow one another in quicker succession, but total numbers were also very high, as was the potential for exploiting the wide range of possibilities that this medium offered the designer.

Even if the special qualities of pottery can be adequately explained by all these arguments, it was, in the end, a trivial reason that gave this sort of discovery such a crucial role in archaeological research. Fragments of broken pots are only surpassed in their imperishability by the remains of stone tools, and in addition, apart from a very few special cases, they have absolutely no value for reuse. Thus the great number of pottery vessels in use at any one time has endowed us with an immeasurable number of pottery fragments from each excavation, which also, for the reasons previously mentioned, presents us with a tremendous breadth of variation.

Of course, we never find anything approaching all the possible ways of shaping pottery at one and the same time. Rather, particular possibilities—according to particular preferences—were selected, and these consequently determine the ceramic repertoire at a given time. Both the wish to make things individual and the wish to follow fashion are limited by the availability of materials, tools, and ideas, which differ from place to place and from district to district, as well as from epoch to epoch. This led to the varied appearance of the pottery that has been found, based on the various elements involved. As a result, we are able to carry out a more or less detailed definition of groups of pottery by contrasting them with one another, and are thus able to organize them chronologically or geographically.

The decision about whether differences in pottery are to be interpreted chronologically or geographically must, however, be guided by additional information. For example, the decoration on pottery vessels obviously had a much greater part to play in the early period than it did later. On the one hand, this was certainly necessitated by the need to close the large pores in clay vessels, which made these containers almost useless for storing liquids, by using finer material, with which the vessels could be decorated in the form of slip or painted. On the other hand, the painting of pots surely resembled older forms of decoration, such as the painting of walls or of the human body, in being an opportunity for artistic expression or for the definition of family or clan identity. Observation of styles of painting and of patterns therefore enables us, for the early periods, to differentiate between countless large and small groups of pots whose chronological and geographical distribution can provide points of reference for a whole series of interpretations.

We must, for example, differentiate between changes affecting a large area—for example, the whole Near Eastern area—and changes that clearly only had an effect in smaller areas at a given time. If we assume that the Near East was, for a long period, a coherent cultural entity, we might suppose that among the changes that would have affected the whole of the Near East, those based on some kind of technical development would have been first and foremost. After all, a cultural entity does imply the same standards, the same problems, and hence the same openness and willingness to take on technological innovations. It should, therefore, be possible to interpret changes that affect a larger area as chronological changes.

Differences in the appearance of the vessels, especially those that can be interpreted as trends in fashion and can be restricted to smaller areas, are, on the other hand, more likely to be the expression of regional or local changes, even if we cannot rule out the possibility that such changes may also be explicable as chronological differences. We shall see that it is possible to make rough chronological distinctions on the basis of technological horizons of development in the pottery of the early periods in the Near East.

It is possible, especially on the basis of ceramic decoration, to identify both large and small groups of pottery down to the smallest subgroups, and at least partially to determine their geographic relationships, as far as our material permits. Relationships whose common denominator can only be rarely given concrete definition can, in general, be described as cultural affiliations. Assuming that pottery groups can be indicative of social groups as a rule, we think of family relationships among the groups who have produced the pottery in question, even if the theory that certain purely organizational relationships may explain the similarities should not be ruled out. It is true that in later periods areas of political control at times coincided with the borderlines of areas of distribution of certain kinds of pottery. This should not, however, lead us to an a priori assumption of some sort of political alliances during the early periods, only because we can show the existence of demarcation lines between specific pottery groups.

An examination of the earliest pottery provides a very good example of the difficulties that confront us in any interpretation of the similarities or differences in pottery. Later on, there was hardly ever so strong a differentiation in so narrow a vicinity as that which appeared when pottery first came into being.

As an example of this, we shall use groupings of characteristic ceramic products from four excavation sites that are all in the northern and central Zagros area (fig. 8). Chronological correspondence is made possible by the fact that at three of these sites, Qal'at Jarmo, Tepe

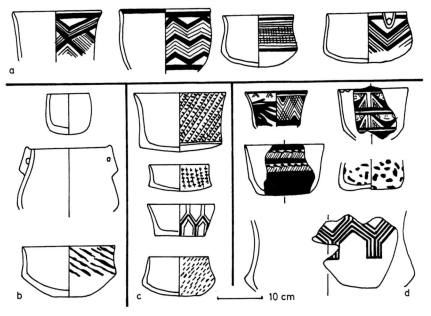

Figure 8. Pottery vessels of the Neolithic period, from the Zagros Mountains: (a) Ali Kosh; (b) Qal'at Jarmo; (c) Tepe Guran; (d) Qal'e Rostam. After (a) F. Hole, K. V. Flannery, and J. A. Neely, *Prehistory and Human Ecology of the Deh Luran Plain.* Courtesy, Museum of Anthropology, University of Michigan; (Ann Arbor, 1979), fig. 44, (b) R. J. Braidwood et al., *Prehistoric Archaeology along the Zagros Flanks,* OIP 105 (Chicago, 1983), figs. 105 and 106. Courtesy, Oriental Institute, University of Chicago. (c) J. Mellaart, *The Neolithic of the Near East* (New York, 1975), fig. 38; (d) H. J. Nissen and A. Zagarell, "Expedition to the Zagros Mountains, 1975," *Proc. of the IVth Ann. Symp. on Archaeol. Res. in Iran* (Teheran, 1976), figs. 4–6.

Guran, and Tepe Ali Kosh, there was an uninterrupted succession from preceramic to ceramic layers, which as the earliest ceramic finds must therefore belong to the same chronological horizon. The sequence at the fourth site, Qalʾe Rostam, did not reach back to prepottery layers, but everything else speaks for its being contemporaneous.

Whereas the shapes and methods of production are similar, the techniques of decoration and the patterns differ widely. Decoration is variously splashed on or carefully painted. Matt colors contrast with gloss, and monochrome with polychrome painting. Some vessels were not treated in any way; others had the outer "skin" highly condensed over the painting (we call this "burnished").

These varied pottery groups were clearly even smaller than might be assumed from the close proximity of the four places mentioned. Although archaeological investigation of the environment of Qalʾe Rostam has produced pottery fragments from a neighboring valley that are similar in almost every respect to the pottery of Qalʾe Rostam, above all in the characteristic principles of composition employed in the painting, they show none of the patterns typical for Qalʾe Rostam, for example, the human face (see fig. 8d, top right). The general similarities confirm our conjecture that these places did perhaps have some sort of connection with one another, but the distinct differences suggest rather that there was a very conscious attempt at making distinctions among themselves.

Thus it is that pottery, the main evidence we have uncovered, fails us precisely in connection with the question of sociopolitical structures. Moreover, study of the distribution of settlements and the relationships of settlements to one another—which is of great help for later periods—is just as useless here. As noted, at this period it was still necessary to be able to ensure subsistence through food gathering, so as to compensate for possible failures in food production. However, because the hinterland necessary to subsist by food gathering had to be very large, the maximum limits of the land area needed for each settlement were so large that individual settlements were still very far apart from one another. Hence opportunities, and the necessity, for making direct contacts hardly existed at all.

In addition to this there is the fact that the natural sites for settlements, for reasons already discussed, lay in strongly differentiated terrain, so that there were also natural barriers in the way of making contacts. In the sense that the formation of settlement systems is seen as a consequence of the existence and intensification of such neighborly contacts, with their inherent conflicts, such systems cannot be expected to have existed during the period we are dealing with here. The fact that we have not really found any signs of settlements with systematic mutual connections from this period in the areas that have been investigated is probably not to be put down merely to the fragmentary nature of our finds.

Other methods of making assertions about forms of communal organization in Neolithic times have also largely proved to be failures. Settlements have hardly ever been excavated to the point where social differentiation can be determined from the layout of the settlement, the form and sites of the houses, the spread of house sizes, or the differentiation and distribution of the finds. The following examples from Çatal Hüyük in Turkey and Umm Dabaghiyah in Iraq do provide some important clues, but do not allow us to recognize any principles and cannot be reinforced by the addition of other examples, so that it is impossible to make generalizations.

Before the settlements mentioned above are discussed in more detail, we must once again stress the significance of the sites, or rather the surroundings, of settlements in this period. Although it is true that, like Çatal Hüyük, Umm Dabaghiyah, and Hajji Firuz, most of these settlements are to be found in regions that clearly conform to the hypothesis of a differentiated hinterland, we also know of the case of the settlement of Bougras on the central Euphrates, whose hinterland does not appear to show the same degree of internal differentiation. However, the river itself, the terrace on which the settlement was located, and the hinterland gave easy access to as many different sources as possible for food gathering there too.

The excavations in Çatal Hüyük, where a densely built-up area of about 440 square meters has been uncovered, provided us with the largest connected complex of buildings. Houses of standard size and all of roughly the same pattern were found packed closely together on an incline (fig. 9a). Neither paths nor other means of communication were found, nor any doors connecting the individual units with one another, so that one can only suppose that communication between, and entrance into, the living quarters took place via the flat roofs.

From the lack of significant differences in house size and structure and the lack of any sign of communal facilities, we must assume that this was a socially undifferentiated community. Although this would not contradict the generally held view of the type of community that existed during the Neolithic period, it must be noted that it was only possible to uncover about one-eighth of the total settlement. As we shall see, moreover, the grave finds point to the existence of social differences.

At least a fifth of the settlement of Umm Dabaghiyah, situated in

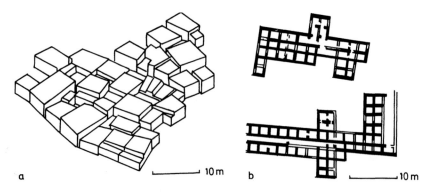

Figure 9. (a) Graphic reconstruction of part of the Neolithic settlement of Çatal Hüyük (Turkey), and (b) plan of the principal buildings at Umm Dabaghiyah (Iraq). After (a) J. Mellaart, "Excavations at Çatal Hüyük, 1962," *Anatolian Studies* 13 (1963), fig. 6, and (b) D. Kirkbride, "Umm Dabaghiyah, 1974," *Iraq* 37 (1975), pl. 1.

northern Iraq, has been uncovered. Within this area, several long rows of small, interconnected rooms on three sides of an open space were found (fig. 9b). The layout and the finding in the rooms of large numbers of onager bones and skins lead us to suppose that these were central warehouses.

Although it was only possible to excavate a few living quarters, we may assume that more of these living quarters continued into the area that has not been excavated. Unfortunately, we cannot say anything about the distribution of sizes among the houses, but it is clear from the site as a whole that, since it possessed buildings that were used collectively, the outlines of an already structured form of organization can be observed here.

Too little of the settlement of Hajji Firuz, in the mountains of northwestern Iran, has been excavated to make possible any statements about the layout of the settlement. It seems that this settlement differed from those mentioned above in that it consisted, for the most part, of individual, freestanding buildings, which could be of slightly different sizes.

It is true that up until now none of the other excavations has provided us with an example of such clear differences in the size of buildings as would point to some sort of social differentiation. However, in all cases the relationship between settlement size and excavated area is always considerably more disadvantageous, so that no conclusions can be drawn from the lack of external differentiation, which could be a consequence of the fragmentary nature of our finds.

Finds such as burials, for example, which otherwise allow us on occasion to make statements about social differentiation, as well as about aspects of religion, unfortunately either do not occur very frequently or are not suitable for this sort of interpretation. In Hajji Firuz, for example, a great number of burial places were found, all under the floors of houses. However, as a rule they are multiple burials, in which the grave goods, which could have told us quite a lot, can no longer be related to individuals; in any case, grave goods were found in relatively few of these multiple graves.

Here, too, the excavations at Çatal Hüyük provide better information. At this site there were also numerous multiple burials, mostly consisting of collections of human bones buried inside the houses underneath benches for sitting or sleeping on, after the dead had presumably been left exposed for some period. Beads or stone tools had seldom been placed in the graves in these later burials.

Besides these burials, there were a few others that were notable for the opulence of the grave goods found in them. Among these were stone and wooden vessels, utensils used for makeup, belt buckles made of bone, and, above all, most exquisitely fashioned utensils made of obsidian and flint. Unfortunately, this clear evidence of social differences must stand alone. The houses that contained these graves do not differ in any way from the others.

Any opportunity we may have for making statements about religious ideas is also limited. The customs of putting food in the grave for the dead, in vessels the dead person was presumably intended to continue to use, and of strewing ochre over the dead person, a red coloring probably supposed to restore the lost color of life, allow us to conclude that they did think about life continuing after death. However, we lack evidence that would enable us to make any more exact statements.

Finds of human skulls modeled over with clay and decorated with shells in the prepottery layers at Jericho do allow us to draw the conclusion that there must have been some sort of ancestor worship, in which the skulls of dead members of the family were honored after some approximation to the way they looked in life had been made in this way. Analogous items are known to ethnologists. Walls, shelves, and "altars" in a few rooms at Çatal Hüyük that appear to be different in shape from other rooms are decorated with bulls' skulls and horns, which could indicate a bull cult, or perhaps the worship of totem animals, with the bull having been the totem of that particular group.

Insofar as we can speak of cult rooms at all, and not merely of a corner set aside for the cult within the normal living area, we notice that such rooms are always directly connected to living quarters. Separate cult buildings—which could be seen as prototypes of later free-standing temples—are not known to us. However, here we must point out that there may well have been simple shrines outside the settlement—either the burial places of the heads of clans, or sacred buildings, or simple huts beside sacred wells or holy trees—just like the ones known to ethnologists as the focal points for cult events.

Although we must avoid making any far-reaching statements about periods for which we can in no way be said to have adequate material, we can say with some certainty that during the periods of time we have been dealing with up to now, from the Palaeolithic onwards, development took place more or less uniformly throughout the Near East. This may not be quite clear without further illustration because, in addition to smaller settlements, we know of at least two settlements that, on account of their size and other special characteristics, seem to belong to a different level of forms of organization, Jericho and Çatal Hüyük.

Both cases point to an extremely highly developed social stratification, which seems just as unusual for the period as does the compact style of building in these settlements. This suggests that there must have been arrangements made for settling the social conflicts that inevitably occur when people live so close together. If in addition—as was the case with Jericho—such settlements were prevented from expanding by a perimeter wall, conflicts could not be solved by reducing the density of the population—that is, by increasing the area covered by the settlement. In this respect, the wall of Jericho not only points to its people's increasing need for protection but must also have had a considerable effect on the development of social relationships within the settlement.

Apart from the pressure for increased internal conflict management, there are two other significant aspects here. On the one hand, the erection of such a wall would be inconceivable without the collective efforts of all the inhabitants, thus exerting pressure in the direction of collective labor. On the other hand, this perimeter wall not only made expansion of the settlement distinctly impossible, but would also have played a crucial role in increasing the differences between the inhabitants of the settlement and people living outside it.

In this type of settlement, sometimes called a "town," a form has in fact been found in this early phase of development that anticipates some of the aspects and problems of the later town, but that differs in one decisive criterion from the later forms: as far as we know, Jericho was not the center of a settled countryside—it was not part of a set-

Figure 10. Tower of the fortifications at Neolithic Jericho. From K. Kenyon, *Excavations at Jericho III* (Jerusalem, 1981), pl. 7a. Courtesy, British School of Archaeology, Jerusalem.

tlement system, but was a river oasis without neighboring dependent settlements.

Neither the excavations in Jericho itself nor any other evidence point to a development that could have led to this early form of "town," or that could have progressed any further from this point. In the ensuing period, after a temporal gap, Jericho once again assumed the character of a settlement just like any other, and it is a very long time before we again find settlements exhibiting external characteristics similar to those of early Jericho.

When they do appear, however, they are coupled with all the characteristics of a real centrality and belong to a line of development that we can trace all the way along through its individual stages. The special development of Jericho and, to a limited extent, also of Çatal Hüyük, in no way therefore changes anything in our general characterization of the period as one of separate open settlements. If Jericho shows anything, it demonstrates how wide the spectrum of possibilities at the beginning of a new phase of development, in this case permanent settlements, can be. However, further development seldom proceeds from the extremes of such a spectrum. Because of special conditions we do not know about, Jericho developed into a special form right on the edge of the spectrum. Hence, further development to higher forms of political organization did not lead via Jericho, Çatal Hüyük, or other similar, but as yet unknown, settlements, but took the very slow way round, via the development of structured relationships between individual settlements and of settlement systems. It will be one theme of the next chapter to describe this course of development.

At this point one can only urge caution in the face of any assumption that the developments of the period can be adequately characterized by these few examples. Above all, it might appear that all the individual developments are to be seen as preliminary stages in the evolution of the following period. However, the problem is that although our material is sufficient for us to assume that there must have been a great variety of living and settlement forms during this period, we cannot yet adequately describe this variety.

THREE

From Isolated Settlement to Town
(ca. 6000–3200 B.C.)

Up to this point there had been more or less constant progress in development throughout the Near East. Toward the end of the period we are now about to deal with, however, considerable differences between individual regions are observable. For example, Susiana now found itself in a preliminary phase of the developmental stage of advanced urban civilization, with centers that stood at the head of multitiered settlement systems. In contrast, other regions, especially the rest of present-day Iran and Anatolia, remained at the level of isolated settlements or at the stage of forming the first centers. Lower Mesopotamia, which was to be an important arena for cultural development in the following period, also remained at the level of isolated settlements, and was still almost completely excluded from the development taking place in the neighboring areas.

The differentiation between individual regions of the area clearly took place at some time during the period at which we are now going to take a closer look. Besides following the general development from isolated settlements to towns, this chapter therefore has the task of attempting to trace the beginnings of the process of differentiation. It is true that we are restricted at more than one point by the inadequacy of our source material, but the question of why different lines of development should have occurred under what seem to have been the same preconditions is of such general and urgent interest that every opportunity, however incomplete, must be exploited in order to investigate it.

During the period treated in the previous chapter, methods of food production and the arrangements made for storing food were already highly developed, so that food production already provided a rather less haphazard contribution ensuring a means of subsistence. Development seems to have progressed toward an economic form in which the proportion of food produced had grown steadily. But it would be deceiving ourselves to think that now, at the time of developed permanent settlements, the mixed economy of the earlier period was given up in favor of a form of economy that relied solely on food production.

39

On the one hand, investigations of animal and plant remains from a whole series of settlements belonging to the close of the Neolithic period have furnished us with evidence that the proportion of hunted and gathered foodstuffs to produced food continued to be relatively high. In addition we even have an example that contradicts the assumption that the proportion of food produced continued to increase.

This was found during the excavations at Ali Kosh, a small site on the Deh-Luran plain, one of the small, marginal western plains of the Zagros mountains. On top of a level that already contained a high proportion of the remains of cultivated plants, deposits were found in which the proportion of wild plants had risen again. That point in time after which man could depend exclusively on the production of food as a guarantee of basic subsistence had clearly not yet arrived. There still had to be a possibility of compensating for failures in food production by greater efforts in hunting, fishing, or gathering—at least to a limited extent.

This is an important observation, insofar as the need to keep open all the options we have mentioned continued to place restrictions on the choice of settlement sites. As before, people were dependent on sites that, as well as being surrounded by sufficient land for cultivation, were also surrounded in very close proximity by the sorts of countryside that afforded opportunities for the acquisition of food by gathering.

Since techniques of food production had apparently come so close to guaranteeing a livelihood that the probability could be ruled out of all the food necessary having to be acquired by gathering if need be, the hinterland required for a settlement could be smaller than was previously the case. However, the surrounding area needed for a settlement was still so large that there were considerable distances between one settlement and another, and there always had to be a large space left before a new settlement, with all its territorial demands, could be founded on a similarly appropriate site. A basic pattern continued to determine the overall picture in which settlements were set at such a distance that although their inhabitants could of course trade or barter with one another, they did not have to develop forms of daily intercourse that extended beyond their own settlements (fig. 11a).

A situation that left all options open, tended strongly to stabilization, and took precautions against every possible risk must be designated as stable, even almost ideal. Further development could emphasize only one aspect—at the expense of the others—of this mixed economy at any given time, thus limiting not only the mechanisms for securing subsistence but also the number of options. The motives for

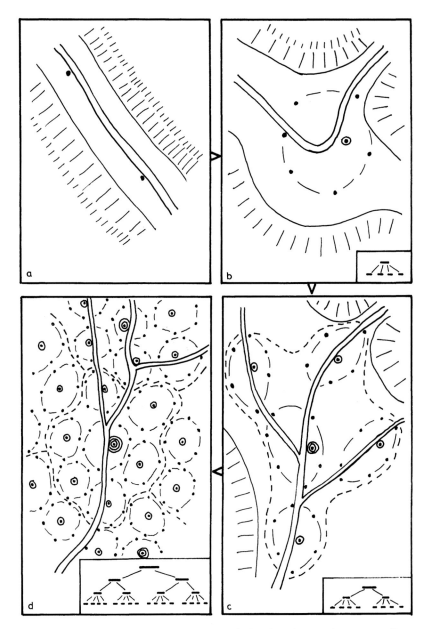

Figure 11. Typology of settlement systems: (a) isolated settlements in narrow valleys; (b) simple settlement system on a small plain; (c) three-tiered and (d) four-tiered settlement systems on larger plains. Author's original.

a development that abandoned this stability must therefore have been very strong indeed.

One explanation—which is, however, insufficient—might be that the possibility of guaranteeing basic subsistence through the production of food became more and more of a reality as experience grew. As they learned to cope with the specific problems associated with crop cultivation and animal husbandry, people were better insured against making mistakes and so there was a greater possibility of managing without the security provided by a careful choice of settlement site.

Growing experience in food production in fact decreased the necessity of obtaining food by hunting, fishing, or gathering, even if this way of procuring food was never completely given up. At a later stage, however, it was not continued from sheer necessity. Even later when the economy was exclusively organized on the basis of food production, texts tell us that a not inconsiderable part of the meat needed by the royal court came from game animals, which were, however, in part kept in preserves.

With the acquisition of a certain degree of security, the absolute necessity of having to settle down on sites that offered the safety net of food gathering gradually decreased. Insofar as people wished, it now for the first time became possible to establish settlements at sites that lay outside the favorable areas previously used. We can only suppose that the prospect of finding more extensive areas of arable land, which would permit the establishment of larger, interconnected fields, must have been an incentive for the early settlers. We shall in fact see that in the following period smaller plains were also inhabited, so that the space for settlements was no longer restricted to the valleys and other particularly prominent sites.

However, the effect of these changes in the area required for a settlement went far beyond mere expansion, for they were the prerequisites for the changes that were now to take place in the settlements themselves and in systems of settlements. To the extent that these small plains greatly exceeded the area of land needed for one settlement, it now became possible for several settlements to grow up within the same ecological unit, and these were now for the first time situated in immediate proximity to one another. Thus we can assume that their subsistence areas may have been contiguous, or at least very close to one another (fig. 11b).

This proximity could be so much closer because increasing experience in the cultivation of plants, besides creating a greater sense of security, involved another effect—the yield per unit of land was also greater. Gathering produces the lowest yield per unit of land, whereas the highest yield is achieved in areas in which, with the aid of irrigation, two or three harvests per year can be produced. With increasing experience in the art of cultivation, the area necessary to feed one person was thus reduced. This meant that the area of land necessary to feed the population of a settlement became smaller, and with increasing security and more intensive use of the land, settlements could move closer and closer together. This is important insofar as the geographical proximity of settlements is a basic prerequisite for the creation of structured relationships between them, in the sense of the formation of settlement systems.

Before we turn once again to the theme of the development of settlement systems, we must here address in a more general sense the problem of the division of labor, for which the creation of settlement systems can stand as one subordinate aspect. For the moment, we shall not concern ourselves with the fact that there was already a certain division of labor among the hunters and gatherers and, naturally, among the groups of early settlers, both according to sex and also among members of the same sex. In the period we are now dealing with there was certainly already a further division. If we proceed on the assumption that at first all necessary tasks were carried out within the family unit, the process of a progressive division of labor among the members of a community can be seen as an increasing autonomy in occupations, at first within and then outside the boundaries of the family itself.

In order to make this more comprehensible, we can undertake a schematic division of occupations according to how frequently they were needed and what level of prior knowledge was required. If we take food production, basic crafts (such as the production of pottery vessels), and specialist crafts (such as the production of valuable jewelry) as the three major fields of activity and plot these occupational groups on a graph, the coordinates of which show how frequently an occupation was used and what level of prior knowledge was required, we obtain a clear picture. We see that the three occupations we have described follow a straight line from, "often used, with limited previous experience" through "little used, with somewhat greater previous experience," to "very seldom used, with many previous qualifications." On account of the high degree of prior knowledge necessary, it might be expected that basic and specialist crafts became autonomous earlier than food production occupations that were engaged in very frequently. However, the fact that the occupations in the field of specialist crafts were only very little engaged in can be set against such a development. For these occupations, the total population must have been very large—large enough to provide a minimum number of customers.

The less frequently an occupation is used, the larger the total population must be before such an occupation can become autonomous, which means that an occupation's becoming autonomous depends on the size of the inhabited catchment area. Basic crafts can become autonomous in relatively small settlements, whereas the autonomy of specialist occupations presupposes the existence of larger living units. The setting up of larger settlements thus makes possible the autonomy of more specialized occupations. In the process, the number of these autonomous occupations increases with the size of the settlement.

Because we must assume that from the moment a few fields of occupation become autonomous this has an effect on other related occupations, the creation of such larger settlements, with the character of centers, means that there is also an incentive for the basic handicrafts. From the moment that there are independent potters or smiths, these occupations are presumably carried on less and less in individual households.

The demand for increased output in these handicrafts can be satisfied in several ways. Either the number of those who practice these occupations independently increases or the occupations themselves or the techniques used in them are changed, with the aim of producing more. One simple way of increasing productivity is to split up a total work process into several small component parts. The number of independent occupations thus becomes greater, but their scope grows smaller. As we shall see, this was clearly the way often followed in the early periods.

Above all, such a development had one further consequence, because now at least a partial attempt had to be made to reverse the dismantling of occupations by splitting them up into their component parts. It was at this point that supervisors or coordinators became necessary. Here it must be noted that with the growth in settlements, with the creation of centers, and especially with their continued growth, the number of autonomous occupations also continued to increase.

Any material we can use to verify the line of development I have just described is very limited because, as I have shown above, of all types of finds, only pottery is available in sufficient quantities and with sufficient differentiation. However, even if we limit ourselves to statements about the production process and the organization of work involved, we can still see a coherent picture, which is sketched in the following paragraphs.

If, in the case of the earliest pottery, we are dealing with products definitely produced in each individual household, we must, at the latest, reckon that the very delicate, finely painted pottery of the so-called Halaf period was produced by specialists. (The period is named after the site where this pottery was found, Tell Halaf in northern Syria.) However, the individually painted vessels from this pottery group, which all took a long time to make, are definitely the work of individuals, who probably carried out each stage of the production process themselves (fig. 12).

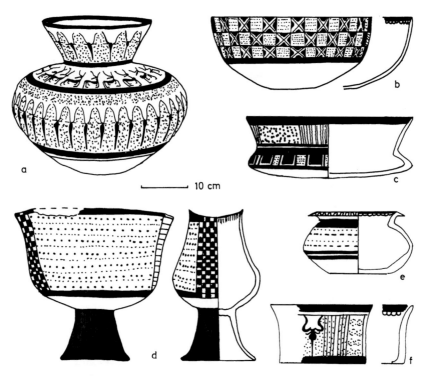

Figure 12. Pottery vessels of the Halaf period, from (a) Tell Halaf (Syria) and (b–f) Tell Arpachiyah (Iraq). After H. Schmidt, *Tell Halaf* (Berlin, 1943), frontispiece, and M. E. L. Mallowan, "Excavations at Tell Arpachiyah," *Iraq* 2 (1935), figs. 62, 64–66, 76.

At the end of this period, which knew other groups of pottery besides the Halaf pottery, there was a very important innovation, the introduction of a pivoted working surface (also called a "tournette" or, erroneously, "a slow rotating wheel"). The most important distinction between this and the actual potter's wheel consists in the fact that this rotating work surface only continues to rotate for as long as someone is turning it. Because it does not have any bearings and is only fixed to the earth through a hole bored by its pivot, it was also probably very hard to turn. However, this new device did make certain tasks easier, including the vertical shaping of pots and, most especially, painting. The painter had neither to readjust the vessel nor to move when the opposite side of a pot had to be painted. With the aid of the rotating work surface, the painter could easily bring the surface to be painted round to whatever position he wished.

However, what had been invented to make work easier soon began to make its impression on the products themselves. The skillful painting of pots in different fields or sections, which had been the usual practice up until then, gradually gave way to simpler styles of painting, which are, on the whole, based on concentric bands round the pots, something now seen as characteristic of the following period, the so-called Ubaid period, named for the site where these pots were found, Tell al-Ubaid in southern Iraq (fig. 13). This new method of decoration arose directly out of the use of the new device, because the concentric bands round the pot were created simply by pressing a color-soaked brush against the rotating pot.

Somewhat more ambitious patterns could be produced in this way, for, by moving the brush up and down, garlands, wavy lines, or herringbone patterns could very easily be applied. Both the production and the painting of pots could therefore be carried out in a fraction of the time formerly necessary.

With the advent of this new technical device, this type of painting prevailed generally throughout a large area of the Near East. Under the influence of the new technique, earlier, more localized, types of decoration underwent such uniform change that the impression could easily arise that this "Ubaid horizon" was the external indication of the spread of the "Ubaid" method of painting to the whole of the Near East from one place as a result of a migratory movement.

Following this easier and quicker way of producing decoration, the proportion of decorated wares found in the total pottery yield increases far beyond the proportion in which painted vessels can still be regarded as luxury goods, as in former times. Because many excavators have concentrated on decorated pottery, details of the pro-

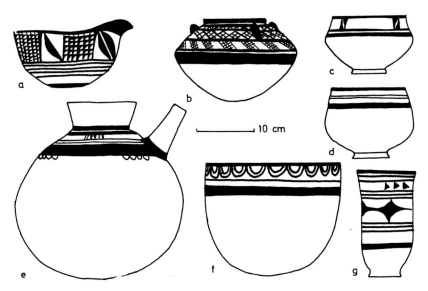

Figure 13. Pottery vessels of the Ubaid period, from (a–c) Tell al'Ubaid, (e–f) Tell Uqair, and (d and g) Ur (all Iraq). After H. R. Hall and C. L. Woolley, "Al-Ubaid," *Ur Excavations I* (1927), pl. 49; S. Lloyd and F. Safar, "Tell Uqair," *Jour. of N. E. Studies* 2 (1943), pl. 21; C. L. Woolley, "The Early Periods," *Ur Excavations* 4 (1956), pl. 18.

portion of unpainted vessels are unfortunately difficult to obtain in most cases. Hence, there is no evidence to support the conjecture that the total number of pottery vessels used at any one time also increased. It was certainly no later than the time at which this sort of pottery was produced that pottery was manufactured by professional potters, and in the process the different procedures were probably the responsibility of different workers.

The next technical innovation was setting the wheel's axle in bearings and hence the creation of an actual potter's wheel, probably at the end of the Ubaid period. The aim of this was probably once again a simplification of the production process. Again there were considerable effects on both the process itself and, more especially, on the appearance of the pottery. Even though these developments belong chronologically to the next chapter, they will be briefly outlined here.

The main changes in pottery after the Ubaid period stem from the different properties required in the consistency of clay when it is worked on a potter's wheel. The potential of the potter's wheel can only be fully exploited if the clay is pliable and does not break off while it is being worked. A great deal more time than before had therefore to be spent in preparing the clay before it was used.

The properties required in the clay could be enhanced by the use of additives, and depending on which of these materials were used, the finished vessels might look totally different from one another. Thus, for example, the addition of substances containing ferric oxide can radically change the basic color after firing. The fact that the basic yellowish color of untreated vessels of the later Uruk period was, in the following period, replaced, after firing, by a reddish-brown background color may be connected with such a process.

Apart from these technical changes, a whole series of other factors, which we are unable to name, certainly influenced the very evident differences between the pottery of the Ubaid period and that of the following Uruk period. Painting was discontinued, apart from a very few examples, and, aside from particular shapes that were given an incised pattern, the pottery is undecorated. An ever-greater role was played by vessels whose shapes indicate that they were used for specialized purposes rather than all-purpose pottery. These changes can in no way be seen as a sign of a change in the population, however, as has occasionally been suggested.

We can, with the greatest certainty, assume that there was an extensive internal division of labor in pottery production after the introduction of the potter's wheel, because we may assume that the long-drawn-out process of preparing the clay was done by others. In addition, it is possible that in larger workshops there were individual potters who specialized in particular forms, a point made probable when finds from the Late Uruk period in Habuba were investigated. Such workshops, which probably also existed in other crafts, could not have carried on working without supervisors and coordinators.

The development just described not only illustrates the evolution of the organization of labor, but it also indicates the connection between specialization and the building of centers. In order to throw more light on this, let us return to a consideration of the development of settlements, or rather of settlement systems.

In the following discussion, this development will be considered especially from the point of view of the thesis that the degree of organization of settlement systems depended on the size of their particular ecological units. As an example I shall choose only one area of the Near East, which offers a practically ideal example of the external preconditions needed to test this hypothesis—the area from Lower Mesopotamia eastwards up to the ridges of the Zagros Mountains. All the external factors required of the natural environment for the different stages of development of organizational forms can be found here in the smallest possible area.

Within this area we find four different zones that can be described as rough ecological units: the narrow valleys of the Zagros; the small alluvial plains in this range of mountains; the alluvial plain of the Karun and Kerkha rivers lying below them, which we call Susiana after the ancient political center of Susa; and, finally, to the west, the great alluvial plain of lower Mesopotamia. These areas are naturally not completely separated from one another and have more or less large-scale features in common. There are, however, also crucial differences. Among the latter are climatic conditions, the prevailing temperatures and the amount of annual precipitation. However, one of the most important differences is the difference in the size of the units suitable for settlements.

In this relatively small section of the Near East, we find all types of settlement, from the first settlements of the prepottery and pottery Neolithic period through the first larger permanent settlements up to all the higher forms of organization, such as the city and the state. Thus, on the one hand, the area offers a wide spectrum of geographical potential, and, on the other, it was the home of such a variety of phases of the development of early civilizations that we might even be tempted to conclude that it played a special part in the growth of early forms of civilization in the Near East.

It fits in very nicely that, at the same time, our chosen area belongs to the part of the Near East for which we have a relatively large amount of reliable evidence about early society. This is not so much related to the actual number of sites excavated but rather to the number of research projects, whose results we are dependent on if we wish to speak about settlement systems and the changes that took place in them. Here we have to rely on projects aimed at surveying, without excavation, all the archaeologically significant remains visible on the surface in a given area. Since settlement sites of all types have left some visible trace behind them, even if it is only, as in most cases, a vast number of discarded pottery shards, it is possible to establish the location of these old settlement sites.

The position and size of all these settlements can therefore be plotted on maps, and surface archaeological finds of many types make it possible to classify these ruined towns by period. In this process, as already mentioned, pottery plays the greatest part because great numbers of broken fragments can be found on the surface of almost every old settlement. In addition, because of the worthlessness of these fragments, we do not have to conclude, in our assessment, and especially

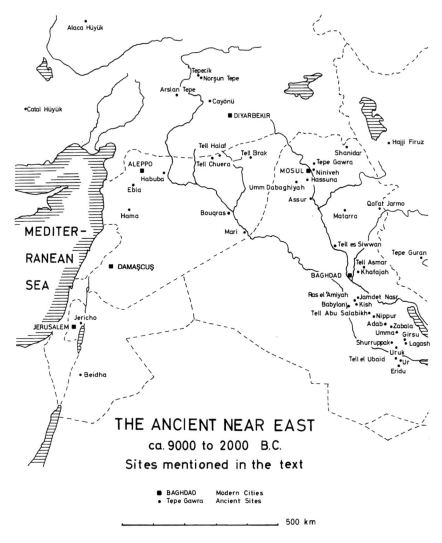

Alaca Hüyük

Tepecik
Norşun Tepe
Arslan Tepe
Çayönü
Çatal Hüyük
■ DIYARBEKIR

Tell Halaf
Tell Brak
Shanidar
ALEPPO
Tell Chuera
Tepe Gawra
MOSUL ■ Niniveh
Habuba
Hassuna
Ebla
Umm Dabaghiyah
Assur
Qal'at Jarmo
Hama
Bouqras
Matarra
Mari

MEDITER-
RANEAN
SEA
Tell es Siwwan
Tepe Guran
Tell Asmar
DAMAŞCUŞ
Khafajah
BAGHDAD

Ras el 'Amiyah
Jamdet Nasr
Babylon
Kish
Tell Abu Salabikh
Nippur
Jericho
Adab
Zabala
JERUSALEM ■
Umma
Girsu
Shurruppak
Lagash
Uruk
Tell el Ubaid
Ur
Eridu

Beidha

Hajji Firuz

THE ANCIENT NEAR EAST
ca. 9000 to 2000 B.C.
Sites mentioned in the text

■ BAGHDAD   Modern Cities
• Tepe Gawra   Ancient Sites

500 km

Figure 14. Map of the Near East with sites mentioned in the text.

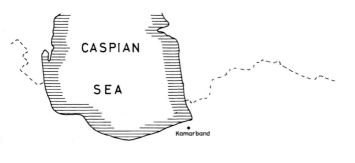

CASPIAN

SEA

Kamarband

■
TEHERAN

Tepe Sarab • Godin Tepe
• • Ganj Dareh

• Tepe Siyalk

■
ISFAHAN

Ali Kosh
Tepe Jaffarabad
• Chogha Mish
Susa

• Qal e Rostam

■
KERMAN

• Tepe Sohz   Anshan •   • Persepolis

BASRAH

■
SHIRAZ

Tepe Yahyah

PERSIAN

GULF

51

in the dating of a complex of finds, that important pieces are missing or that the whole complex was disturbed in its composition at a later date. In the majority of cases where verification is possible, it has in fact been shown that the finds on the surface provide us with a rough, but faithful, picture of what an excavation would produce for purposes of dating. It is self-evident that such investigations can be no substitute for excavations, if only because of the fact that hardly anything else except pottery fragments is ever found on the surface.

The results of such archaeological surface investigations are maps that show the location and size of the settled sites divided up according to periods, such as, for example, those shown by the maps in figure 20. However, this is precisely the basic information we need to arrive at statements about settlement systems and the changes that took place in them.

For the area in which we are interested at the moment, we have this type of survey for the great plains of Babylonia and Susiana, as well as for a few of the smaller plains and valleys in the neighboring Zagros Mountains. From these we obtain the following picture: not only the sites with settlements from the pre-pottery Neolithic period, but also the earliest sites from the pottery Neolithic period, such as Tepe Guran, Tepe Sarab, Ganj Dareh, Qalʾat Jarmo, and Qalʾe Rostam, are all situated in valleys of the Zagros or at the exits to such valleys to smaller plains. They were all isolated settlements, each situated far away from other sites of the same period.

It is only during the following period that we find individual settlements advancing into smaller plains. Local peculiarities, which we can no longer identify in detail, must certainly have guaranteed the necessary breadth of potential for exploitation. We may treat Tepe Jaffarabad or Chogha Mish in Susiana or Ras-al ʿAmiyah and Eridu in Lower Mesopotamia as examples of such settlements that had advanced further, although here we still seem to be dealing with isolated settlements.

Completely developed settlement systems can, for the first time, be identified in a period we call the Late Susiana period, based on the order of the layers at some sites in Susiana. Clearly, this is not meant to imply that in the previous period there were no systematic relationships among settlements, but between the previously mentioned phase of isolated settlements and the one from which we now first know of settlement systems, there is a period for which we have hardly any information at all.

These earliest developed settlement systems were located on small plains amid the Zagros Mountains. The plain surrounding the modern

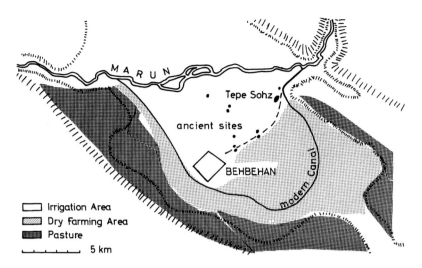

Figure 15. Settlements on the plain of Behbehan around 4000 B.C. and zones of probable land use. Author's original.

town of Behbehan can serve as an example (fig. 15). Here the different places settled during the early period were all abandoned within a very short space of time during the Late Susiana period and were never settled again. Hence, the remains from the early period were directly visible on the surface, and there was extremely informative material available for evaluation.

The plain lies at the junction of two natural routes through an otherwise impassable mountain area. The first of these is the most important east-west passage, which is not only used today for roads between the modern towns of Ahwaz and Shiraz, but was also already an essential section of the "King's Road" of the Achaemenids. The other route, which uses different longitudinal mountain valleys and the passes between them, connects the area a little to the south at the head of the Gulf with the Isfahan region of the central Iranian plateau.

This route is difficult to follow and is of almost no importance today, but it clearly was of great importance during the Middle Ages. The early settlements certainly took advantage of it, because the relationships we can prove to have existed at that time between the civilizations west and east of the Zagros must have made use of this route. It is then easy to suppose that Tepe Sohz, by far the largest site, had a part to play on this connecting route, about which, for the time being, we cannot be any more specific. However, the location of this site near the spot where the Marun River flows into the plain shows that its primary importance had a different basis. Because of its location, the site was in a dominant position for an irrigation system that drew its water from the Marun, a little to the north of Tepe Sohz.

It is true that today the old canal is no longer readily identifiable in an area used intensively for agriculture, but the location of most of the ancient places on a line parallel to a modern irrigation canal that extends from Tepe Sohz is evidence enough. Because of its size and location, Tepe Sohz, with a surface area of almost twelve hectares, was undoubtedly the center of the group of smaller settlements, each of which hardly occupied more than two to three hectares of land. There is no doubt that we are dealing here with a simple settlement system.

Since we know of similar situations on other small plains of this type, we may assume that for the chronological horizon of the Late Susiana period this was the normal form of organization. Interestingly enough, this does not appear to have been true of the Susiana plain immediately to the west. Although there is evidence of sites from this

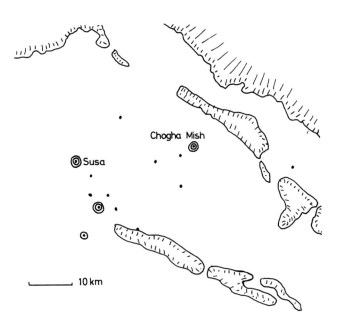

Figure 16. Distribution of settlements in Susiana in Late Uruk times. After G. A. Johnson, "Early State Organization in Southwestern Iran," *Proc. of the IVth Ann. Symp. on Archaeol. Res. in Iran* (Teheran, 1976), p. 196.

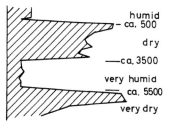

Figure 17. Results from deep drilling in the floor of the Persian Gulf: proportions of organic matter (hatched) in the sediments and inferences regarding the ancient climate. After W. Nützel, "The Climatic Changes of Mesopotamia and Bordering Areas, 14,000 to 2,000 B.C." *Sumer* 32 (1976): 20.

period there, they do not appear to have had such close communications with one another. In this case, it is to be hoped that the publication of research done a long time ago will have more to teach us.

In the next phase we find completely developed settlement systems in the Susiana plain, with centers, such as Susa, that exceed in size anything else we know of up to that time. In addition to this, it has been possible to identify a network of relationships among these settlements that points to a multilevel hierarchy of importance. We are probably not wrong in assuming that here, for the first time, we are dealing with three-tiered settlement systems.

Before we now turn to Lower Mesopotamia, the last great geographical unit of the area outlined above, we must first provide an introduction. This is because it is astonishing to discover that, at a time when the areas just to the east had developed centers of a higher order, we find nothing in Lower Mesopotamia that points to any stage beyond that of isolated individual settlements. Recent research does, however, permit us to give an explanation for this curious state of affairs.

The period with which we were concerned before, the beginning of the fourth millennium B.C., was clearly one that witnessed considerable climatic changes. The evidence for this was provided partly by the findings of a voyage by the research ship *Meteor* in the Gulf during the winter of 1964/65. Tests of the sediment that forms the floor of the Gulf, especially the discovery of the respective proportions of organic materials, revealed astonishing changes in its composition. With the help of individual carbon 14 measurements, it was possible to fix the points chronologically on a graph produced in this way (fig. 17).

Because the percentage of inorganic materials increases with the quantity of water flowing in from a river, a low proportion of organic material in the substances carried by a river and later deposited points to a large amount of water—that is, to high precipitation in the drainage area of the river, and therefore to a damp, humid climate. The consequences are of great importance to us because the span of time for which particularily conspicuous changes are evident corresponds partly to the periods of interest to us here.

The profile reproduced in figure 17 shows that roughly in the middle of the fourth millennium B.C. what was probably a slight, but noticeable, change of climate must have taken place, leading to slightly cooler and dryer average conditions. According to the evidence provided by a graph of the variations in sea level in the Gulf, reconstructed with the help of other observations, the sea level was almost three meters higher at the time when the climatic changes began than it is today.

The effects of climatic changes are visible in the gradual drop in sea level, as well as in the fact that, because they carried less water, the rivers that flowed into the Gulf also carried and laid down less sedimentary material. Here it is significant for us that the reduction in precipitation that was the cause of this affected the whole drainage area of these rivers, so that this climatic fluctuation was not just a localized affair but must have involved the whole of the region drained by these great rivers and their tributaries.

Of course these climatic changes also had an effect on the mountainous regions we have been discussing and on the plains that lie among them. However, it would seem that there was no change in one important respect. These regions definitely remained within the area in which there was sufficient precipitation for plant cultivation.

In contrast, the effects on Lower Mesopotamia were far-reaching. A prolonged period in which only very scattered individual settlements existed was suddenly followed by a phase in which the land was clearly so densely settled that nothing like it had been seen even in the Susiana of the previous period. With the help of information from the *Meteor* research project, an explanation for this development in Babylonia is now possible. The land, which had been unsuitable for settlement owing to the high sea level in the Gulf or the large amount of water in the rivers, had at first supported only a few island sites, but from the moment the waters began to recede it was open to much more extensive inhabitation.

The question of developments in the other regions of the Near East mentioned earlier can, unfortunately, be answered very quickly. There, the sites investigated are always very much farther apart from one another and cannot therefore furnish as much information as the area discussed above. The places investigated in the latter area are in each case so close together that we cannot avoid assuming that there was a direct linkage in space and in time, whereas elsewhere in the Near East we almost always find ourselves in a situation where we have to bridge huge gaps. The interpolations necessary for this must, however, inevitably lead to false assertions, because such a method of proceeding always tends to obscure existing differences. This means that an important point such as the beginning of local differentiation will certainly keep being covered up.

Let us select one obvious example of our helplessness. We have already seen that the period named for the finding of Halaf pottery also produced other pottery groups. The most characteristic of these other groups is called "Samarra" pottery, after the site on the central Tigris where it was first found. Like Halaf pottery, it, too, belongs to the painted types of pottery, which are remarkable for their great wealth of patterns. However, the differences between these two groups are there, staring us in the face. Samarra pottery tended to simpler shapes and circular patterns, which, moreover, were applied in matte colors, as opposed to the glossy paints used on Halaf pottery.

For a long time it was assumed that these two groups, which were easy to differentiate, followed one another chronologically. However, several excavations have provided evidence that they could also have occurred simultaneously.

Then it was thought that the differences could be explained geographically, Halaf pottery occurring more in Anatolia, Syria, and the western part of northern Mesopotamia, and Samarra pottery occurring more in the eastern and southern regions of northern Mesopotamia, as far as the Zagros. The overlap of the sites where these pots were found is, however, very large, if one can talk of a dividing line between the sites at all.

The next attempt at an explanation was based on the assumption that the two pottery groups conceal different population groups, each with different ways of life, the one made up of cultivators and the other of livestock farmers. Apart from the fact that the preceding survey has shown that these pure forms probably did not yet exist as opposites at this period, it would be amazing if, given the regional differentiation that has been partially substantiated for the area in question, there were not also quite different ways of life in existence.

We shall certainly not succeed in finding an answer to this question until the number of places investigated has increased considerably, just as only an increase in this field of research will allow us to make any assertions about the relationships that must surely have existed between the different settlements. It is small comfort that, even if no positive statements can be made, at least nothing has appeared that would contradict the picture drawn above of the general process of development.

If we now return to the question, posed at the beginning of this chapter, of the reasons for the beginning of regional differentiation in the Near East, one explanation seems to be in the forefront. The differences seem to be between regions that fulfil the spatial requirements for the development of more complex settlement systems and areas that are too small in scale for this. It is clear that this explanation on its own can hardly be considered satisfactory. Otherwise, why did broader areas of the Near East, the wide plains of northern Mesopotamia and northern Syria, not develop forms of organization similar to Susiana? The size of the ecological unit cannot be the reason for regional differentiation—or at least not the only one.

In looking for other criteria to differentiate Susiana and Lower Mesopotamia—which was soon to be central to developments here—from the other plains of the Near East, we soon come upon a further basic factor: the difference in the availability of water. Since the most recent evidence available on climatic development and climatic correlations indicates that the relative climatic structures and, above all, the relative frequency of precipitation in these regions were hardly any different from what they are today—that is, that the gradation of the individual regions in relation to one another was about the same—we may assume that, in contrast to the other areas for which early settlement activity has been established, the great plains of Susiana and Babylonia did not have enough precipitation even then to guarantee continued plant cultivation.

Today, Lower Mesopotamia is completely outside the area in which dry farming can be practiced, whereas at least part of Susiana is in an area in which it is highly probable that sufficient precipitation can be expected. Crop cultivation without irrigation is thus possible only in parts of Susiana, and it is not possible at all in Lower Mesopotamia. This difference between the main regions of the Near East has been repeatedly cited as the main reason for the difference in development. According to this older view of things, the rise of Lower Mesopotamia can be explained by the fact that to carry out any irrigation, and especially to maintain the technical facilities necessary for it, larger organized associations of all those who participated in such an irrigation system became necessary. This view would only be correct, however, if in the days when the settlement of these great plains was taking place, it was necessary to irrigate in the manner we know from texts of later Babylonia: with the help of long feeder canals from the Euphrates, the waters of which—valuable because always insufficient—had to be carefully distributed among those who lived on its banks. However, as we shall see below, such irrigation systems, although they did in fact require a complex administrative system, belonged to a later stage of development. The existence of complicated irrigation systems can definitely be ruled out for the early periods.

This derives from the observation that the sea level in the Gulf was high before the climatic changes, so that large areas in the extreme south of Lower Mesopotamia were submerged, while at the same time the rivers were carrying so much water that in the critical seasons large sections of the rest of the alluvial plains were also flooded. Even if the change in climate did, in the end, mean that large areas of the country were no longer under water and so could, to a large extent, be settled, this can only mean conversely that for a long period of time there was so much water in the country that large areas were available for cultivation at a time when there was still sufficient water on hand in a profusion of small, even minute, creeks and waterways. Wherever artificial irrigation was necessary, there was, therefore, water available,

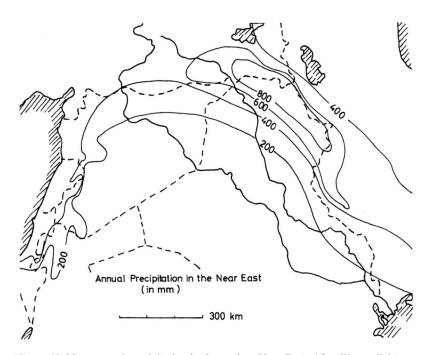

Figure 18. Mean annual precipitation in the modern Near East. After W. van Zeist. "Reflections of Prehistoric Environments in the Near East," fig. 3, in P. J. Ucko and G. W. Dimbleby, (eds.), *The Domestication and Exploitation of Plants and Animals* (London, 1969).

without any great effort being needed to obtain it. Hence, the thesis, attractive enough in itself, that it was the need to administer water supplies that encouraged the rapid development of Susiana and in Babylonia no longer coincides with our knowledge of the situation.

However, the main argument is correct. Even if the presence of artificial irrigation does not automatically mean that this necessarily had to take place in the context of a larger organization, there is a considerable difference between this type of agriculture and dry farming. Not only did more physical energy have to be invested; the intellectual challenge was also greater. The ground can be much more intensively farmed with the help of irrigation—that is, greater yields can be achieved from a given area of land than by dry farming. In addition, the increase in yields could be strengthened by the fact that barley, which in its uncultivated state has two rows of grain, had reacted to the complete change of milieu brought about by cultivation using artificial irrigation with a considerable increase in its six-row mutants, and that selection in favor of the six-row variety was thus a rapid success. This variant seems to have spread in a very short space of time throughout the whole of the Near East. Although the grains of two-row barley do appear to have been larger than the ones of the six-row variety, so that the increase in yield does not amount to an arithmetical 300 percent, the average yield was at least half as much again when the six-row variety was planted.

Different factors thus united to allow a higher yield to be obtained and made it possible to feed more people from the yield of a given area. Or, to put it another way, the area of land surrounding a settlement that was necessary to feed a given population could become considerably smaller. The consequence was that in regions with irrigation, the settlements could move much closer together than in areas where the cultivation of plants depended only on natural precipitation.

This difference, however, had far-reaching consequences. Increased proximity encourages cultural and economic exchange, but it also encourages the development of conflicts, or an increase in their intensity. If, in addition, they occurred in areas that were as a whole densely populated, such conflicts could not be resolved by the people moving away from one another—a method by which they might even have been avoided in the first place.

Living together in such close quarters meant that conflicts had, rather, to be actively controlled, leading to the setting up of rules for resolving conflicts. As we have already seen, situations where people lived together in close proximity could only arise in the intensively cultivated irrigation areas. Thus it was also the inhabitants of these areas—that is, especially of Babylonia—who found themselves confronted by these challenges and had to find answers to them. The need to establish rules enabling people or communities to live together is far more important in encouraging the higher development of civilizations than the need to create purely administrative structures. Hence, we can cite the specific characteristics of the great southern plains, particularly their size and their need for irrigation, as the reasons for the uneven development of parts of the Near East.

The fact that these different regions still had much in common at the end of this period in spite of this can be shown by the spread over most of the Near East of the technique of painting we name for the place where it was discovered in southern Iraq, Tell al-Ubaid, to which we have already referred. After what were at times very distinctive and detailed styles of painting in the earlier periods, Ubaid painting was increasingly restricted to concentric bands, garlands, wavy lines, or other all-round patterns. This trend took hold of almost all the regions of the Near East simultaneously, with greater or lesser intensity. We have already noted that this basic trend cannot be put down to the migration of a particular population group or to some other sort of grouping, but is rather the visible sign of the introduction and spread of a new technical device, the pivoted work surface.

Our main interest here is the idea that the spread of a technological innovation is tied up with specific preconditions; the acceptance of such an innovation is only conceivable when we can reasonably expect that it will help solve particular problems. Hence, the introduction of this new device over wide areas of the Near East at almost the same time means that, at least in the areas involved in the production and use of pottery, the problems were the same or similar. As previously observed this innovation aimed at an increase in productivity and must be seen as an aspect of the evolving division of labor. Its introduction signals a higher degree of professionalization. These are definitely processes that go beyond the narrow limits of pottery manufacture and that can shed light on contemporary Near Eastern economic organization as a whole. In the areas that took on this technical innovation, very similar economic problems and needs probably existed in other spheres as well. Hence these economics were very similar. It should be noted, however, this is not true for the Ubaid period itself, but for the phase before that, which appears to have been a period where, from our observation of the forms of settlement, no clear differentiation had as yet taken place among the regions of the Near East.

We do, however, have an example from the Ubaid period with a similar thrust, which has also already been mentioned: the introduction of the potter's wheel equipped with axle bearings, which followed that of the pivoted surface. This appeared in the latter part of the Ubaid period and was basically responsible for the obvious difference between the pottery of the Ubaid period and that of the following Uruk period.

This innovation, too, was certainly connected with the progressive division of labor and with the demand for greater specialization and increased productivity. Hence it, too, was clearly tied to the obviously increasing needs of a specific form of economy. Unlike the rotating work surface, the potter's wheel did not spread rapidly over large areas of the Near East. It could only make a breakthrough in the more highly developed regions.

The decoration of pottery, especially painting, which is often at the very center of the discussion, can hardly be approached in an unbiased way since, all too often, the distribution of a particular style of painting or a particular range of patterns is linked to reflections on the distribution or the migratory patterns of population groups.

The discussion of the Ubaid painting style has probably best illustrated the difficulties inherent in such a manner of proceeding, as has also our earlier discussion of the problem of the simultaneous existence of Halaf and Samarra pottery. Any interpretation of the relationships between different pottery groups should therefore be subject to strict limits, which can only be defined where statements can be made that go beyond the stage of talking about contemporaneity or noncontemporaneity. Even if, in the following paragraphs, specific conclusions are drawn from one observation, it is only because the statements are of a very general nature.

Our discussion is concerned with the question of how many different, well-defined pottery groups there were for each respective period in the Near East, and how their relationships to each other changed over the years. The result can be quickly sketched if we take the beginnings of pottery production as the start and the Ubaid horizon as the end of the period under observation. At the beginning we come across a situation where, although there are common factors in production techniques, the groups of decorative patterns are so different from one another that, for example, pottery can differ from one small area to the next in the Zagros Mountains.

After taking a great leap, we do see at the end of this development that, although there are still definitely recognizable local differences, common characteristics predominate. The developments in the period in between—to the extent that we know about them—do not contradict the assumption that what we have here is a continuous development.

The units within which we can talk of pottery types that are closely related grow larger and larger as time goes on. This development is astonishing, because we would be more likely to think of greater unity coming at the beginning and of individual groups differentiating themselves from it at the end. We cease to be astonished, however, if we set this development in its proper relationship to development in general.

First we should consider possible reasons for decorating pottery vessels with different patterns. If it is true that pleasure in decorating useful objects played a part in this, it is at least as important that here was an opportunity to introduce differences, to set oneself apart from other large and small groups or other individuals. Differentiation between the families of one settlement, and also between the larger units who live together in a settlement, has great significance for the life of every community. Hence it is no wonder that, in a period for which we must assume that the main structures in society were based on family relationships, we find that one element of differentiation is especially clearly defined.

In the following period, other aspects besides the progressive division of labor by the formation of hierarchies and social differentiation—neither of which can manage without status symbols—determined the course of social development, which was increasingly dependent upon the exchange of raw materials, and also of finished products and experience. If, on the one hand, the regions were drawn closer together by this, on the other, the painting of pottery lost its role as the main method of demonstrating social differentiation. In a society beginning to organize its social differentiation according to quite different criteria, the possibilities of expressing this differentiation must of necessity also have been different. It is highly probable that these other forms of differentiation hardly ever existed in a form as easily accessible for us as the painting of pottery. The assertion that there were direct relationships between developments in the types of pottery and social conditions may anticipate the next chapter. In the above sense it is indeed only consistent that, after the largely insignificant painting of the late Ubaid period in Lower Mesopotamia, which is almost exclusively content with concentric bands, the pottery of the following Uruk period should have no, or almost no, painting. It is certainly no coincidence that this is the first period where we can point to a form of society we can call "stratified."

In the light of these facts, it is clear that we must be extremely careful about interpreting both similarities (or "relationships") and nonsimilarities in pottery types, in the sense of the relationship or nonrelationship between the groups responsible for making them. We are confronted here with a very concrete warning, which may be generalized beyond the field of research into pottery. In the course of the rest of this study, we shall come up against yet other concrete cases that render dubious the linking of archaeological relationships and ethnic units.

By the end of the period dealt with in this chapter, the switches had been set for further differentiation. This took place both from a geographical point of view, in that the regions of the Near East had begun to grow even further away from one another, and from a social point of view, inasmuch as an even stricter articulation of society continued in the direction already taken. Favored by the climatic changes noted above, Lower Mesopotamia became the main scene of action for the developments that followed.

FOUR

The Period of Early High Civilization
(ca. 3200–2800 B.C.)

The term "early high civilization" comes from a period when research into the history of the Near East had advanced to the point where the external chronological parameters and some of the specific characteristics of the individual periods had become clear, but the details that would have allowed us to understand the internal connections of the society in question were not yet known. The fact that cylinder seals, writing, monumental architecture, and art—all of which played such an important role in the later development of the Near East—emerged in Babylonia within a short space of time led people to conclude that this era represented a particular high point in history. They likewise felt justified in assuming, from the sudden emergence of these achievements, that the culture of the previous period had been at a notably low point of development. "Early high civilization" is moreover, a term that stems from a period in which people had no difficulty imagining that the emergence of a new ethnic group made possible the scaling of new peaks of cultural development.

Since then, there have been developments that have obliged us to reappraise assertions about any ethnic group's unique talents. At the same time our knowledge of early periods has grown to the point where we are better able to recognize the developmental patterns underlying the complex we have grown used to calling "early high civilization." If we continue in spite of all our many reservations to use the term, "early high civilization," it is because useful, well-established terms should not be abandoned unless this is absolutely unavoidable.

Earlier, we pointed to the special role played by Babylonia which makes it necessary to consider this geographical area as a separate entity. The archaeological record speaks for itself. In all areas of the Near East, we see a trend toward gradually denser settlements and, simultaneously, the rise of structured relationships between the settlement sites. In Susiana, it even seems that a multilevel pattern of settlement had been developing, whereas the growth of settlements in Babylonia seems to have occurred considerably later than in the surrounding areas. Throughout this first, longer, period, the density of

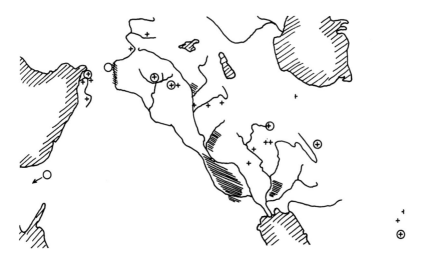

Figure 19. The Near East during the Late Uruk period. Hatched areas: the Late Uruk civilization in Babylonia, and its direct offshoots; circles: finds of cylinder seals; crosses: finds of bevel-rimmed bowls. Author's original.

settlement also never surpassed that of the first phase, and the settlement sites continued to be so far apart that, as far as we know, no possibility existed for structured relationships among them.

This picture changes completely for the period we designate as the beginning of early high civilization, the so-called Late Uruk period (named after the site of Uruk in southern Babylonia). The hinterland of the city of Uruk, one of the most intensively studied areas to date, is eminently suitable for use in studying changing settlement patterns. Within this area more than ten times as many sites appear than before, most of them so close to one another that we can easily recognize connections between them—that is, settlement systems.

These systems were not merely at the same organizational level as that already reached in Susiana, but had, in all likelihood, surpassed it by advancing a step further toward a higher level of organization. Instead of a three-tiered system, we now have a four-tiered hierarchy, with Uruk at its head (see fig. 11). With no apparent transition, Babylonia moved from a phase of individual settlements to one characterized by the most complex organization yet seen. Until recently, this sudden change remained an enigma, but it can now be explained with some degree of probability. Of course, the conclusion had already been reached in studying the evolution of the Babylonian flood plain—as an alluvial deposit at the Tigris and Euphrates—that what had at one time been an area of lagoons and swamps had only gradually been trans-formed into dry land. However, this did not explain the relatively sudden appearance of large-scale settlement, since such a silting-up process must have required a considerable amount of time, so that any growth in the amount of land suitable for habitation would have been a slow one.

The results of studies of the ancient climate and of changes in the amount of water in the Mesopotamian river system and in the Gulf, as outlined above, now present us with a clearer picture of developments in southern Babylonia. The climatic changes documented for the middle of the fourth millennium seem, within a space of two to three hundred years, to have stemmed the floods that regularly covered large tracts of land and to have drained such large areas that in a relatively short period of time large parts of Babylonia, particularly throughout the south, became attractive for new permanent settlements.

However, in saying this we must continually bear in mind that, given our telescopic view of history, a "relatively short period" can still mean thirty to fifty, or perhaps even a hundred, years. Thanks to the experience in food producing techniques gained beforehand in neighboring areas and to the organizational structures developed there, this "new land" could immediately be occupied on full scale. Hence, the development of settlement systems, to mention only this one aspect, could begin immediately at the stage already reached, for example, in Susiana. In these circumstances, we suddenly see the number of set-tlements increase more than tenfold from one period to the next and the aggregate settlement area jump from 60 to 440 hectares (fig. 20). In this case, aggregate settlement area should be understood simply as the sum of the surface areas of all sites occupied at any one time. Assuming that, on the average, the number of inhabitants per unit area remained roughly constant, the total area of settlement is a useful gauge by which to measure changes in population, without, however, the possibility of giving actual numbers of inhabitants.

The allure of this new land certainly also brought new population groups into the area, even if the growth in population resulted not from a single wave of immigration but rather from a combination of factors. One possibility may have been an internal population shift. If we com-pare maps of settlement areas in Babylonia as a whole during the Early Uruk period, which preceded the period of early high civilization, with those of the Late Uruk period in which we have noted the great increase in the number of settlements, we can see that in the earlier period the majority of settlements were clearly located in northern Babylonia.

In the following period, the number of sites in the north decreased,

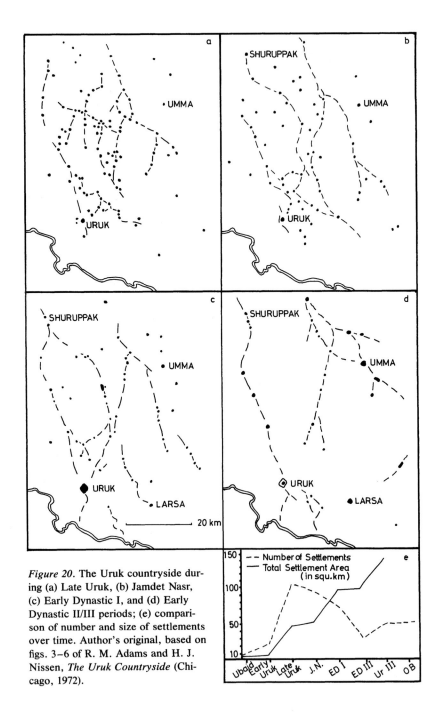

Figure 20. The Uruk countryside during (a) Late Uruk, (b) Jamdet Nasr, (c) Early Dynastic I, and (d) Early Dynastic II/III periods; (e) comparison of number and size of settlements over time. Author's original, based on figs. 3–6 of R. M. Adams and H. J. Nissen, *The Uruk Countryside* (Chicago, 1972).

68

whilst the number of sites in the south far exceeded the number that had previously existed in the north. Along with probable adjustments in settlements between the different parts of the country, it is therefore likely that by the Late Uruk period other groups had also entered the area. If there is any moment in time to which we can assign the arrival of the Sumerians with a high degree of probability, it is this first period of settlements in large areas of the southern Babylonian plain.

The net result was that Babylonia was now much more densely settled than any other part of the Near East had ever been in the previous period. This was one result of the necessity to employ irrigation, the basic techniques of which had long been known, but which never previously had to be used so systematically. As noted, however, irrigation in the earlier periods looked quite different from the way we usually imagine it to have looked in Babylonia. Even though by this time the water had receded so much that the land had become habitable, there was nonetheless for some considerable time so much water still available that nearly every arable plot had easy and direct access to it. This fact, together with Babylonia's extremely fertile soil, must have produced a "paradise," with multiple, high-yield harvests each year.

Aided by these external conditions, the amount of cultivated land necessary to support an individual had become extremely small, so that the area around a settlement needed to support its population could be smaller than ever before. In what follows we shall see how this high productivity, coupled with the high density of population it afforded, posed problems for Babylonia, the solution to which finally brought about the complex we call early high civilization.

Despite the fact that research has progressed in certain decisive respects over the past few years, our clearest examples still come from Babylonia, and there primarily from the excavations of the city of Uruk in the southern part of the region. Occupation of this site probably goes back to the very earliest period of settlement in Babylonia and, from at least the Ubaid period onward, has provided information about the chronological sequence of phases of settlement that overshadows all other evidence about Babylonia. As noted, the archaeological investigation of the countryside around the city has been almost as important as the excavations within it.

Stratigraphic excavations at Uruk and other sites in Babylonia have yielded a sequence of pottery types that have proved to be characteristic of particular periods, and that can now be used to date pottery found out of context at other sites. There are numerous sites in the area around Uruk, today mostly desert, that can be identified as ancient settlements on the basis of the visible remains of walls and, more

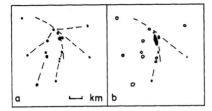

Figure 21. Group of settlements northeast of Uruk, during (a) Late Uruk, and (b) Early Dynastic I periods. Settlements abandoned after the Late Uruk period are shown as circles. Author's original, based on fig. 14 of R. M. Adams and H. J. Nissen, *The Uruk Countryside* (Chicago, 1972).

commonly, large quantities of potsherds on the surface. Given a knowledge of the ceramic sequence, it is possible to determine in which periods most of these sites were inhabited. With this information it is then possible to draw distribution maps of the area showing all the sites inhabited in any given period (fig. 20). The comparison of these maps allows us to draw certain conclusions about possible changes in the settlement of the area in question, and has thereby provided us with information that could not have been acquired through excavation. These complementary methods of research—excavation and surface survey—are particularly important in the case of Uruk, since they provide an abundance of information relevant to the problem of the interdependence of center and surrounding area.

On the basis of developments in architecture, pottery, seals, and writing, the period of early high civilization can be divided into three subperiods, conventionally known as the Late Uruk, Jamdet Nasr, and Early Dynastic I periods. Site distribution maps can be drawn for each of these three periods, and their comparison has yielded extremely informative results, showing clear developmental trends. Thus, while the absolute number of settlements decreased markedly between the Late Uruk and Early Dynastic I periods, the average size of individual settlements increased so much that a considerable overall expansion of the inhabited area can be seen if we take into account all the areas inhabited at the same time. Thus there was an increase in population, although this was probably not as spectacular as that which characterized the first phase of settlement in the period of early high civilization. The basic mechanism by which the number of sites decreased and the area of settlement increased can be inferred from several cases in which, during the Late Uruk period, we find a number of small sites clustered around a central one which, by the Early Dynastic I period, had grown much larger and remained virtually the only site in the area still inhabited (see fig. 21).

Though surely too vague, it must be noted that we nevertheless use as our basic assumption that the number of inhabitants per unit of settled area remained roughly constant. As noted above, the expansion or shrinkage of a settlement is taken to indicate an expansion or reduction in population size. It would, in fact, be possible to quote absolute figures if we based our estimates on an average, which has from time to time been suggested, from one to two hundred inhabitants per thousand square meters of inhabited area. Yet, to stay on the safe side, only the specification of relative changes from one period to the other seems in any way acceptable.

Perhaps the most impressive example of the developmental trend we have mentioned is afforded by Uruk itself. The exact limits of the site at any one time are still difficult to determine, because the survey of a city area that was continuously built upon can naturally only provide us with incomplete data. Almost the whole of the surface of the city of Uruk has, however, been subjected to a detailed investigation, so that certain trends do become visible. On the drawings shown here (fig. 22) of the plan of Uruk, only those areas that were definitely inhabited in the different periods are shown. Therefore, for each respective period they only show the minimum dimensions of the area covered by the city. The general tendency is, however, already clear: the city area grows continually into the Early Dynastic I period when its extension is delineated by the city wall, built in this period. This wall enclosed an area of some 5.5 square kilometers. In addition, not all of the area inhabited during this period lay within the wall, since

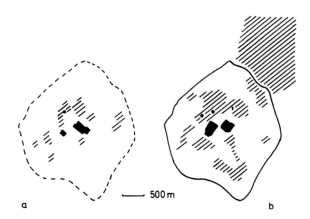

Figure 22. Minimal extent of the settled area of Uruk during (a) the Late Uruk and (b) Early Dynastic I periods, on evidence from excavations (black) and concentrations of surface finds (hatched). Author's original, using additional information provided by Dr. U. Finkbeiner, Tübingen University.

sherd scatter indicates that habitation extended a further two to three kilometers beyond the northeastern section of the city.

However, this underlines not only the general trend toward an increase in the size of settlements that characterized the period up to Early Dynastic I, but also the more general fact of the extraordinary size of Babylonian settlements. Athens, after the expansion under Themistocles, covered an area of about 2.5 square kilometers—not even half the area of Uruk. Jerusalem, after its extension under Agrippa I around A.D. 43, reached the size of 1 square kilometer. Even the metropolis of Rome at the time of the emperor Hadrian in the first century A.D. was only twice as large as Uruk had been three thousand years earlier. Having said this, it should be noted that the size of Uruk was by no means exceptional, since two subordinate settlements in the Uruk hinterland covered an area of nearly 1.5 square kilometers, which, in other parts of the world, would have been regarded as considerable even for capitals of large regions (fig. 23).

By comparing the maps shown in fig. 20 we can observe gradual changes in the system of water courses. In the Late Uruk period we see a network of small water courses of different sizes spreading out in an irregular fashion and then coming together again, a good illustration of the situation that existed in an area that had just been freed from the problem of a surfeit of water. By the Early Dynastic I period,

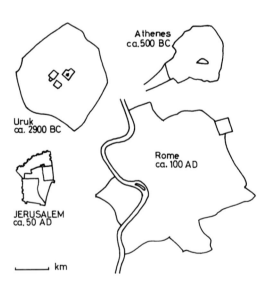

Figure 23. Comparison of the sizes of some major cities of antiquity. Author's original.

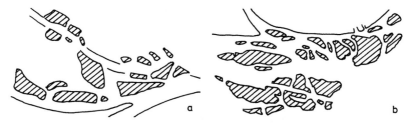

Figure 24. Marsh settlements in lower Iraq of (a) Jamdet Nasr times in the vicinity of Uruk, and (b) today (Segal in the Hor al-Hammar). Hatched areas were heavily covered with potsherds or mark the settled areas; in the modern case, the intervening spaces stand for water courses. After (a) R. M. Adams and H. J. Nissen, *The Uruk Countryside* (Chicago, 1972), fig. 12, and (b) S. Westphal-Hellbusch, *Die Ma'dan* (Berlin, 1962), plan at the end.

the picture had changed completely. In this final phase of the development of early high civilization, water was restricted to a few main courses, a pattern that was to characterize the later periods of Babylonian history, when the countryside was traversed only by the major rivers and a number of large artificial canals. Yet this development in the period of early high civilization also fits into the general picture, for the effects of the climatic change initially responsible for the drainage of certain parts of Babylonia continued, causing the ever-increasing recession of the waters from the land.

One example typifying the situation as a whole is that of a site from the Jamdet Nasr period located roughly ten kilometers north of Uruk (fig. 24a). This site was undoubtedly a marsh settlement, as a comparison between its plan and that of a modern village in the marshes of southern Iraq indicates (fig. 24b). This means that, at a time when, according to our maps, water was beginning to fall back into the limited number of river courses, certain parts of the countryside were still under water. However, the settlement did not survive into the following period, part of a trend in which this region was almost entirely abandoned. The existence of far fewer water courses in the Early Dynastic I period leads one to conclude, among other things, that considerably less water was available than previously and, above all, that large tracts of land could no longer be reached by water.

We hardly need emphasize how great the effects of such a diminution in the available water supply must have been for agriculture, and consequently for the entire economy. In fact, the continued decline in the supply of water during the following periods posed the greatest problem for society. However, for the time being this development only seems to have led to a greater concentration of land used for agriculture

Figure 25. Cylinder seal and impression from the representational group. Courtesy, Vorderasiatisches Museum, Berlin.

along the main water courses, as we can see from the fact that there was a tendency to transfer the growing settlements of the Early Dynastic I period to the remaining waterways, or, preferably, to expand sites already located there.

But let us turn back to the beginnings of early high civilization. Strata from the Late Uruk period have, for the first time, brought to light those things we consider characteristic of Mesopotamian culture in general: writing, cylinder seals, large-scale works of art, and monumental architecture. In the last two cases we should bear in mind that there may be examples from the earlier period that have not yet been found only because the older strata that have been uncovered are very limited in size. However, if cylinder seals and writing had existed before, they would have had to have been discovered. Both at first appear to belong to the artistic or literary sphere, but were in reality concrete components of economic administration, a fact established in both cases by an analysis of their use.

Unfortunately we possess only relatively few original cylinder seals from the Late Uruk period, though there are numerous seal impressions on clay. A cylinder seal is a stone cylinder, with a hole bored through it lengthwise, on the surface of which a pattern has been engraved in negative relief. When the cylinder is rolled over a plastic material, the result is a raised relief (fig. 25, 26). The material over which such seals were rolled was a specially prepared, highly plastic clay that dried and hardened quickly in the hot, dry air of Babylonia and preserved a true impression. This clay was used to seal all manner of things. It could be molded over the knot of a bundle bound with

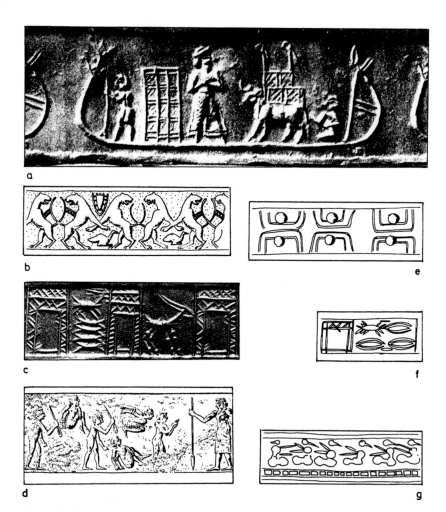

Figure 26. Seals of the Late Uruk and Jamdet Nasr periods, from Babylonia. From (a) E. Heinrich, "Kleinfunde aus den Archaischen Tempelschichten in Uruk," *Ausgr. der Deutschen Forsch. gem. in Uruk-Warka* 1 (Leipzig, 1936), pl. 17a.; (b) *Uruk Vorbericht* 5 (1934), pl. 26b; (c) H. J. Lenzen, "Die Tempel der Schicht Archaisch IV in Uruk," *Zeitschr. f. Assyriologie* 49 (1949) pl. 3, 5; (d) H. Frankfort, *Stratified Cylinder Seals from the Diyala Region,* OIP 72 (Chicago, 1955), no. 31. Courtesy, Oriental Institute, University of Chicago; (e) E. Porada, *Corpus of Anc. Near Eastern Seals in North American Collections: The Pierpont Morgan Library,* New York, 1948, no. 29; (f) Frankfort, *Stratified Cylinder Seals,* no. 49. Courtesy, Oriental Institute, University of Chicago; (g) Porada, *Pierpont Morgan Library,* no. 15.

75

rope or around the neck of a jar that had been covered with cloth and tied with string, or it could seal the rope fastening of a door.

In all cases, it was supposed to prevent unauthorized people from gaining access to what had been sealed. If the seal used bore an unambiguous representation by which anyone could recognize its owner, it is clear that there was a direct connection between the act of sealing and a particular person. If this person was the one in charge of the particular economic sphere in question, then by virtue of the authority of the seal, any tampering with what had been sealed could be ruled out.

Cylinder seals were better suited to this type of sealing than the commonly used, earlier stamp seals because they could ensure the inviolability of a much greater surface area. In fact, the bands of cylinder impressions are often so close to one another on the clay that there is not a single piece of the sealed object that does not bear an impression. Seals, then, were instruments of economic control that could be used effectively to guarantee the supervision of proceedings, even more when the amount of information exceeded what a single individual was capable of surveying, or remembering. Representations on cylinder seals therefore served two purposes. First, they had to fill up the field so that after the seal was used every part of the surface

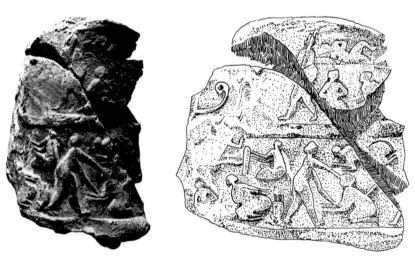

Figure 27. Photo and graphic reconstruction of a fragmentary jar cover, from Uruk. Courtesy, Deutsches Archäologisches Institut, Abteilung Baghdad. (Cf. *Uruk Vorbericht* 15 [1959], pls. 28a and 30a).

76

Figure 28. Cylinder seal and impression from the abstract group. Height 2.4 cm. Collection of the Seminar für Vorderasiatische Altertumskunde, Freie Universität, Berlin. Photo M. Nissen. (See U. Moortgat-Correns, "Die ehem. Rollsiegel-Sammlung E. Oppenländer," *Baghd. Mitt.* 4 [1968], no. 14.)

would contain recognizable traces of the original. Second, they had to permit the identification of the person who, by the act of sealing, wanted to be sure that something would remain intact.

By looking at the types of representations found on earlier cylinder seals, we can go on beyond the general observation that seals had an economic function. The fact that the representation on a seal also served to identify the seal's owner means that the breadth of variation in seal designs had to be great enough to ensure that every seal owner could be unmistakably identified by a particular design. In fact, we find that the majority of seals have designs that allow for a large amount of variation. These are mainly figurative representations composed of various human and animal forms engaged in a variety of activities (see, for example, figure 27). The fine elaboration of detail also served to increase the number of possibilities for variation (fig. 26a–c). The number of major themes—worshipping at a temple, processions of boats, prisoners before a ruler, the feeding of animals, rows of animals, and battles between wild and domestic animals—seems to have been limited. But by a change in just one detail an unmistakable original was created for each individual case.

There is, however, a large group of contemporary cylinder seals whose representations do not fit into this pattern (fig. 26d–f). These seals differ from those mentioned above in a number of ways. They are predominantly much smaller and have different proportions, and the ratio of the length of the cylinder to its diameter is 1:1, whereas for the former group this relationship is for the most part close to 2:1. More important, however, is the fact that these seals feature almost unrecognizably abstract symbols or geometric patterns, so that the seal impressions are so alike that it is very hard to imagine identifying the seal's owner on the basis of the pattern alone.

A further fundamental difference between the two groups of seals has to do with their manufacture. Whereas the representations in the figurative group were carved with extreme attention to detail, from clothing and jewelry to finely defined aspects of physique and hairstyle that could only be achieved with the finest tools, the "abstract" patterns were made exclusively with mechanical tools such as drills or cutting wheels. These are only capable of producing rough shapes—semispherical indentations and straight lines—that produce barely distinguishable patterns.

Cylinder seals from this "abstract" group could be made in a fraction of the time it would take to prepare a "figurative" seal. To attribute the differences between the two groups of seals merely to differences in the owners' social status is not an entirely satisfactory explanation, however, particularly since it is difficult to understand why lower-level administrators would not also need some means of identification.

Perhaps the answer lies in a slightly different direction and can be expressed in terms of "individual seals" versus "collective seals." To put it more clearly, we may assume a difference in the use to which the seals were put. In the one case, the kind of business needed the responsibility for its transaction, respectively a guarantee, to be ascribable to an individual. In the other case, responsibility was assumed exclusively by the administration or a branch thereof. The act of sealing could thus have been undertaken by any number of representatives of that administrative unit. An unusual archaeological situation could fit in with this assumption. Numerous clay fragments with "figurative" impressions on them (more than two thousand from the excavations in the so-called archaic levels at Uruk alone) have been found, but hardly any original seals. On the other hand, many original "abstract" seals have been found, but very few remains of sealings. Whatever the explanation may be, the two types of seals were evidently used in different ways and in different places. Unfortunately, almost all our sealings and original seals come from rubble levels, so that it is impossible to assign them to particular spheres of activity.

In the next phase, the Jamdet Nasr period, the visible differences between the two types of seal are less apparent, in that the figurative seals, formerly so detailed, were now made with the help of mechanical tools, making the reproduction of detail less and less possible (fig. 26g). However, the basic distinction remains. It is only in the following phase, the Early Dynastic I period, that new criteria come into play. The representation of one theme of the figurative seals—rows of animals—becomes, under the influence exercised on design by the cutting wheel,

Figure 29. Seals of the Early Dynastic I period, from Babylonia. From (a) H. Frank-fort, *Stratified Cylinder Seals from the Diyala Region,* OIP 72 (Chicago, 1955), no. 448. Courtesy, Oriental Institute, University of Chicago; (d) no. 236; (c) after L. Le-grain, "Archaic Seal-Impressions," *Ur Excavations III* (London, 1936), no. 431. Courtesy, Oriental Institute, University of Chicago; (b) E. Heinrich, *Fara* (Berlin, 1931), pl. 54c.

a highly decorative basket-weave, which fills the whole surface of the seal in a most ingenious manner (fig. 29d), though in these "brocade" seals we find none of the breadth of variation that distinguished earlier representations of this theme. Whereas "abstract" seals still remained in use (fig. 29a; fig. 26d–f, h), a new group of "figurative" seals arose at this time, which, although they almost exclusively represent the theme of "fighting animals" in a new style, maintain the desired range of variation, thanks to a great delight in detail (fig. 29b).

For the sake of completeness, yet another group of seals from the Early Dynastic I period should be mentioned here, even though it cannot be included in the above development. This group, which will be discussed later, is known to us only from seal impressions. The actual seals were apparently very large and had, as their sole decorative motif, rows of artistically rendered cuneiform signs spelling out the names of a varying number of Babylonian cities (fig. 29c). These seals must certainly be attributed to a third functional category.

In addition to the examples already mentioned, we have further evidence leading us to the assumption that the highly developed eco-nomic organization during the period of early high civilization required not only abstract methods of control but also other organizational aids. Given a highly developed division of labor and a well-defined hierarchy in the administration, the professions, and the political leadership, the

Figure 30. Cylinder seal and impression of the linear style group. Height 1.5 cm. Collection of the Seminar für Vorderasiatische Altertumskunde, Freie Universität, Berlin. Photo M. Nissen. (Cf. U. Moortgat-Correns, "Die ehem. Rollsiegel-Sammlung E. Oppenländer," *Baghd. Mitt.* 4 [1968], no. 5.)

stage of the village economy had been abandoned long before. In addition to the seals already referred to, further examples of this high level of development are provided both by one of the oldest pieces of written evidence and by the site of a former workshop area in the city of Uruk.

Among the most ancient written documents, which appear at the end of the Lake Uruk period, we find a fragment of a text known in its more complete form from many copies made during the next phase (fig. 31). From then on, up to the period of the Akkad Dynasty, this text was so carefully and repeatedly copied that we have an unbroken text tradition spanning more than seven hundred years. The text takes the form of a list, and is a collection of groups of signs that, as far as we know, represent the titles of officials and names of professions. Although, for the time being, we do not understand all the entries, the principles behind the arrangement emerge clearly. First come the signs of the holders of the highest offices, followed by those of officials, priests, and the specialist professions; not until the end is there a series of symbols for simple occupations. If this sequence clearly points to a hierarchical way of thinking, in which there seems to have been considerable consciousness of a fixed division of duties and offices according to rank, this impression is only further underlined by the fact that there is evidence for internal subdivision within the individual offices and professions. Three or four different ranks can be defined for one and the same description of a particular office or profession, where the top rank is, in every case, referred to as "Head X." Hence, not only are the different offices arranged in a specific order with regard to one another; there are also clearly separate ranks within each of the offices and professions.

The second example can be found in the site of a manufactory excavated in Uruk (fig. 32). On a gently sloping, smooth area of ground

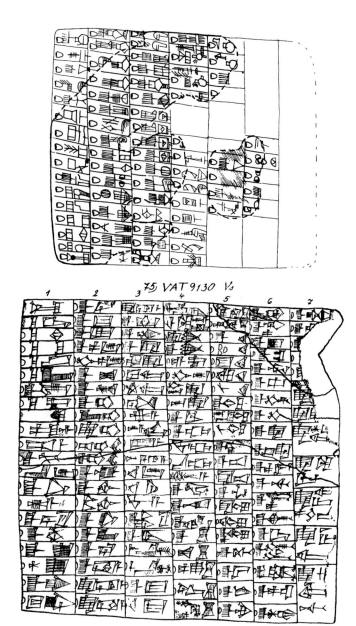

Figure 31. Copies of the Standard Professions List A: (a) dating to the Jamdet Nasr period, from Uruk; (b) dating to the end of the Early Dynastic II period, from Shuruppak. From (a) author's original, and (b) A. Deimel, "Schultexte aus Fara," *Wiss. Veröff., der Deutschen Or. Ges.* 43 (1923): 71.

81

whose surface has been baked to a gritty, brick-red, consistency by high temperatures, U-shaped channels with a cross section of about twenty by twenty centimeters have been dug out parallel to the gradient. Along the sides of the channels are rows of oval holes, eighty by forty centimeters in area and about fifty centimeters deep, whose walls have also been subjected to high temperatures. Like the channels, these holes were found to be filled with the remains of ashes when excavated.

The remarkable thing is that these fire holes, which are spaced in two or three concentric rows around the channels, are staggered in the direction of the channels. This means that there was unimpeded access to a part of the channel from each fire hole. Unfortunately, the excavations provided no direct indication as to what was produced or processed there. The only thing that is unambiguously clear is that the work involved very high temperatures. This is also suggested by the greasy black ash, which proved to be the burnt-out residue of bitumen, which lay around everywhere as cakes of fuel in the open areas that were part of the layout.

The idea that there was a metal smelting works here must unfortunately remain pure conjecture. A highly restrictive disadvantage of that period—the fact that only very small quantities of metal could be smelted at one time—could have been circumvented by pouring many such small quantities into the previously heated runoff channels, thus combining them to cast larger objects. This would fit in quite well with the fact that a whole series of Uruk texts from the period of early high civilization deal with metals and metal objects.

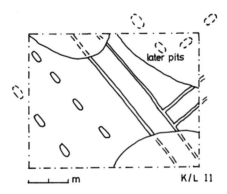

later pits

K/L 11

Figure 32. Fire troughs and fire pits of a workshop area in Uruk, dating to the Late Uruk period. Author's original. (See H. J. Nissen, "Grabung in den Quadraten K/L XII in Uruk-Warka," *Baghd. Mitt.* 5 (1970), pl. 6).

Even if we consider this interpretation too daring, there were quite clearly a number of people here doing the same job with a common aim. What we have here, therefore, is a classic case of intensification of labor, characteristic of a highly structured division of labor in the society in question.

On the basis of these two examples, it seems valid to speculate that the economic units of the Late Uruk period were rigidly structured; notwithstanding that for the present we have almost no direct evidence about what must surely have been the largest components of such units—that is, about agriculture and animal husbandry. However, it must be remembered that all of our examples come from the center of Uruk, and here, too, only from the central area of the sanctuary of Eanna, because hardly any other levels of this period have been reached. If we continue with the above train of thought and assume that these economic units must have been of a considerable size, or even that they were central to a city's economic activity, we must still concede that in the countryside there may well have been totally different forms of organization, of which we are ignorant only because no research has been done in that area. For the time being, therefore, this is no subject for generalizations.

In Uruk itself, it was clearly the very large economic unit of Eanna (fig. 38) that controlled not only agriculture, animal husbandry, and the crafts, but also trade, and that was responsible for delivering raw materials to this land that was so poor in them. Clearly, it was also responsible for the building and maintenance of the temple complex, as well as for the organization of religious festivals and the supervision of sacrifices. We find evidence for this in the numerous lists of allowances for festivals and sacrifices found among the texts of this period.

The size of the economic units is also substantiated by another type of find, which, at the same time, allows further advances in our knowledge of the character of economic organization in Uruk. Isolated examples of ceramic bowls differing considerably from other pottery of the same period had already been found in levels from the Early Uruk period. The bowls in question have a sloping edge and were made out of some very coarse, and therefore extremely porous, material. Among archaeologists, they are known as "bevel-rimmed bowls" (figs. 33, 36e). Some consideration of how these vessels must have been produced led to the observation that, unlike all the other pottery of this period, they were molded. These vessels appear in such large quantities from the beginning of the Late Uruk period onward that sometimes more than three quarters of the total amount of pottery found on any one site is of this type.

Apart from occasional larger and smaller versions, the majority of these bowls are all of the same size, with little variation. This type of bowl is, therefore, clearly so special, given the properties we have mentioned above, that we are forced to assume that it had a rather specialized function. Cheap and rapid mass production of millions of bowls of uniform size suitable only for use as containers for solid matter immediately leads us to think of a characteristic of economic organization that is not, however, actually shown to have existed until over six hundred years later.

We know from written texts of later periods that the enormous armies of workers in large economic units were paid in kind—that is, in daily rations. The major part of these rations was made up of grain. Unfortunately, at the moment we still do not know whether this kind of payment was also customary in the Late Uruk period, and if this were the case we would still have no precise knowledge about the method of distribution.

Nevertheless, not only do all the special characteristics of these bowls point to their being containers for the distribution of the grain ration, but the capacity of one of these vessels corresponds almost

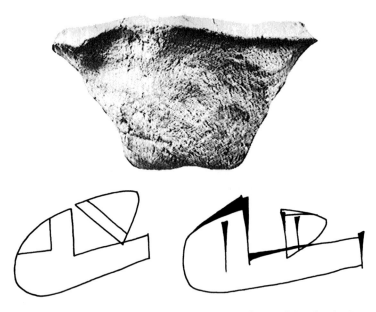

Figure 33. Bevel-rimmed bowl and the stage IV and III forms of the sign for "to eat." Author's original.

exactly to what we know to have been a laborer's daily ration. In addition, this is supported by the theory that the symbol for "to eat" in the most ancient texts is made up of the pictorial reproduction of a human head and a bowl that has the same shape as the "bevel-rimmed bowl" (fig. 33). Consequently, these bowls not only provide direct evidence of one aspect of economic organization, but are also indirect proof that units of measurement were already fixed some time before the period when standardization of units of measurement, which must certainly have also existed in other fields, can be included unequivocally among the methods of economic control (a development that can be irrefutably confirmed with the aid of the earliest written documents).

It seems almost incredible that what was obviously already a very complex administration should have managed to survive for long using simple methods of control we have been dealing with up to now. Hence we can well imagine that an attempt would have been made to expand the system of methods available to facilitate control.

In fact, during the Late Uruk period, we see the emergence of several different methods of this kind, until finally, at the end of this era, writing appears in its first form. In this case, too, the relevant discoveries are almost exclusively from the excavations of Uruk, although they all come, unfortunately, from old rubbish heaps in the central area of the city.

Tally stones are one ancient method of aiding the memory while counting (fig. 34c). While a herd of animals was being counted, for example, a stone was thrown on a pile or dropped into a container for every tenth or *x*th animal. By this method only the number can be fixed, and this only for as long as the stones or tokens are kept together. Every other aspect of the process, such as the kind of animals, the place, the time, or the people involved, must be obtained by recourse to the memory of the people taking part.

This system, whose "stones," already in earlier times—especially in Babylonia where there were no stones—had been made of clay and could thus easily be made into different shapes, was refined by having "stones" of different shapes represent different counting units: something numerous finds attest to. A further step was taken by shaping some of the pieces of clay to help one to recognize what was being counted. If such pieces of clay were kept together in containers, it was possible to carry out something like the simplest form of bookkeeping, although this clearly still meant going without a record of all the other important information involved.

The next step, shown by the material we have found, combined this token method and the system of cylinder seals, which had been

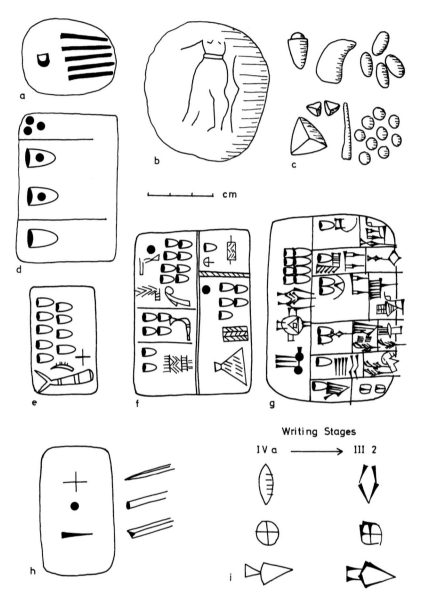

Writing Stages

IVa   ⟶   III 2

Figure 34. Examples of the early development of writing, from Uruk: (a) tablets with numerical signs; (b) and (c) sealed clay bullae and clay tokens; (d) subdivided tablet with numercial signs; (e) simple and (f) complex economic tablets of Late Uruk date (stage IV); (g) complex economic tablet of Jamdet Nasr date (stage III); (h) differently shaped styli and their marks; and (i) their influence on the shape of the signs. Author's original.

set up in the meantime. The precise number of clay pieces collected together for a specific operation were now encased in a lump of clay that was moulded into a ball, the outside of which was then covered with impressions, mostly from only one seal (fig. 34b). In this way, two important further aspects could be recorded: (a) since it was possible to identify the seal of a particular person, it became possible to name those who took part in or were responsible for an operation; and (b) here, for the first time, there was a protection against manipulation. It must, however, be conceded that this method was exceedingly laborious, which meant that it was scarcely of use for all the operations involved in economic administration.

However, there is a direct line of development from here on, insofar as in some cases there are oblong impressions on the outside of such balls that represent numbers, to judge from further developments, and that were intended to make visible on the outside the numbers encased within the ball.

The next development is linked with this one because now, for the first time, we see the emergence of flat clay slabs with the oblong signs for numbers on their surfaces, which may be completely covered by impressions of cylinder seals (fig. 34a). The same matters could now be dealt with in a much simpler way than with the use of the sealed balls. And there was an added advantage, which would later be one of the most important preconditions for the formulation of lengthier texts—with the help of simple incised lines such clay tablets could be subdivided into compartments, each of which could hold a different number (fig. 34d). This meant that several operations could be recorded on one tablet. Obviously, what was actually being counted and the time, place, and so forth still had either to be retained in the memory or distinguished by the use of particular storage places for the tablets.

After so many attempts to expand, in so many directions, the extent of what could be recorded—and there were certainly many others of which we know nothing because they have left no traces—it seems an almost logical conclusion that finally a universal means of control—writing—should have been invented, with the help of which everything could be recorded that seemed worth recording. Thus it was not only possible to record numbers and what was being counted, as well as place, time, and the persons involved. It was now also possible to describe processes that had previously evaded a uniform treatment, either because of the complexity of what was being counted, the greater numbers of people or things involved, or differing aims.

The length of this phase of preliminary testing, which leads us to the conclusion that the inadequacy of the earlier methods must have

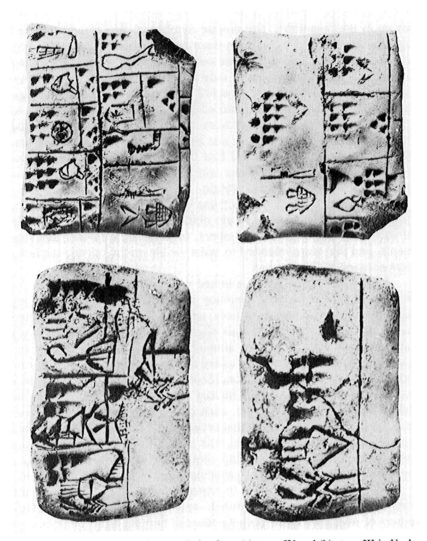

Figure 35. Complex economic texts dating from (a) stage IV and (b) stage III in Uruk. The number on the reverse results from adding up all the numbers on the obverse (round impressions = 10, elongated impressions = 1). Courtesy, Deutsches Archäologisches Institut, Abteilung Baghdad.

been very directly felt, certainly led to a situation where, after the idea of writing arose somewhere in the administration, its value was immediately recognized and it was developed into a functional instrument in the shortest time possible.

In fact, writing, in so far as it is identifiable, appears in our finds to be well developed from the outset (fig. 34e–f). Theories that the earliest writing we know of must have had more primitive predecessors can only lead to error if one searches for more primitive signs on, for example, less durable material. As we have seen, there were in fact precursors of writing, but on a different level.

This is also the case if one wishes to pursue the theory that the written sign was merely the two-dimensional transcription of pieces of clay given the shapes of the objects being counted. It may be assumed that some of these forms were taken over in writing. An example of this process of transcription is the reproduction of a container for rations as part of the symbol for "to eat." However, these tokens should in no way be seen as a sort of early form of writing.

It is not only the existence of writing that bears witness to the complex structure of economic administration. The texts themselves that describe almost exclusively economic processes also come to our aid. We are not yet able to understand these completely; but, even without knowing the contents in every case, we can make some assertions on the basis of the organization of the tablets. Thus, we find numerous tablets where the information is clearly separated into different units. On the obverse we find many different entries in the shape of numbers, together with written symbols that may stand for what was being counted, but might also be personal names. In a second section, the same entries are grouped according to specific criteria, recognizable by the partial addition of individual numbers. In the example illustrated in figure 34g, the total (8) is written in the lefthand column of the tablet. In a third section, usually on the back of the tablet, the subtotals are added up to make a final total. Here, too, we see a strict bookkeeping mentality, and there is no difficulty in matching this to the examples already quoted.

Even if we are still unable to read them in their entirety, many texts can be categorized according to their contents. Thus, for example, we can distinguish between texts concerned with the allotment of sustenance and lists of sacrifices, with the partition of fields and the keeping of herds of animals, and—of special importance to us—with the organization of metal and textile manufacture. The latter texts have a role to play when we come to deal with the commercial links between Babylonia and the surrounding countries.

Until the texts of this period have been completely analyzed, it is not possible to say very much more about economic conditions during the following two phases of the era of early high civilization, the Jamdet Nasr period and the Early Dynastic I period. As far as we can tell, there was a tendency to simplification and acceleration of operations in every sphere. For example, as already mentioned, time-saving mechanical tools such as drills and the grinding or cutting wheel were now increasingly being used in the production of figurative cylinder seals (fig. 26g).

This can also be discerned in a similar way in the production of pottery, where first the technical and then the organizational requirements were satisfied in order to facilitate mass production on the potter's wheel. It is true that the potter's wheel was already known in the Uruk period, and that in fact a great deal of the pottery of this period was produced on the wheel. However, in essence, the process involved meant that the amount of clay necessary for each vessel had to be thrown upon the wheel, after which the vessel was completed and then cut away from the clay remaining on the wheel. Then, for the next pot, a new clump of clay had to be thrown. True, there was a need for mass-produced pottery already in the Late Uruk period, but the process described above was evidently too slow. This is the reason why the vessels mass-produced in the Late Uruk period, the "bevel-rimmed bowls," were produced in molds and not on the potter's wheel.

The next innovation took place at the beginning of the second phase of the era of early high civilization, the Jamdet Nasr period. A much larger amount of clay was thrown onto the wheel and formed into a cone, and the individual vessel was produced only from the top part of the cone, so that a shape like an hourglass appeared on the wheel. After the top part of the cone had been cut off just below the narrowest section of the "hourglass," the production of the next pot could begin at once. We can draw this conclusion from the fact that from now on in many cases, and especially in the case of the so-called "flower pots" (fig. 36f), the base of the pot—formed from the tip of the lower part of the "hourglass"—is slightly extended to make a flat surface on which the pot can stand.

This technique made possible such an acceleration in the production process that the type of pots that succeeded the "bevel-rimmed bowls," the abovementioned "flower pots," could now be produced on the wheel. These new, mass-produced pots were so similar to the "bevel-rimmed bowls" in size of vessel, numbers produced, and in every other respect except for method of production that one must assume that they also fulfilled the same function.

This new way of working clay, especially the swift drawing out of the vessel from a rotating cone, demanded an intimate knowledge of the properties of clay. It was only through the creation of a special consistency in the clay that it was possible to avoid any cracking occurring during the process. This different method of preparing the clay was obviously now used to provide the basic material for all the other sorts of pottery as well, and this meant that all the pottery of this period acquired an appearance that distinguishes it from the pottery of the previous period.

In the case of writing as well, this tendency to simplification can be recognized, in that it was changed within a very short space of time so that it became much easier to use. This was achieved more than anything else through a change in writing techniques. The signs that made up the first stage of writing, from the end of the Late Uruk period,

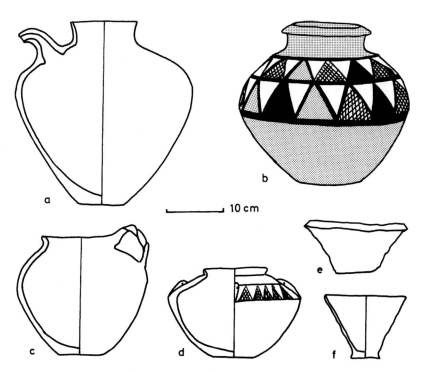

Figure 36. Pottery vessels of the Late Uruk (a, c–e) and the Jamdet Nasr periods (b, f); (e) is a bevel-rimmed bowl, (f) a conical cup. Author's original; (b) after E. Mackay, *Report on Excavations at Jamdet Nasr, Iraq* (Chicago, 1931), pl. 78, 1.

which were in part still highly pictorial, had been incised into the surface of clay tablets with a pointed stylus. In a few isolated cases, short, straight lines were impressed on the clay within the sign by holding the stylus faced at an angle. Making impressions of this sort with a stylus faced with a triangular point now became the main writing technique, which of course made it much faster to write than was possible by the old technique of incising (figs. 34h, 53).

Although the same symbols were used, and certainly the same language was being reproduced by them, many of the symbols were completely changed in their form because of the new writing technique, since not only were all superfluous details now omitted, but the fact that this kind of impression allowed only for straight lines also led to all the lines that had previously been rounded being replaced by short, straight lines (figs. 34i, 53). In addition, this new method of making slanting impressions in the clay meant that these straight lines now received a "head," which was more deeply impressed and therefore wider. Thus, the lines developed a wedge shape that was to give this type of writing its name, "cuneiform script" (fig. 53). As a parallel development, writing was also made easier by the fact that a whole series of complicated symbols were eliminated.

The changes in the way writing was used may also well have had their basis in the increased need an expanding economy must have had of scribes. Analogous further developments extending into the Early Dynastic I period also suggest indirectly that for this period, too, there must have been further developments in the field of administration. However, we have no direct evidence of this because there is a gap in the research that has been done.

The discovery of the introduction of a new building material in the Early Dynastic I period brings us to a further chapter in the changes in the socioeconomic sphere. On account of its cake-shaped, domed upper surface, this technically rather strange building material is called the "plano-convex brick" (fig. 37). This form of brick remained the standard Babylonian building material for every kind of building for almost five hundred years. The introduction of this type of brick, which is specially suitable neither for laying in normal flat courses nor for bonding, is really most curious, especially since flat bricks that were, to some extent, suitable for bonding had already been in use for thousands of years. The Late Uruk period in particular had developed, in the so-called *Riemchen,* a long, thin brick that was almost square in cross section, a building material that not only served to construct very stable walls but also made possible the multitude of patterns on the

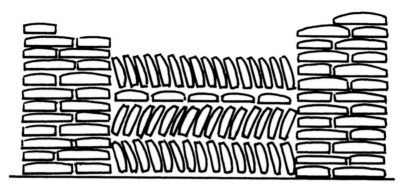

Figure 37. Shape and employment of the plano-convex bricks of the Early Dynastic period. After P. P. Delougaz, "Plano-convex Bricks and the Methods of Their Employment," *Stud. in Anc. Or. Civ.* 7 (1933), fig. 23.

facades of public buildings that were so greatly favored during this period.

One clue as to a possible explanation for the development of this new form of brick arises from the ways in which it was used, which, like the brick itself, diverge completely from the norm. Whereas the structurally important parts of a building, such as the corners or the door frames, were built up in columns made up of flat layers with the aid of a lot of mortar to fill the gaps, the sections of wall in between were constructed with the bricks set at an angle, resulting in courses that were less stable, but much quicker to construct. The bricks were laid at alternating angles. The overall impression produced by this sort of building technique is the characteristic herringbone pattern. The one convex side, which offers only a thin area of contact to the flat underside of the next brick makes it possible—because of this curved shape—to correct the direction of the brick at any point in the construction. The height of the layer of bricks can also be corrected, so that normally this type of bricklaying can be carried out very quickly and completely without attention to detail. The fact that a greater amount of mortar is necessary and that this can easily be smeared into any hollow spaces makes the speed of construction of these portions of wall even greater. This restriction of major effort to the building of the structurally important parts fits in completely with the picture sketched above. If, in addition, it is assumed that this technique made it possible for experienced and inexperienced people to work hand in hand, we would have yet another example of an expansion in the division of labor.

Although detailed evidence about economic conditions is not yet available, the examples mentioned provide a very good general impression of the state of development. Unfortunately, our information about the social sphere is far more limited. Here again, we can only exploit the previously mentioned examples, which support our assumption of a rigidly stratified society. Thus, the idea that extended families or clans no longer played a decisive role, as they must probably have done in earlier periods, is an attractive one. A wish to show this in detail, or any attempt to define individual groups or classes within the population, would place far too heavy a burden on our material.

Living quarters from this period, which could tell us something about daily life, have not yet been excavated, and the texts from this, the earliest stage in the development of writing, which would most likely tell of the functions and offices held by members of the upper class, are still not completely comprehensible to us. The only thing that is definitely clear from the examples we have mentioned is that an upper class must have existed.

Naturally, one possible way to arrive at a more exact classification of the different social strata would be to attempt to apply the social relationships we know of from a later period to this society. Here, however, we must take warning from a few instances in which, although clearly the same title is used in the early period as in the later one, its meaning is obviously different. There are also examples where we have evidence to show that different titles were used for the same office. So, for example, the titles "*en*-priest" and "*lugal*" do appear in the early texts, and both can later be used to designate the highest representatives of a city-state or a state, but they appear in isolated cases and in situations where, according to the context, they can only mean a functionary among other functionaires. In addition, in one case they both appear on the same tablet, although they later appear to be mutually exclusive as titles.

On the other hand, the aforementioned list of names of professionals and officials (fig. 31) begins with a title—not yet completely decipherable—which, in a word list of a very much later date is translated by the word for "king." Hence the titles of the higher offices were probably subject to certain changes during the period between the earliest texts and the later historical texts, which we cannot yet define because of our lack of material. Probably it was not merely the titles that changed, but above all the offices themselves. Here we must take special note of the fact that in the professions list a title appears among the highest functionaries that, at a later date, means "leader of the council." If this also applies to the period of early high civilization, what function would the council have had, and who belonged to it? These are all questions that we are unable to answer for the time being.

We have noted that the need to resolve social conflicts produced by living together in close proximity in towns and cities triggered further developments in the way the life of a community was regulated. Such conflicts must naturally be expected on a large scale, especially in a developing, stratified society that was at the same time subject to cramped forms of communal life. But it is equally self-evident that we can expect to know very little about this development.

The best example for such conflicts comes to us from the Gilgamesh epic, which, although it was put down in writing at a later date, surely contains a very much older tradition. It is highly probable that Gilgamesh was a ruler of Uruk in the period we call Early Dynastic I, so that some of the episodes recounted in the epic most likely belong historically to the last phase of the era of early high civilization. At the beginning of the poem, we are told how Gilgamesh had to suppress the people of Uruk in order to be able to erect the city wall (fig. 22b), which is described as a wondrous feat of building. This wall, the length of which was established as 9.5 kilometers, with at least nine hundred semicircular towers, has actually been identified in excavations as being a new structure in the Early Dynastic period because it was built out of plano-convex bricks.

In addition to this there are other examples of the need for forced labor on the part of the population during the construction of larger-scale buildings. At the end of the Late Uruk period, an enormous terrace was constructed in the west of the holy district of Eanna, which completely covered up the more ancient shrine of the so-called Anu Ziggurat. The excavators of this terrace have calculated that its construction would have employed 1500 people working ten hours a day for five years. This must definitely have required strong centralistic measures.

The organization of labor probably proved extremely useful in the solution of a problem that became increasingly urgent for Babylonia: the growing shortage of water. As we have already seen, in the beginning the recession of the waters, triggered by a mild change in climate, had nothing but beneficial effects. As the recession continued, however, it must finally have had a tremendous effect on an agricultural economy that relied exclusively on artificial irrigation, so that during the Early Dynastic I period settlements were no longer scattered over wide areas of the whole country, but assembled along a few water courses. In addition the river courses not only seem to run in a straightened line but, in some cases, water courses branch off from them that are so straight that they resemble, for the first time, lines of canals (fig. 20c).

If we move on to further development, we see that, from the moment we have more comprehensive textual evidence, we find unequivocal proof that the land was now no longer supplied with water exclusively from natural water courses. There were also artificial canals bringing water to areas that would otherwise have remained waterless. It may be seen as a matter of luck in the development of this area that at the moment when it became necessary to build the sort of huge canal systems that could only be constructed by great collective effort, society had already developed suitable methods for the organization of labor.

This precondition holds good, in a less unambiguous manner, for the construction of the other great works of the period of early high civilization. The enormous buildings of the precinct of Eanna in the Late Uruk period spring particularly to mind. Buildings with a surface area of 80×50 meters set the tone for the excavated part of this central area of the city of Uruk (fig. 38). Unfortunately, in spite of large-scale excavations, the organizational relationships between the different buildings in Eanna are not yet clear. Even for the buildings of the last phase of the Late Uruk period, which we know best, we can hardly say any more than that judging by their position, they were clearly related to one another in some significant way.

The older the levels, the less it has been possible to uncover, so that we are inadequately informed about the beginnings of the central area. With some reservations we may assume that large public buildings already existed in Eanna at the beginning of the Late Uruk period. This is because extensive heaps containing color-coated clay cones were discovered in the deposits from this period. This type of cone was used in Eanna for fixing and decorating the external facades of public buildings.

The first time we come across the ground plan of such a large building is in level V and even this is, unfortunately, incompletely preserved. Its foundations were constructed from limestone slabs, a building material unusual for Babylonia because it had to be transported a long way from subterranean limestone inliers sixty to seventy kilometers further west, like the one that can be seen today, for example, in the Euphrates bed near Samawa.

However, the quality of this stone is so bad that it could not be

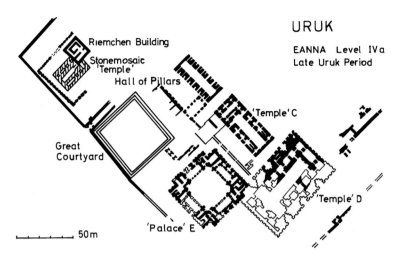

Figure 38. Plan of the level IVa buildings in the precinct of Eanna in Uruk. After H. J. Lenzen, *Uruk Vorbericht* 24 (1968), pl. 27, and *Uruk Vorbericht* 25 (1974), pl. 31.

used as a raw material for the many works of art or vessels made of stone that we know of from the period of early high civilization. For more demanding work in stone, the raw material was more likely to have been brought from the neighboring zone to the east, the central Zagros area, or, later, from the mountains of Oman.

This "limestone temple" from Archaic Level V in Eanna reveals the same plan as that of "Temple C" reproduced in fig. 38. There was a "head" part of the building, whose long, central room lay at right angles to the longitudinal axis of the building and was surrounded by small rooms, and a main part that follows the same plan in its layout but that determines the main direction of the building with its very much larger central room. A few of the rooms surrounding the main part were used for stairwells. These buildings point to an overall concept that can be found again and again in almost all buildings of the Late Uruk period.

Both this building and the buildings of the following level, Archaic IV, were clearly not destroyed by catastrophes, but had to give way to a new plan for the whole area. For this purpose, the walls of the buildings were removed until only a short stump was left and the rooms and courtyards were filled in with demolition material in such a way that a gigantic, flat area was produced.

97

One consequence of this planned demolition was that not a single trace of the original furnishings of the buildings was to to be found in them. The only things that can be connected with the function of the buildings are specially shaped fireplaces in the middle of each of the large courtyards or central spaces. Thus we can find out next to nothing about the function of each of the buildings individually.

Because of their monumental size and the fireplaces, these buildings have been designated "temples" by excavators, whereas another large building, which has a square ground plan, has been given the name of "Palace E" (fig. 38). However, since we know so little about the system of political leadership in this community and nothing can be said about the function of the buildings based on internal evidence, they really ought only to be designated "public buildings." The results of excavations in a residential area in Syria from this period, discussed below, suggest caution. These buildings with the same ground plan and similar fireplaces to the so-called temples of Uruk were found to be the respective centers of residential complexes. Therefore, this type of building could quite clearly be a standard building unit, which was only endowed with its specific function through position, size, and other characteristics as yet unknown to us.

During Archaic Level IVa—that is, the last level of the Late Uruk period—there are in the central area of Eanna, besides the buildings that correspond to the type of plan already mentioned, a number of buildings that were obviously based on different notions. For example, the enormous dimensions of the pillars of a building northwest of "Temple C" lead us to conclude that there must once have been a very high, perhaps vaulted, building here. The so-called Hall of Pillars was open on all sides, and on the individual pillars there was a complicated mosaic decoration of colored clay cones.

The "Stone Cone Temple" seems to have been a very special building with its own perimeter wall inside the long perimeter wall that circled the whole precinct of Eanna. This can probably be traced back to the fact that it predates the period in which the perimeter wall round the precinct was built. Here, the mosaics on the walls of the building and on the wall itself were made of cones made out of different colored stones.

To the southeast of this was a large, square sunken courtyard with a bank all around it in which, apart from the remains of a water pipe, there is nothing that allows any conclusions to be drawn about the purpose it once served.

Finally, in our catalogue of the different types of buildings, we must not forget "Palace E," which has the largest central space, oc-

Figure 39. The so-called Stone Mosaic Temple at Uruk. From E. Strommenger and M. Hirmer, *5 Jahrtausende Mesopotamien* (Munich, 1975), pl. 13. Courtesy, Hirmer Photoarchiv, Munich.

cupying 30 × 30 meters. All these buildings demonstrate such characteristic properties that we are forced to assume that they served specific purposes. Unfortunately, these functions cannot be defined. But the fact that they all appear to be related to one another, and their variety, makes it clear that all the activities in this area of Eanna obviously sprang from very differentiated concepts.

It is certain that the buildings that served the actual cult ceremonial were also in this central area. This can be inferred from the fact that the writing tablets of the time, which, in part, deal with matters connected with the cult, were all found in the precinct of Eanna. As noted, we are still not in possession of evidence that would enable us to determine the function of the buildings. If one does not wish to regard the buildings that have been excavated as belonging to the cult, it should be pointed out that large areas of Eanna have still not been investigated and that we can certainly expect to find other sorts of buildings there. On the one hand, this conclusion can be drawn from the fact that the area which later on was the midpoint of the central precinct has not been accessible to excavation because of the later building over, in the form of the temple on a stage tower, the Ziggurat. On the other hand, we feel justified in making this assumption because thus far we know of no structures that can unambiguously be identified as warehouses or commercial buildings. However, it is precisely this sort of building that we could expect to find in Eanna because the thousands upon thousands of broken clay tablets and sealed fastenings that ended up on the old garbage heaps of Eanna definitely came from the rubbish cleared out of such administrative buildings.

For the time being we are also dependent on very few clues for our knowledge of the field of religion itself because, although the texts repeatedly quote the names of gods, and especially the name of the goddess Innin, who is later described as the city goddess of Uruk and the Lady of Eanna, these are hardly ever placed in a clear and unequivocal context. Numerous examples of well-defined local cult traditions in Babylonia may well support the thesis that Innin already played a role in Eanna in the early period, if not the dominant role.

Unfortunately, the probability of cult traditions for other divinities cannot be shown in the same way. We would especially like to know more about the god of heaven, An, who played a very significant role in Uruk at a very much later period and seems even to have exceeded the old city goddess in importance then. During this late period, the main cult center of the god An was situated in a gigantic new temple complex rising up above the terrace whose construction in the Late Uruk period has already been mentioned. Because this terrace had buried the earlier high temple in the western part of the city, it was assumed for a time that there was a cultic tradition in this place, and, for this reason, the old, enclosed high temple was linked with the cult of the god An. This is why this high temple in the western part of the city of Uruk is called the Anu Ziggurat. (*Ziggurat* is the term for the stepped pyramidal mounds surmounted by a high temple that were the cultic centers of almost all Babylonian cities at a later period.) However, a bridge of almost three thousand years would have to be reckoned with because we have no remains from the area in question for such a long period.

Excavations in this western area of Uruk, which we may perhaps call by the place name known to us from later texts—Kullaba—have unfortunately only extended a little way beyond the temple terrace itself. So we know nothing about its placement within a larger context. Research has, however, shown that a shrine in the form of a temple standing on a high terrace with steep sides, already existed during the Ubaid period, and that from that time on the terrace was always only repaired, given a new exterior, and raised. The remains of the old temple were sometimes included in the raising of the surface upon which the new temple was then constructed. Not only are the origins

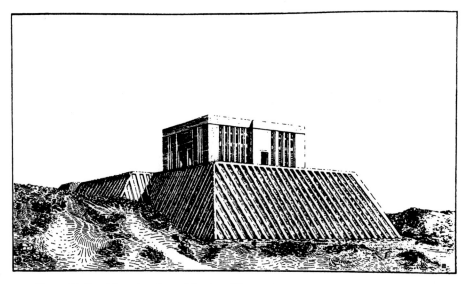

Figure 40. Graphic restoration of the Anu Ziggurat in Uruk. From A. Nöldecke, *Uruk Vorbericht* 7 (1936), fig. 5.

of this shrine considerably older than those of the larger buildings in Eanna, they are older than all other remains in Eanna which, lying at the foot of a deep shaft, turn out to be the remains of reed and mud huts. One may rightly regard the western area as the kernel of the whole great settlement of Uruk.

Whether or not An can be shown to be the god of the western temple area, we can, in any case, deduce from the completely different layout of the two shrines in the Late Uruk period that there must have been greater differences here than can be expressed merely by the assumption that we are dealing with different divinities.

While in the western area, a terrace that was a good ten meters high, on which stood a high building visible from afar, the precinct of Eanna was completely differently organized. All the buildings were erected upon flat ground without the slightest elevation. Whereas in the western area it was already impossible, from the point of view of building, for there to be more than one cult building, the layout of Eanna does not exclude the possibility that several such cult buildings were in use simultaneously. This difference in external organization can definitely be traced back to differences in the organization of the cult and can thus also clearly be traced back to different basic religious concepts.

The development into the following phase shows how far removed we still are from grasping these basic ideas. The whole of the central area, both the earlier western part and the eastern part, was now, at the end of the Late Uruk period or the beginning of the Jamdet Nasr period, so altered that no part remained untouched. For the last time, all the buildings standing in Eanna were razed, in the manner we have described above, and the stumps of the walls were covered over so that an expanse of enormous size was created. At the same time, the gigantic terrace to the west of Eanna, which was so high that it buried the high terrace, including the temple on top of it, within itself, was constructed. The former shrine in the west of the city was thus removed from view once and for all. Now, in place of the diverse buildings of the Late Uruk period, a high terrace, such as was formerly only to be found in the west, arose in Eanna. Presumably it also had a temple on top of it, the remains of which are, however, just barely accessible in outline under the dominating edifice that makes up the later Ziggurat of Eanna. From now on, instead of two cult areas, the city of Uruk had only one, which was laid out in the same way as the "buried one."

Figure 41. Find situation in the "Riemchen" building in Uruk. From H. J. Lenzen, *Uruk Vorbericht* 14 (1958), pl. 34a.

Here, too, it is unfortunately impossible to trace the directions of the change that lay behind this building program. Possibly it happened as the result of a political consolidation. It is at the very least obvious that changes must have taken place that had a tremendous effect on the religious and political life of the city. This situation, in which the only central cult area in the city had as its focal point a terrace surmounted by a temple, remained from that moment—for almost three thousand years—the determining element in the city, until, finally, late in the first millennium B.C., two new temple complexes were built in the western part of the city.

As we have said, all buildings, including the possible cult installations, were completely emptied before they were razed. In only one case has pure chance provided us with a small building that was constructed underground, the so-called *Riemchen* Building, made of the special kind of elongated bricks characteristic of the period. This was in the immediate neighborhood of the so-called Stone Mosaic Temple and was clearly designed to act as a repository for the former inventory of this or some other temples (fig. 38).

Unfortunately, we cannot reconstruct the exact arrangement of the findings at the original place, but we do at least get a good idea from the finds of the composition of such fittings. In addition to a great number of sometimes unusual pottery vessels and large containers made of colored stones, there were countless pieces of stone inlay that originally served as a decoration for furniture and—the most important find—fragments of a larger than life-sized human head made of stone. The latter are, of course, especially interesting, although they can no longer be pieced together because many pieces are missing. They must already have been fragments when they came into the building. Apart from the fact that these are the earliest remains of large human sculptures in Babylonia, there was a special interest in the observation that on a fragment of the hairline there seemed to be traces of a flat bump, possibly traces of a horn. If substantiated, the fragments could have belonged to a divine statue, as later horns always served as a mark of the gods in human form. Yet, neither could the observation be confirmed, nor can we be sure of the validity of that mark of distinction. Accordingly, we cannot be sure whether some figures on cylinder seals and on the "cult vase" from Uruk should be recognized as representing images of gods.

The so-called cult vase, a large vessel made of limestone, decorated in relief, is one of the most splendid pieces from the period of early high civilization (fig. 42). In spite of a certain amount of damage, the thematic relations between the four friezes are sufficiently clear.

In the lowest frieze, stylized plants or ears of grain are shown standing above water, which is represented as a wavy line; in the band above this one, goats and sheep looking to the right alternate with one another. In the next frieze, a row of naked men can be seen looking to the left, carrying in front of them gifts in baskets and in open and closed vessels. On the top frieze, the main direction of the figures is changed once more. In the left half of our figure, it is still possible to discern the remains of three human figures turning to the right. They are also carrying gifts in front of them, or something that has come to be referred to as a "cult fillet." In front of them, and looking in their direction, stands what is probably a female figure in a long coat, who previously wore a tall headdress, of which, because of some ancient damage, unfortunately only a small part is still recognizable. Certain traces could suggest a pair of horns, which would identify the figure as a goddess. But even without the horns this figure can be designated the main personage in the whole composition, as may also be seen from the objects reproduced behind the figure. Among these, special note

Figure 42. Form and decoration of the "cult vase" from Uruk, dating to the Late Uruk–Jamdet Nasr period. From E. Heinrich, *Kleinfunde aus den Archaischen Tempelschichten in Uruk,* (Berlin, 1936), pls. 2, 38.

must be made of the two so-called reed-ring bundles, the original door posts in the traditional reed architecture of the country: in the loops on either side of the door opening hang the poles around which the rush mats that served as door curtains were wound. These can probably be interpreted here, as later, as symbols of the goddess Innin, the city goddess of Uruk (compare the second sign in the first box in the lefthand column of text in figure 34f). On two small tables shaped like rams there are small human figures, certainly statues, which, like the objects and vessels shown behind them, could have belonged to any cult inventory. The whole sequence on the cult vase represents a procession whose leaders are being received by the goddess or by a priestess. It is interesting that two of the vessels portrayed in the uppermost frieze have exactly the same shape as the cult vase itself, from which conclusions about the function of the relief vessel itself may perhaps be drawn.

Apart from the content of the friezes, we are interested in their composition, the strict ordering of which can be explained by a belief to which we have found repeated references. It is not only by their external framing—for example, the gradually increasing heights of the friezes—that the pictorial strips make the uppermost inevitably appear to be the most important. The water, plants, animals, ordinary people, and people of higher rank in the strips are arranged in such a way that the sequence must, of necessity, illustrate a view of the world that carefully fits man's own existence into a hierarchy by comparing him with all the surrounding phenomena. Here, perhaps, the intellectual roots of the conversion of all areas of life into a hierarchy are most clearly visible.

We possess numerous works of art from the period of early high civilization, mostly however objects in isolation, torn from their context, so that we can say nothing of their function or intent. The question of whether they had a cultic connotation or not would probably in any case not be the right one to ask in this form, since we are not even in a position to answer the question of whether there was a distinction of any sort made between cult and noncult objects. On another level, the question of whether there were differences between public and private art can also not yet be answered, because, up until now, the interests of the excavators have only been directed at the public areas of these settlements, and hence private houses in Babylonia from this period are unknown. Most of the objects known to us probably do, therefore, come from this public sector of the community.

We are left with more open questions than positive answers. We can, however, still conclude that in the period of early high civilization communal energies were evidently released to such an extent that

Figure 43. The "Lady of Uruk" and the "Little King," both from Uruk, dating to the Late Uruk–Jamdet Nasr period. From A Nöldeke, *Uruk Vorbericht* 11 (1940), pl. 1; H. J. Lenzen, Uruk *Vorbericht* 16 (1960), pl. 17a.

speedy and comprehensive changes took place in all fields of life. This energy was so great that the rate of change increased rather than decreased in the following two to three hundred years during which a development took place in Babylonia that influenced the course of history more enduringly than many another.

The discussion has thus far centered on Uruk and its hinterland because hardly anything is known about other places in Babylonia, such as, for example, Ur, Lagash, Nippur, and Kish, during the period of early high civilization apart from the fact that they were inhabited. The things found there have such a direct connection with the finds from Uruk that we can certainly assume that there was the same cultural context throughout Babylonia. We should like to know more about mutual relations between the larger centers, but our material is inadequate for this.

If we assume, for the time being, that Babylonia was subdivided into a number of political entities, each of which—as was the case with Uruk—consisted of a center with a surrounding hinterland, then this corresponds to a picture that, it is true, matches situations of a later date, but that so far is not confirmed by anything at all. As we shall see, considerable expansion of trade took place, radiating outward from Babylonia, above all during the Late Uruk period. This expansion proceeded in all directions in the Near East and was connected in part with the setting up of "colonies," and in part simply with a strong cultural expansion, for which—in addition to economic necessity—a political imperative must also have been operating. Was every center active on its own, or was there—perhaps for this purpose alone—something like a supraregional political alliance?

Epics, which were admittedly written later, but which in part describe events from the period of early high civilization, allow us to assume that the initiatives proceeded rather more from individual cities. Thus, for example, the Enmerkar epic tells us about the economic relationship between Uruk and Aratta, a city in what is today central Iran that has not yet been located. No other centers in Babylonia are mentioned as being linked with the outside world in this way, but we lack the basic evidence to say anything more definite on the subject.

Though linkage must, of course, always have existed on a more general level, the first signs of some sort of institutionalization of the relationships of these political units with one another are from the last phase of the period of early high civilization, the Early Dynastic I period. These are the cylinder seal impressions found in many different places in Babylonia, especially at Ur, that bear nothing but the written symbols for various cities (fig. 29c). The theory that in this case we are dealing with the official seals of economic unions to which the cities mentioned on the seals all belonged is a very plausible one. Unfortunately, this period has left us so little information about itself that this theory cannot at present be supported by anything else. Further discussion will, however, show that such unions would fit in completely with the general picture of development.

Susiana, the foremost of Babylon's neighboring regions, had seen a diversity of new developments in the period preceding the early high civilization period. Physically, this region is very similar to Babylonia. It, too, was an alluvial plain created by rivers in a section of the large rift valley whose southern part is now covered by the Gulf. However, one difference has already been mentioned, namely, that Susiana lay in an area where, for the larger part, dry farming was still possible.

According to the previous chapter, it might be expected that, of all the areas in the Near East, Susiana would be most likely to show the same development as Babylonia. The fact that this assumption does not hold true must be explained in detail. First of all, however, we must give a short sketch of Susiana's development.

Situated in the direct foreland of the Zagros Mountains, Susiana was probably never marshland, except for its southern part, which

107

even today has hardly been settled. Thus, from the most ancient time on, Susiana represented a large coherent tract of settlement land that awaited exploitation as soon as the organizational and technical preconditions came into being. In the previous chapter we saw how this led to a continuous development of settlement in Susiana, which, in the Middle and Late Susiana phases, that is, at the time of the Ubaid period in Babylonia, had led to a relatively dense settlement of the land. The complex settlement systems, with the creation of centers, that grew up under these conditions contrasted with the widely separated isolated settlements in water-logged Babylonia. However, on the whole, both areas formed parts of a greater unity. The surprising thing comes with the changes that led to the next phase.

Unlike the development in Babylonia, where a slow change took place from the painted pottery of the late Ubaid period to the unpainted pottery—made on the potter's wheel—of the Uruk period, with some repetition and parallel developments in the intermediate phase, in Susiana, the richly painted pottery of the Late Susiana phase was followed directly—with no noticeable transition—by unpainted pottery, thrown on the wheel, of the sort we know from the Uruk period in Babylonia. This observation suggests that this clearly recognizable pottery was developed in Babylonia and taken over by Susiana.

This statement can be expanded. In Susiana, it was not only the special way of producing pottery that was taken over, but also almost all the other developments we have learned of in Babylonia. Thus, for example, we again find all the details previously assembled in trying to build up a picture of economic conditions. On the one hand, we have the mass appearance of bevel-rimmed bowls; on the other, tally stones, sealed balls, cylinder seals from both of the large groups, clay tablets that only have impressions of numbers on them, and, finally, writing. It is no easy task to define an independent development in Susiana at this time. Since the excavations in Susa and in other places that reveal strata from this period have not led to the uncovering of such large areas as in Uruk, we have to regard the absence of large buildings and of monumental sculpture as pure chance; but other differences may justifiably be regarded as significant.

One important argument in favor of the idea that, in spite of all the things they had in common, there must also have been fundamental differences, is provided by an examination of the writing. It seems to emerge in its usable form somewhat later in Susiana than in Babylonia. It is true that it corresponds exactly to Babylonian writing in the materials used and in the technique and elements of writing, but it uses different symbols and most probably reproduces a different language.

Unfortunately, efforts to decipher these tablets have not yet been successful. Close inspection also reveals differences in the things represented on the cylinder seals. In Susiana, these are drawn from a wider thematic area than in Babylonia and, judging by the way they are put together, may well be based partly on different concepts. Thus, whole series of seals show scenes connected with the theme of the siege and conquest of a city or scenes representing the erection of buildings, themes that were of course actualities in Babylonia too, but were apparently not depicted there. The common factors mentioned above were therefore probably more related to economic and other forms of organization. We can deduce this from the fact that all the things necessary for organization, such as all means of control, even including

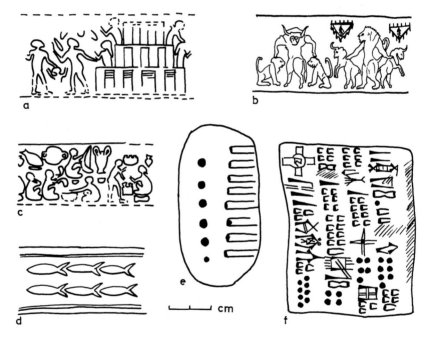

Figure 44. Cylinder seals and protoelamite tablets from Chogha Mish (a,c) and Susa, dating from the Late Uruk–Jamdet Nasr period. After (a, c) P. P. Delougaz and H. J. Kantor, "New Evidence for the Prehistoric and Protoliterate Culture Development of Khuzestan," *Vth Congress of Iranian Art and Archaeology* (Teheran, 1972), pl. 10b, d; (b) L. Legrain, *Memoirs de la Del. Arch. en Perse* 16 (1921), no. 330; (d) P. Amiet, "La Glyptique de l'Acropole," *Cahiers de la DAFI* 1 (1971), fig. 43.10; (e) A. Le Brun and F. Vallat, "L'Origine de l'écriture a Suse," *Cahiers de la DAFI* 8 (1978), fig. 4; (f) V. Scheil, *Mem. de la Del. Arch. en Perse* 17 (1923), pl. 7, no. 45.

the system of ration containers, had been taken over. Each area's own cultural traditions were probably largely untouched by all of this and took their own shape as soon as an opportunity presented itself.

This strong mutuality seems to have lasted for a relatively short time, that is, only during the Late Uruk period. The extent to which this mutuality had already begun to dissolve in the following phase is shown, for example, by the fact that from the Jamdet Nasr period on, the system of distributing rations using special containers was no longer maintained, at least not according to the Babylonian pattern. The earlier mass-produced types of bevel-rimmed bowls, which were just as numerous in Susiana as in Babylonia, had no successors. Among the subsequent types of pottery found in Susiana there is no type that can in any way be described as mass-produced, whereas the development in Babylonia during this and the following period was characterized precisely by the spread of mass-produced wares.

On the other hand, one aspect of the complex from the Uruk period, which probably fell victim to new forms of organization in Babylonia after the Late Uruk period, survived in Susiana—the car-

Figure 45. Protoelamite seals, from Susa. From L. Delaporte, *Musée du Louvre, Cat. des cylindres orientaux I* (Paris, 1920), (a) pl. 24.8, (b) pl. 26.7.

rying out of business transactions with faraway regions, insofar as this can be perceived through archaeological methods. Tepe Sialk, Tepe Yahya on the central Iranian plateau, and Shahr-i-Sokhtah in distant Seistan are probably examples of such outposts that retained their connections with Susiana.

Similar differences to those we have mentioned before can be observed in writing. From the sort of rapid changes that took place in Babylonia the conclusion can quite unambiguously be drawn that the aim was to make writing more readily usable, so that the range of uses for writing obviously became larger. However, in Susiana the form of writing remains remarkably static. During the period that in Babylonia brought far-reaching changes in writing techniques, and thus in the appearance of writing, there is no sign of any internal changes at all in writing from Susiana. After a short time this so-called "proto-Elamite" writing even ceased to be used. This happened at a time when writing in Babylonia gradually found itself on the way toward the stage of development that, for the first time, allowed complicated texts to be written down in faithful detail.

It is almost superfluous to point out that changes in building techniques because of the introduction of the plano-convex brick, which we referred to when discussing the sphere of development of socio-economic conditions in Babylonia, also did not occur. Here, the normal building material remained the flat brick, which had been in use for a very long time.

In Babylonia a culture was constantly expanding both internally and in relation to the outside world. In place of this, in Susiana during the period contemporary with the Early Dynastic I period in Babylonia, we find a form of economic and cultural life that, in its outward expression, was rather more similar to what we know of in Susiana before the assumption of the civilization of the Late Uruk period. Things we have seen to be essential yardsticks for the further development of civilization, such as writing and cylinder seals, were no longer developed independently here, and only art found a new sphere of activity in its old medium, the painting of pottery, which had ceased to be practised in the intervening period.

This whole development is remarkable because, as noted, conditions and opportunities in both areas were, at least for a time, so similar that one might reasonably expect that forms of economic organization would also be similar or the same. There must, therefore, be an explanation for the fact that this form of civilization could expand and develop further in Babylonia, but collapsed in Susiana. However, here we must remind ourselves that this form of civilization grew up

111

in Babylonia and was merely taken over by Susiana. Thus we are, once again, thrown back on the question of why this form should occur in Babylonia and not in the neighboring areas.

We have already given a general answer to this question by pointing to the relatively sudden opportunity for settlement that arose in this large, coherent habitable tract of land, to the necessity of providing the land with artificial irrigation, and to the greater density of settlements that this made possible. On the other hand, the fact that, in spite of the absence of these criteria, the civilization of the Late Uruk period could be taken over almost in its entirety by Susiana shows how low the threshold must have been that prevented Susiana from achieving the same degree of organization by its own efforts.

The greater the change in organizational forms suited specifically to conditions in Babylonia, the higher this threshold grew, so that with the sharp pace of change in Babylonia, the time soon had to come when new organizational structures created there no longer had any meaning for the management of living conditions in Susiana, because of differences in scale. Then the answer could no longer lie in a retention of the forms that had been taken over, but in a return to forms of organization more relevant to Susiana's own conditions. This development allows us to return to one of our former lines of thought, because we can hardly think of a better example for the proposition that in the Early Period the size of the interconnected economic and settlement areas was closely related to the degree of complexity of forms of organization.

On account of this fundamental difference between the two great plains, it is in no way possible for us to fill in the gaps in our knowledge about conditions in Susiana by using our information about Babylonia. We can find no evidence for Susiana to confirm what has already been said about the state of the division of labor and the strict hierarchy, or about forced labor as a means of carrying out a great collective project, though we cannot on this account rule out these forms of organization. The fact that we know of high terraces, which must definitely have originally been surmounted by temples, as the only form of cult buildings, a form that has its equivalent in Babylonia, still gives us no right immediately to draw conclusions from this about common factors in the field of religion. But we also find no material from the early period that would support the assumption that religious concepts differed greatly, as they did in the later period. At points like this, when we already possess a considerable number of pieces from the original mosaic, gaps in our knowledge become more apparent than in other places.

As we said earlier, up to this time the Zagros area was always in the front line of developments. After a dense pattern of settlement had spread out during the Late Susiana period by creating settlement hierarchies in valleys and on small plains, the changeover to the phase that corresponds roughly to the Uruk period in Babylonia is even more striking. In rare agreement, all surface investigations of these valleys and plains in the Zagros Mountains have shown that the number of settlements shrank considerably, if indeed any one of these settlements survived into this period at all. One impressive example of this is the small plain of Behbehan, which has already been mentioned (fig. 15), where there is not a single pottery fragment to indicate that the rich settlement tradition of the previous period was carried on. It is only on very few such plains that at least one settlement remained alive.

Although we are far from being able to explain this phenomenon at the moment, we must at least compare it to the observation that some of the places that remained developed in a particular manner. At Godin Tepe in the northern Zagros region, for example, in an area that had also always displayed markedly local development in earlier periods, the changes are especially clearly visible. On the plain on top of the settlement hill, formed by several meters of the debris of earlier settlements, is a complex distinguished by its architectural form, that in addition provided finds that not only contrast with the characteristics of local development but can also be connected with the sort of inventory we know from the Late Uruk period in Babylonia and Susiana. Clear evidence for the fact that here we are dealing with a rather different phenomenon to the relationship between Babylonia and Susiana is provided by the appearance, within an otherwise local context, of architectural forms; cylinder seals; clay tablets with perhaps rudimentary, but nonetheless clearly recognizable, written signs; and pottery that, although it does not correspond exactly with that from Babylonia and Susiana, resembles it more than it does the local pottery.

Too little research has been done to make a generalized observation that settlements at one time retreated to fewer, but larger, sites, and that in addition these were subject to considerable external influence. Even so, similar observations can be made in places as widely separated as Tepe Sialk on the eastern slopes of the Zagros Mountains or even in Tepe Yahya in southern central Iran, near Kerman. In addition to the local milieu, there is clear evidence of some alien influence.

Although some objects found can be recognized mostly as alien, the peculiarities are, unfortunately, hardly so pronounced as to allow us to reconcile them with the finely differentiated sequences in Ba-

Figure 46. View of the citadel of Godin Tepe (Iran). Courtesy, T. C. Young.

bylonia and Susiana. It is therefore, at the moment, impossible to fix exactly the point in time when this process of reaching out into the neighboring regions to the east and northeast began, apart from the fact that it took place during the Late Uruk–Jamdet Nasr period.

An exact identification is only possible in one case, and that is with Tepe Malyan, a site on the eastern side of the Zagros Mountains at some considerable distance from the western lowlands. The small border plain on which Tepe Malyan lies is known more than anything else for the fact that the monumental structures of Persepolis were later erected there. Tepe Malyan reveals a long period of common interest with Susa. Thus the inscriptions dating from a later period that were found there made it possible to identify the site with Anshan. Anshan later became well known as a fixed part of the political entity of Elam. Afterwards, in the historical periods, Elam clearly politically linked areas that were geographically separated from one another by the traverse mountain chains of the Zagros area. A close similarity to Susa can also be confirmed for the early period, so that here too, we must consider the possibility of political affiliations, even if we have no further information to confirm such an assumption for the early period.

The reduction in indications of direct relations between the mountain regions and the lands to the west of the Zagros—with the exception of the cases already mentioned—and even the extensive abandonment of land that had earlier been heavily settled, is not therefore to be taken with any certainty as an indication of an actual retreat from large-scale relationships, but as a sign that the style of living in these regions was subject to drastic changes and that communication took place on a different level.

The use of cylinder seals and writing even beyond the confines of central Iran is certainly a sign of economic changes. However, this is definitely not meant in the sense that complex economic organizations such as could be found in the lowlands were now to be reckoned with here, but rather that these means of control were all parts of a cultural complex that was taken over as a whole. After all, it was not only the will to take over such a package that must have existed, but also the opportunity.

In these areas of what is today Central Iran, we see, in a more sharply defined way than in Susiana, how little these means of control provided answers to their own urgent problems. This is because these signs of closer direct relationship disappear as quickly as they came, without leaving behind any evidence of aftereffects. At all the sites in question, it is only for a short phase that relevant finds are available. At the very latest during the period we call Early Dynastic in Babylonia, there is not a single trace left in the rest of the Iranian area of cylinder seals, writing, or pottery showing a western influence.

Here, too, it would be a mistake to draw the conclusion that this meant a breaking off of all relations. This is because we know that Tepe Yahya, for example, was a center of production for a specific kind of vessel decorated with relief designs and made from chlorite, a stone found nearby. Products from this center were clearly sold over wide areas, including Babylonia, where such vessels have been found in levels of the Early Dynastic period. Once again, it was only the kind of relationship that had changed. We can only regret that these relationships increasingly took on forms that did not find expression in archaeologically tangible details—or took on forms we simply cannot understand.

If we now turn our attention to the lowlands to the west of the northern Zagros area just discussed, we once again find ourselves confronted with different conditions. This area has played a considerable role in providing us with information about the development of the early phases of civilization in the Near East, with sites such as Qalʾat Jarmo, Umm Dabaghiyah, and Hassuna. The northern Mesopotamian plain, with the mountain zones bordering it on the north and east, was a showplace for varied developments in the following period as well. Unfortunately, for this region too, it must be stressed that, for the time being, the evidence is still completely inadequate.

Figure 47. Fragment of a vessel made of steatite, from Bismaya (Iraq). From W. Orthmann, *Propyläen Kunstgeschichte* 14 (Berlin, 1975), fig. 76.

Thus it can be little more than conjecture, or, at least, almost inadmissible generalization, to think we can distinguish between the phases of independent change here and the far more numerous and longer phases in which northern Mesopotamia was merely an integral part of the larger settlement area that stretched from the Mediterranean to the mountains. This holds true for the whole of the early period, when, as we have seen, this region played a part in supraregional changes in pottery production, if it was not actually the center of those developments.

Just as we had seen in the other regions of the Near East, up to a phase corresponding to the so-called Ubaid Horizon, simpler forms of pottery were preferred in northern Mesopotamia. Decoration with simpler, concentric bands did not, however, totally replace the older type of painting that covered the whole surface of the vessel. Here, too, we see the tendency to shift older activities, which had not hitherto been carried out centrally, to larger working units, thus simultaneously satisfying a greater demand.

This trend continued into the following phase, which corresponds chronologically to the Late Uruk period in Babylonia. There was even less painting on pottery, and the forms of vessels are also even more restricted. This becomes very marked in the pottery we know from a total of twenty levels in the long sequence from Tepe Gawra, in the center of the northern Mesopotamian piedmont of the Zagros Mountains. Here, at the time of early high civilization, particular techniques in decoration, such as the impression of stamps on the necks of vessels and particular indented patterns, were added to the repertoire. Without the slightest difficulty, this can be seen as a completely normal development from the pottery previously dominant in the region. Thus we can regard this pottery sequence, which also turns up at other sites in the region, as a normal local development. Apart from the general trend toward simplification, it has nothing in common with developments in Babylonia or Susiana.

However, the general trend we have referred to and the discovery of a large number of stamp seals do show that here, too, we are in no way dealing with a static civilization. These seals quite obviously had the same function as cylinder seals. A less developed economy required different sorts of controls, however, and most probably needed fewer

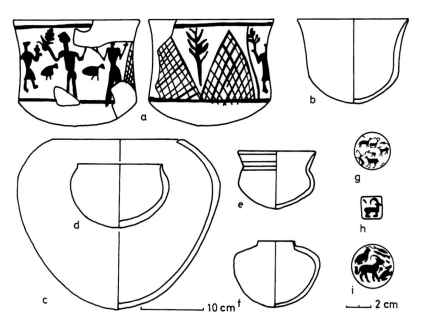

Figure 48. Pottery vessels and stamp seals from Tepe Gawra (Iraq), dating to the Late Uruk period. After A. J. Tobler, *Excavations at Tepe Gawra II* (Philadelphia, 1950), pls. 145, 147, 159.

117

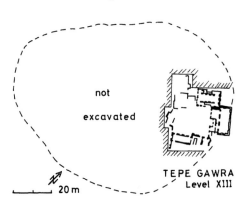

Figure 49. Probable original size and excavated area of Tepe Gawra (Iraq), level XIII, dating to the Early Uruk period. Author's original, based on A. J. Tobler, *Excavations at Tepe Gawra II* (Philadelphia, 1950), pls. 1, 11.

of them. This meant that the Babylonian forms of control, which were the most effective, but also much more complicated to use, were not necessary here. At the same time we must also bear in mind that this region was completely in the area of dry farming, and that furthermore irrigation was possible at only a few places, so that we can assume there was extensive agriculture and animal husbandry, with settlements at relatively few, widely dispersed sites.

This does not rule out the creation of centers, as is shown by the example of Tepe Gawra. There, during a somewhat earlier period, a public precinct had grown up on the already ancient settlement mound, whose sides had, in the meantime, become so steep that only limited building was possible (fig. 49). This precinct was made up of a large square surrounded on three sides by buildings that, according to everything we know, may be referred to as temples. This public area took up almost a quarter of the total surface of the mound that could be built on. Since this can hardly be said to correspond to the normal size ratio between public and residential areas, we may rightly suppose that the importance of this central area of the settlement extended beyond the limits of the site itself. Unfortunately, we know of no sites in the direct environs of Tepe Gawra that could have belonged to a settlement system with Tepe Gawra at its center. This can surely be put down to the limited archaeological research done in the region.

Though the development of pottery as we know it from Tepe Gawra is to be seen as the norm for northern Mesopotamia, it was not the only kind produced. Here we find several places that, though they did produce pottery of the type known from Tepe Gawra, also produced things typical of late Uruk civilization in Babylonia in far greater numbers. Thus, in the deepest levels of ancient Nineveh, which have, unfortunately, been only very inadequately excavated, we find numerous cylinder seals and seal impressions, bevel-rimmed bowls, and a series of other vessels typical of the Late Uruk civilization.

It is impossible to say anything about the exact chronology of these levels in comparison with developments in Babylonia or in Susiana because the finds have hardly been examined in detail. In these finds, we do however possess irrefutable evidence of the fact that there was direct influence from the civilization of the Late Uruk period in Babylonia in northern Mesopotamia as well, though it did not embrace the whole region as it did in Susiana. Rather, it affected islands in an area that continued to develop culturally in a different way.

The very limited excavation work done in the old city of Nineveh does not allow us to make any statements about the architecture. It would be a miracle if large works of art had in fact been found there. A few other sites in northern Mesopotamia have been just as inadequately excavated, above all the ones situated in the border zones of the mountains to the east. Even so, similar collections of finds are known to us from these places as from Nineveh, even though they are not in context. From these finds we can draw the conclusion that a direct connection with the south was not an isolated phenomenon.

Given the fact that a normal local tradition and a tradition that mostly shows parallels with the south of Mesopotamia existed side by side, one is forced to draw different conclusions about relations between the northern Mesopotamian area and Babylonia and those between Babylonia and Susiana. The partial correspondence we have confirmed here cannot be interpreted as meaning that the economic situation in both geographical areas was the same or similar. In the case of northern Mesopotamia, we must consider rather the existence of two different economic systems, of which one had a greater similarity with the south than the other. We can hardly assume that with settlements of the "Nineveh type" we are dealing with external support bases. For the following period, the Jamdet Nasr and the Early Dynastic I period in the terminology of Babylonia, the evidence from Nineveh and from Babylonia is far too vague for us to be able to say whether, and how, the situation changed.

During our tour through the areas neighboring the two lowland plains, Babylonia and Susiana, we have already come to know of different ways in which the local variations of a civilization reacted to what were clearly very attractive influences emanating from the lowland plains. In the Syrian area, we now encounter yet another variant. In a completely independent local development, individual settlements were founded that are absolutely identical with what we know from Babylonia and Susiana, down to the last pottery sherd in the inventory. Communication, which must have taken place in some way, can only be detected to a limited extent in the inventory of objects found in the Syrian settlements. There does not seem to have been any traffic in the opposite direction. If, in addition, we consider that these alien types

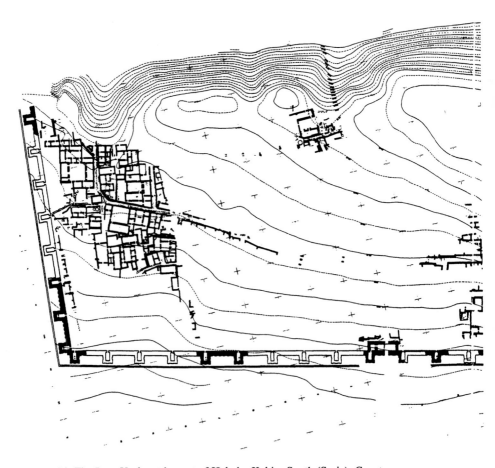

Figure 50. The Late Uruk settlement of Habuba Kabira South (Syria). Courtesy, Dr. E. Strommenger, Berlin.

of settlement were all either directly on the Euphrates or on its tributaries, there seems to be a relatively simple explanation for the whole situation. We are most probably dealing here with settlements established by people who came there directly from the southern lowland plains. Without doubt, the securing of trade interests had a part to play here—the Euphrates and its tributaries had always been the preferred trade routes—and no other motivation has been revealed to us. Of these settlements, we know one—Habuba Kabira South—very well;

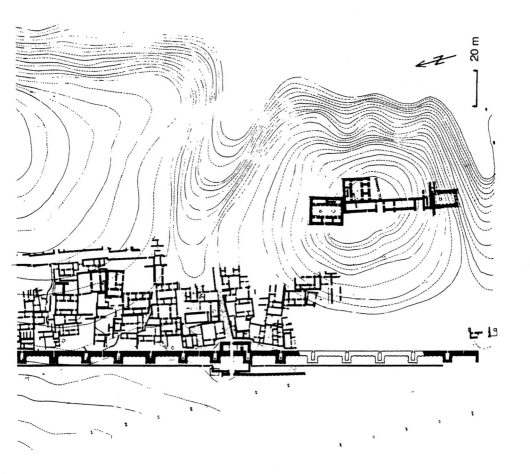

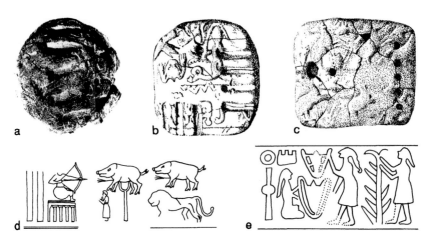

Figure 51. Finds, from Habuba Kabira South (Syria): (a) sealed clay bulla; (b, c) sealed tablets with numerical signs, (d, e) drawings of seal impressions. Courtesy, Dr. E. Strommenger, Berlin. Cf. E. Strommenger, *Habuba Kabira, Eine Stadt vor 5000 Jahren* (Mainz, 1980), figs. 55, 56, 58.

the other, on the Jebel Aruda, we know about at least as regards its public area. Both settlements appear to have been set up within a very short space of time. The Habuba settlement has even been provided with a large perimeter wall, and both towns were equipped with large public buildings. These settlements were surely built to last, but the fact that only two levels of habitation can be differentiated shows that they hardly survived more than fifty years.

Thanks to the complete agreement between the inventory and the changes that took place in Babylonian settlements of this period, it is possible for us to define exact chronological boundaries here, at least for the termination of these settlements. We have all the "forerunners" of writing—cylinder seals, sealed clay balls, and even clay tablets that show only signs for numbers. In the case of Babylonia, we were able to show all these as being characteristic of the period directly before the appearance of writing itself. However, given the fact that no written signs appear here, we can tell the precise point in time when this settlement was abandoned. In the terminology of the sequence of levels in Uruk it must come before level IVa, the phase in which the first written documents are found. If we count the two generations of the settlement at Habuba backwards from this point in time, we find ourselves with a date for the establishment of these settlements that is still within the Late Uruk period. As has already been shown from observations in other regions, we must consider the Late Uruk period to have been a phase of expansion.

Information about local developments in Syria is, on the one hand, rare and, on the other, generally limited in scope, as at sites with a protracted local continuity of settlement, layers of this period are buried deep beneath later layers, and it has therefore only been possible to excavate small areas of them. Only pottery is known in adequate quantities, and we have scant information about architecture and the structure of settlements in particular.

The pottery is completely within local traditions of production and decoration, which, as might be expected, were quite different from the traditions of the new arrivals. The only argument that can be offered beyond this is that in contrast to the pottery of the foreign groups, the pottery from the local tradition was without exception produced without the aid of the potter's wheel. This allows us to conclude that there must have been differences in the rest of the technology too. The possible range of variation with this local and older method of production was very much greater, and hence there was not even the beginning of a trend such as the one in Babylonia that led to a gradual growth in mass production.

At this point, however, one reservation must be made. An examination of the situation points to the fact that specific needs must have existed that made it seem desirable to borrow certain features. In Babylonia, as already mentioned, there was a demand for mass production, which could not be satisfied with the aid of existing technology. This resulted in the use of the technique of making pots in moulds. In its turn, this led to the production of bevel-rimmed bowls, a type of pot that required the least expenditure in terms of material and techniques and hence represented far and away the cheapest containers (see p. 84). As such, they were already used for a multitude of purposes in Babylonia, quite apart from their original one. Although they clearly could not be used for every purpose because of their special properties, as the simplest of all containers, these vessels, and the way they were produced, became part of the local repertoires of most of the areas neighboring Babylonia, without, however, bringing in their wake other aspects of early high civilization (see fig. 19).

Occasionally, and certainly not always in conjunction with bevel-rimmed bowls, there have been finds of Babylonian artifacts in excavations in Syria, and even in sites further west. Cylinder seals of the abstract group from the tradition of the Babylonian Late Uruk–Jamdet Nasr period have come to light in the sites in question without their having a substantive relation to their environment, thus giving the impression of being exotic, isolated pieces. Unfortunately we can also obtain no information from the wider context in order, for example, to answer the question of whether it is of any significance that only abstract and never figurative seals, and only original seals and almost never impressions of seals have been found. Only one thing seems certain: the appearance of such isolated pieces can hardly prompt us to suppose that economic conditions at these sites were of the same type as the ones that led to the invention of cylinder seals in Babylonia.

In spite of all these reservations, the seals and the bevel-rimmed bowls mentioned above are a very welcome aid to dating. Although earlier estimates sought to assign all of these seals to the horizon of the Jamdet Nasr period, we have in the meantime learned that they already belonged to the inventory of the Late Uruk period. We are indebted for this piece of knowledge to finds of such seals in Habuba Kabira South and Chogha Mish, at both of which sites the period of settlement, as we have said, concluded before the end of the Late Uruk period.

The expansion of Babylonian civilization along the Euphrates to the north, which led to the establishment of the settlements on Syrian territory, did not come to a halt at the borders of the great plain. It then spread along the course of the river into the mountain regions, where the type of understanding arrived at with the local civilization was clearly different from that in the area of the Syrian plain. Here we are more able to recognize parallels with the situation in northern Mesopotamia, and above all in the Zagros area.

As in the Zagros area, we encounter relationships between finds here that are clearly not local and unambiguously show influences from the sphere of the Late Uruk period civilization. However, they are very far from showing such direct correspondences as, for example, in Habuba. What are probably the most impressive complexes of finds have been furnished by Arslan Tepe near Malatya and Tepecik near Elazig in the Keban reservoir area. This last-named place is of special interest to us here because it has been possible to show that local pottery and foreign-influenced pottery existed on the same site, but in different places. The situation corresponds to that of Godin Tepe in reverse. The pottery made under foreign influence came from a residential quarter that established itself on flat ground in front of a settlement—represented exclusively by locally determined pottery—built on a settlement mound that was already elevated.

Unfortunately, we know far too little about this region too, especially about the aspects that go beyond merely enumerating and sorting out the pottery. Here, too, the local pottery was still shaped by hand without the aid of the potter's wheel, but here this is largely also true of the pottery that shows foreign influence.

This excursion through the neighboring regions has provided new understanding of the nature of the influence Babylonia had over these areas. Whether we talk of "expansion" or "attraction," however, we shall obviously not get any closer to an explanation if we see only either trade or imperialist expansion behind this influence, or even if we assume that it was a quasi-inadvertent expansion. It is possible that two factors went hand in hand in this development. On the one hand, there was the fascination on the part of the "underdeveloped" areas when faced with the complex way of life and the knowledge of Babylonia; on the other, Babylonia needed to organize the import of raw materials, and perhaps also the export of manufactured goods, to satisfy a rapidly expanding internal economy.

Here, the archaic texts from Uruk will certainly be of further help as soon as they are completely comprehensible. Thus, for example, the texts about metal will throw light on an important branch of imports, while texts about textiles are concerned with products that possibly played a role in exports. However, the evidence for a relationship between local people and strangers that was not always without its problems cannot be overlooked. The existence of a "citadel" such as Godin and a walled settlement such as in Habuba shows that the relationships were not always free from conflicts.

One other observation is almost more important, because it affords us a glimpse into an area normally closed to us because of the shortage of primary information. The fact that from the east across the whole northern area and into the west, all the neighboring regions were in one way or another incorporated by Babylonia either directly or indirectly into a network of relationships stronger than there had ever been before shows that this extension of influence was not aimed directly at one region, but spread out in all directions.

If individual local civilizations reacted differently to this expansion, it may be because different approaches were used according to region. However, this seems rather to mirror differences in the local civilizations.

In view of the special affinity between Susiana and Babylonia, Susa's assumption from Babylonia of the whole complex of Late Uruk period civilization does not come as a surprise. The other regions, in spite of all their internal differences, may be divided into two groups, the plains and the mountains. In the case of the plains—Syria and northern Mesopotamia—what strikes us as a common aspect is the fact that newcomers established their own settlements, sometimes in conjunction with older settlements, as was the case with Nineveh, and that in these settlements they led the existence to which they were accustomed in their homeland in every detail and with all the facilities they were accustomed to. In the archaeological material we have found, we have hardly any evidence of reciprocal influences between these settlements and the local ones.

In the mountain regions the local differences were greater. Here, too, however, a common denominator can be seen in that the settlements established by strangers could be directly connected with local settlements. Above all, it is clear that reciprocal influence was considerably greater and much more in evidence here. To explain the different reactions by merely attempting to trace them back to different topographical features would certainly be too short-sighted a way of looking at things. On the other hand, we shall be stretching our limited material too far if we attempt to give any more extensive explanation. Thus, the only fact we are left with is that the neighboring areas, which, because of our lack of material, all appear to loom up at us out of a sort of fog of uniformity, were differentiated amongst themselves.

While we can probably call the Late Uruk period the beginning of this cultural expansion—and this is roughly true everywhere—the date at which it ended seems to be more uncertain. The only date we can fix with certainty is that of the ending of this influence in Syria/Anatolia—that is, for the area of the upper Euphrates—as the finds from Habuba make clear. The settlements there were already abandoned before the end of the Late Uruk period and it is highly likely that this also signaled the end of the expansion into Anatolia. A similar date seems to hold good for northern Mesopotamia, where very little has been found that has to be categorized as belonging to the Jamdet Nasr period.

The situation in Susiana and in the Iranian hinterland is obviously different. With the creation of its own variants of early writing and of other developments, the tradition of the Late Uruk period was carried on into the Jamdet Nasr period in a Susiana that was still only very thinly populated. This description also fits Tepe Malyan, on the other side of the Zagros Mountains. In other places, such as Godin Tepe and Tepe Yahya, it is, for the moment, difficult to decide when the end of direct influence came about. But it was surely before the beginning of the Early Dynastic period in Babylonia.

Up until now, one region has been left out of our discussions because conditions were completely different there—the Gulf region. Any evaluation of this area must be an especially cautious one, because archaeological research work there has only just begun. It may look for the moment as if this region was only connected to the larger cultural network of the neighboring regions from time to time and on a temporary basis, interrupted by longer or shorter phases for which no coherent cultural evidence is available. However, this is clearly in part the result of inadequate sources of information. Therefore, for the time being, we have no evidence at all for the existence of a well-defined local civilization, let alone for a Babylonian-influenced civilization of the Late Uruk period.

Finds from graves in Abu Dhabi and Oman throw a sudden and powerful light on the subject. There, we find weapons and pottery that so clearly resemble those of the Jamdet Nasr period that there can be no doubt that these objects came from Babylonia. Their presence is easily explained, since the rich sources of copper in Oman were obviously already known and exploited before this time. It is, however, harder to explain why there is not a continuous sequence of evidence for this. For the time being, the context of these finds is completely obscure.

Whether or not this phase of Babylonia's direct influence was of varied intensity and lasted for different lengths of time in the different neighboring regions, it must be noted that in all these areas, including Susiana, the phase was a relatively short one. In addition, it hardly left behind it the kind of long-term impressions that would speak for a permanent connection with Babylonian development. In the Early Dynastic I period, which introduced a new and important phase in internal political development in Babylonia and was connected with a further consolidation of economic and social processes, only local traditions survived in the neighboring areas, a continuation of what had—as it seems to us—continued to exist side by side with the alien influences. Here, too, however, we are once again warned to be cautious because of the far too limited material available to us. In the later Early Dynastic period such centers as Assur in northern Mesopotamia and Tell Huera and Ebla in Syria call attention to themselves through well-established complexes of objects that are clearly in the mainstream of the Babylonian tradition. Like the ones in Ebla they can at this time even demonstrate a phase of their own further development of what they had taken over, so that we would at least like to assume that a certain openness was created by the earlier, more direct relationships.

The era of early high civilization between ca. 3200 and 2800 B.C. was the period in which the different regions of the Near East developed furthest away from one another. In this context, Babylonia was, without doubt, the region that produced the most complex economic, political, and social orders.

FIVE

The Period of the Rival City-States
(ca. 2800–2350 B.C.)

As was the case with the previous period, it is difficult for us to give any one reason for the beginning of this period that would be similarly applicable throughout the Near East. Here, too, the names we give and our definition of chronological limits are tailored to fit the area that made the most striking progress, and that therefore provides us with the most obvious opportunity for chronological differentiation. If this means that the title of the chapter also seems, at first, to apply only to Babylonia, it may nonetheless, in a limited sense, be valid for other areas of the Near East. There, at the end of this period, the first recognizably larger units emerged and came into political contact with one another and with Babylonia. So that even if this period of time is defined rather more by Babylonia than by other regions, its chronological limits cannot be clearly fixed even for Babylonia, because there we have a completely unbroken, continuous development.

This applies to the economy, the social structure, and to architecture and art. However, at the same time, political developments become apparent that were clearly qualitatively different from any previous ones. There were problems caused by further environmental changes and, above all, by internal changes in the society. There would continue to be problems, with a continual striving for solutions.

There were two changes in particular, one long-term and one short-term, but both concerned with the provision of water, which encouraged the speeding up of development. In chapter 4, it was made clear that the waters continued to recede, as indicated by the fact that the water level in the Gulf continued to fall. In the first half of the third millennium B.C., the level of the sea continually sank, and at the same time the rivers held less water.

These changes must have had at least two effects on the economics of the water supply in Babylonia. One was that, as a whole, less water could be used to irrigate the land. The other was that the lowering of the sea level in the Gulf meant that the lower courses of the rivers dug more deeply into the land and thus had the collateral effect of drawing even more water from the surrounding land. From now on, because of the shortage of water, more and more effort had to be expended in transporting water to the places where it was most needed. As we have seen, this necessity had clearly led to the construction of canals as far back as the Early Dynastic I period. Thus, the first steps had been taken that, in the following period, would lead to the building up of the enormous Mesopotamian canal system that became so well known from later literature.

We shall see how the further receding of the waters involved continual refinement of the irrigation system and how, finally, measures had to be taken to use and even to store—with the aid of ingenious arrangements like reserve basins—that part of the water that, even in an intensive irrigation system, flowed past the fields and was not used. We must also note here that this unleashed one of the greatest countrywide catastrophes, the progressive salinization of the soil.

However, the changes in the water supply did not only affect agriculture. They also affected the settlement structure of the land, as has already been mentioned for the Early Dynastic I period. Considered from the general point of view that settlements could only survive on a permanent basis if they lay on a watercourse that provided water throughout the year, the gradual receding of the water into fewer watercourses must have involved a gradual linkage between the settlements and these few remaining watercourses. We have already seen this happening in the previous period, where the tendency began to emerge for settlements to concentrate around the courses of the larger rivers, while the area between the rivers became increasingly empty. This tendency can also be observed in this period.

In addition, as it had done previously, it led to the tendency for a few settlements to grow larger at the expense of the others. In the hinterland of Uruk, which has thus far been used in our discussion as a control area, the number of settlements decreased from sixty-two to twenty-nine by comparison with the Early Dynastic I period. However, at the same time the average size of the settlements increased to thirty-eight hectares. If we apply our rather rough measurements here, we discover that during the later part of the Early Dynastic period—the period we are now dealing with—the main body of the population was concentrated in such urban centers, while small settlements out in the countryside had almost ceased to exist.

This fact becomes even more pronounced if we add together the areas of all the settlements of less than thirty hectares ("rural settlements"), and set this against the relevant number of settlements of more than thirty-one hectares ("urban settlements"). If we compare the surface area of the large sites with that of the small ones, we arrive at a ratio of 2:8 for the Late Uruk period. Approximately six hundred years later, during the Early Dynastic II period, the ratio had been reversed and now stood at 9:1 in favor of the larger sites. According to our rough estimates, this would mean that approximately nine-tenths of the population lived in settlements larger than thirty hectares.

Let us now return to an earlier idea. A greater concentration of people living closely together created social conflicts within any city whose size was limited by city walls. The resolution of these conflicts provided the impulse for what we call the development of civilization. In the processes mentioned above, we already have enough evidence to support the theory that even during the Early Dynastic period there was enough impetus to provide for further rapid development in Babylonia; however, there was an additional source of conflict.

Assuming that what we have been discussing up to now lay within the sphere of the long-term change I have mentioned, something happened at the end of the Early Dynastic period that aggravated the situation in a decisive fashion. Because of a change in the course of the river, an arm of the Euphrates that lay farther to the east replaced the old main channel of the river—which had developed out of a jumble of side channels during the period of early high civilization, on which such places as Nippur, Shuruppak, and Uruk lay—as the new main river. Sites situated along this new main course, such as Adab, Zabalam, and Umma, blossomed during the following period and were able to achieve great political significance in the way Umma did at the end of the Early Dynastic period. The importance of places on the old main course of the river decreased, sometimes at a faster and sometimes at a slower pace. The city of Uruk was clearly hardest hit by these changes, since the density of population within the city walls was considerably reduced after the Early Dynastic I period.

The development that stands out most clearly for us in this connection is the rapid increase in size, importance, and power of Umma, which was probably directly set in motion and made possible by the change in the course of the river. This had far-reaching consequences. In order to understand these in detail we must, in what follows, speak a little more fully about an observation made during the evaluation of the research done in the hinterland of Uruk. If we take the relationship of Uruk to its hinterland during the period from Late Uruk to Early Dynastic I as an example and determine—on the basis of the distribution of settlements around Uruk—something like a sphere of influence around the center, which is hard to define, and then do the same for other centers contemporaneous with Uruk, like Nippur or Girsu, we find that at the times under consideration the supposed areas of influence were far apart (see the areas sketched in around the sites in fig. 52 and the period maps in fig. 20).

After the new situation due to the change in the course of the river had arisen, the settlement of Umma, which lay between the old spheres of influence, could at first develop unhindered, without intruding upon the claims of anyone else. However, the point when considerable encroachment occurred must have arrived, at the latest, when Umma reached a size similar to the previously mentioned places and could thus lay claim to a sphere of influence of a similar size. The emergence of conflict zones was thus preordained, since the territory available between the original areas was not large enough to grant Umma the sphere of influence that was its due.

The validity of this hypothesis depends on whether we can successfully define the rather vague term "sphere of influence." If we look more closely at maps of the country around Uruk (fig. 20), we notice that the dispersion of settlements over the whole hinterland is uneven, but that almost concentrically around Uruk, at a distance of twelve to fifteen kilometers, there is a strip two to three kilometers wide with no trace of settlements at all (roughly represented by the strip between the two shaded areas around Uruk in fig. 52). This zone is especially important because the situation of the settlements in the area between Uruk and the strip changed in a different way from that of those beyond the strip. Here we can refer to what was said above in connection with the concentration of the settlements (pp. 70–72). On closer examination, this development toward fewer, but larger, settlements cannot be confirmed for the whole hinterland, but only for the area outside the strip mentioned above. In contrast, in the area between Uruk and the strip, the number of settlements did decrease, but the remaining settlements did not become any larger. Instead, the center, Uruk, reached the greatest size of its entire history in the course of the Early Dynastic I period (see fig. 22a–b).

The difference between the areas on the two sides of the strip can probably be traced back to the differing strength of relationships with the center. The fact that a strip that was empty of settlements marked the separation provides us with further evidence for this. Such situations are not unknown to settlement geography; they occur where specific competing central influences have affected noncentral settlements.

If such a settlement lies within the "force field" of two neighboring centers, this can have positive as well as negative effects on the settlement. The opportunities for exploiting the competitive situation in the economic sphere are completely positive, since a lower price for goods that are needed or a better offer for one's own products can be sought. From this point of view it is advantageous if facilities for transportation are, wherever possible, equally good in both directions. The ideal case is when the settlement is situated exactly midway between the two centers.

It is a different matter if questions of administration or political power have a role to play, because then a settlement situated midway between two centers would very soon find itself being torn apart. In

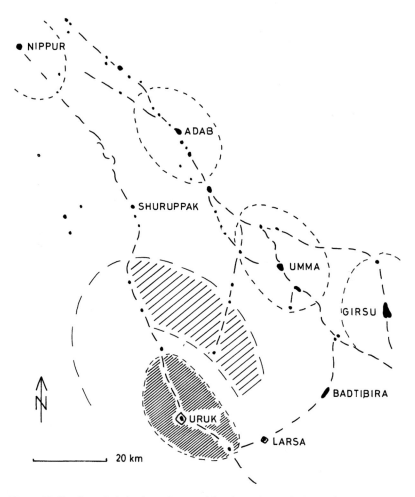

Figure 52. Southern Babylonia at the transition from the Early Dynastic I to the Early Dynastic II period. The closely hatched area around Uruk stands for the zone of direct influence, the widely hatched area for the zone of indirect influence. Author's original.

such a case, the creation of an unequivocal relationship with one center alone would be the only solution. To put it concretely, the settlement must not be at a site in the area between two centers if both centers can lay claim to the site: it should be in an area that clearly belongs to one center. If the main emphasis of the relationship between center and hinterland is preponderantly in the administrative or political sphere, a zone empty of settlements emerges.

In the case of Uruk, we are not faced with exactly the same situation, in that the development outside the strip that was empty of settlements was not caused by another center. However, the situation is comparable, in that the development in the outer region, with the formation of larger settlements and, thus, the creation of new potential centers of power, did not really correspond to the intentions of the original center. This development did not, after all, take place within the narrow sphere of influence of the old center. Thus, the areas both inside and outside the strip that was empty of settlements can now be called a zone of closer or direct influence and a zone of indirect influence. It was clearly important for the inhabitants to relate unequivocally to one or the other area; in contrast, the area where relations were not clearly defined was avoided.

This results in our being able to fix on two statements. There was clearly such a thing as a sphere of influence, whose borders, in the case we are dealing with, may have lain between twelve and fifteen kilometers away from the center. Beyond this, there was a sphere of less direct influence. At the same time, this special ordering of the settlements in the hinterland of Uruk shows us that in the relationship between center and surrounding area, the administrative or political component plays an important, if not the most important, role.

The creation of spheres of influence was, of course, not restricted to Uruk, but took place automatically as settlements grew to sizes comparable with those of Uruk and other older centers. Thus it was obvious that this process should also accompany the growth of Umma. Restrictions on the spheres of influence and thus an increase in sources of conflict must then have affected relations with, in particular, the old center of Girsu. This is true above all if we imagine an area of external influence around Umma and Girsu like the one around Uruk (fig. 52). In contrast, the potential of the relationship between Umma and Uruk for conflict would have been much smaller. Because of the change in the course of the river that led to Umma's rise, Uruk itself had declined considerably in importance, and since it did not lie on the same river course as Umma, contacts between them also did not have to be especially close.

The relationship between Umma and Girsu, whose surroundings were, for the most part, irrigated by the same eastern arm of the Euphrates, led to permanent conflict between these two cities. According to the written sources of the later Early Dynastic period, it was a question of borderlands and border canals. This conflict, which continued to surface throughout many generations, was thus brought about by the changes in water supply and settlement structure. It is tempting to assume that all the other numerous conflicts between Babylonian cities mentioned in texts from the Early Dynastic III period can be traced back to similar causes. At that time, Girsu was, after all, only the main center of the city-state of Lagash, which took its name from a more ancient main center buried to the southeast of Girsu in the al-Hiba mound of ruins. The rulers who lived in Girsu continued to call themselves rulers of Lagash right down to a much later period.

We do not, it is true, have any evidence about other such long-lasting conflicts, and we have only isolated reports about individual disagreements, but this is certainly because it was only in the case of Umma and Girsu that the conflict caused by the new situation took on such dimensions that it seemed worthwhile to record in writing.

The changes in the distribution of water, such as those concentrated at the end of the Early Dynastic I period, can thus broadly be regarded as the cause of a qualitative change in ways of political coexistence. In spite of all our reservations, we must concede that a new phase does commence with the beginning of the Early Dynastic II period. From now on, conflicts between individual centers were incorporated in the political system of Babylonia.

Wars and conflicts between these centers, which, judging from the written sources of the Early Dynastic III period, must have had a determining influence on the character of this period, should not be seen as merely the work of power-hungry rulers. That it was not possible to solve these conflicts by military expeditions is indicated by the fact that at the end of the Early Dynastic period the whole political system changed completely, which seems to be the logical outcome of the development we have described.

Unfortunately, we have practically no written evidence available to us from the Early Dynastic II period, the period in which the above mentioned conflicts arose. An inadequate number of finds, not a decrease in the use of writing, is clearly responsible for this. On the other hand, the visible effects of these political changes probably ended up below the level of what is archaeologically tangible to us. When the great find of tablets from Fara, ancient Shuruppak, comes into view at the end of the Early Dynastic II period, the forms and use of written signs so clearly represent a further development of writing from the group of tablets we know from Ur in the Early Dynastic I period that we must assume that writing and its uses developed further during the Early Dynastic II period (cf. fig. 31b). They are not such comprehensive changes as took place at the outset of the development of writing, but an acceleration of the tendency, already noted, toward making writing easier and more universally useful (fig. 53). A further reduction in the number of signs, along with further abstraction in their form, is part of this process. Although it may appear as if the signs from the Fara texts had become more complicated—and in fact they do, at times, use more impressions of the stylus in order to write a sign—these individual impressions all lie within a narrow segment of the possible directions the writing stylus could, theoretically, take on the tablet. This restriction means that as few changes of direction as possible are demanded of the hand doing the writing.

Thus the alleviation of the task of writing lay in the fact that impressions requiring considerable twisting of both tablet and stylus were replaced by ones that lay in a more consistent direction. This meant that the speed of writing could be increased, in spite of the fact that from time to time the scribe had to make a larger number of impressions. The appearance of the writing as a whole can be seen as indirect evidence of the fact that the demand for scribes had increased.

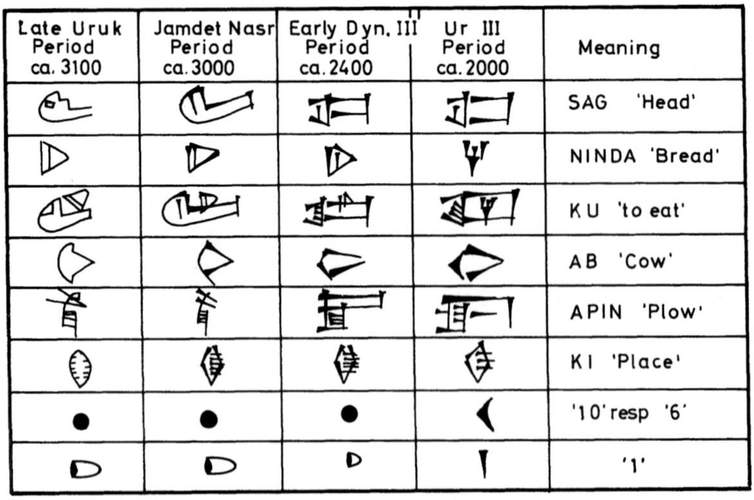

Late Uruk Period ca. 3100	Jamdet Nasr Period ca. 3000	Early Dyn. III Period ca. 2400	Ur III Period ca. 2000	Meaning
				SAG 'Head'
				NINDA 'Bread'
				KU 'to eat'
				AB 'Cow'
				APIN 'Plow'
				KI 'Place'
				'10' resp '6'
				'1'

Figure 53. Development of some signs of the Babylonian cuneiform script. Author's original.

Though there are variations in the way the individual signs are written, their number grows markedly fewer vis-à-vis earlier periods. This very uniform writing technique, which distinguished in each case between certain deeply impressed wedges, others that completed the outline of a sign, and the very light impressions drawn within the sign, must, as a whole, have been the result of a very highly formalized and strict training of scribes. This, in its turn, points to the necessity of making the training course more rigid in order to make it accessible to more students.

However, the process described above may be seen in yet another context. Up until that point, the words necessary for transmitting a piece of information could be placed next to one another in a random fashion. The texts from Shuruppak ushered in a development that, a short time later in the Early Dynastic III period, led to writing that reproduced the whole flow of speech exactly, so that now historical, political, or religious factual content could be transmitted. For this, two changes in the system of writing were necessary. One was the extension of the existing capacity to reduce signs for whole words to signs for syllables, and the other was the use of these not only, as previously, to write further words for which there was no special sign but also for the rendering of grammatical elements. If, previously, "sentences" had consisted of a stringing together of nouns, with possibly a few verbs, where the reader had to derive the syntax from the context, now it was possible for the first time to represent syntactical relationships in their entirety. Whereas previously—in order to avoid too great an ambiguity—writing had had to restrict itself to indicating simple syntactical relationships (and in recording economic processes there are hardly any others), now it was possible to fix for the reader in an unmistakable way the complicated speech structures, such as attributes, apposition, relative clauses, and so forth, that were of course present in the spoken language.

Starting with the most ancient texts, moreover, we find the remarkable fact that within a case representing the smallest sense unit, the signs used to express the information could be written down in an order that was clearly not yet fixed. Even in the texts from Shuruppak, which are the first in which grammatical elements are written down, this can still be seen to a certain extent; more developed are the inscriptions of the ruler Ur-Nanshe of Lagash shortly after the period of the Shuruppak texts. (These are the earliest texts of the type we call "royal inscriptions," in which, from then on, rulers give us lengthy, but certainly not always complete, reports of their deeds.) The tradition of writing words and grammatical elements according to their spoken

Figure 54. Obverse and reverse of an economic text from the end of the Early Dynastic II period, unknown provenience. Private collection; copyright of the author.

order first began in the period of Eannatum of Lagash, a younger son of Ur-Nanshe. It was only after this step had been taken that writing was able to convert all aspects of language to written form. It is no wonder that from this time on more and more fields of spoken language were drawn upon and fixed in writing. Writing, which by then, about 2500 B.C., already had a six-hundred-year history behind it, was only made into the universally useful instrument we know by these changes.

In attempting to answer the question of why these changes in writing took place precisely at this time, we come across another phenomenon: although written in the language we call Sumerian, certain texts contemporary with those from Fara, but which come from the site of Abu Salabikh near Nippur in central Babylonia, were composed by scribes who mostly had Semitic names. Now, notwithstanding that the language of the early texts was, for the most part, Sumerian, it also contained elements of one or several other languages. Like Sumerian itself, these languages cannot at present be defined with regard to their origins or relationships. However, one thing that is certain is that Semitic languages did not play any role in this. Yet here we suddenly find people who clearly belong to a Semitic group in positions that were probably the prerogative of the leading classes in the community at that time. Thus, a Semitic population—perhaps only in certain areas of Babylonia—must have won for itself an important position in society in the period shortly before these texts were written. For the time being, the political aspect of this is not our main interest, but only the fact that from now on the necessity arose to write down the totally different sort of language spoken by this new group. As was also the case in such situations later on, the writing system was, to a certain extent, able to cope with this task without any great changes. Signs representing whole words were simply read and pronounced in the Semitic language rather than in Sumerian. However, not only is this process more difficult when words are written syllabically (that is, with the aid of several syllable signs), but the totally different construction of the Semitic language also required a new organization of writing.

Whereas, in agglutinative Sumerian, the word stem always remains the same and specifications such as person or time are expressed by the use of prefixes or suffixes, the Semitic languages are inflected and can also change their word stems. They are therefore highly dependent on syllabic writing.

As noted, syllables were already being depicted in writing, probably because from the beginning the script was under pressure to do more than reproduce only Sumerian. When it now became necessary to transcribe yet another new language, this part of the writing system could be rapidly expanded. The use of syllable signs liberated from word meanings now formed an important part of the writing system. It is not difficult to see this development, together with the expansion in writing's capacity to reproduce speech, as a direct consequence of the fact that writing had to be capable of being used for the reproduction of languages other than the one for which it was originally developed.

Economic texts, which now become slightly more explicit, and the category of word lists, which are also well known at an earlier date, can henceforth be set beside historical and literary texts and what we subsume under the heading of legal documents. Now, for the first time, we hear something about the succession of rulers, about the extent and importance of their realms, about conflicts between these realms, and about changes in the power structure within the country as a whole, as well as about the way conflicts were resolved both between the individual realms and the inhabitants of different towns or cities. We receive substantial details about political, religious, and economic conditions and the changes that occurred in them. However, we learn almost nothing about one of the most severe conflicts, which was at least in the offing, and probably in full swing, in this period: the conflict between central and noncentral power. At times we might be tempted to call this a conflict between "religious" and "secular" power, were it possible to use this pair of concepts at all.

The evidence to support the thesis of such a conflict between "king" and "priests" seems to be very clear, because in the texts of the later Early Dynastic period there are several terms for the highest representative of a political structure. There is the title *en,* or, somewhat later, *ensi,* whose bearer can be shown in every case to have had a strong relationship to the gods of each of the centers in question. In addition to this, there was the *lugal*— literally speaking, "the great man"—for whom this unequivocal relationship to the gods does not seem to have existed. For reasons to be discussed later, it was formerly assumed that in the early period the whole city, its inhabitants, and all the land that belonged to it were the property of the supreme god of the city, and that it was administered by the high priest or high priestess of the god. Thus it seemed plausible to see this representative of the god in the *en,* who in fact generally proves to have been the high priest of a city god, and who would thus simultaneously have been the highest political figure. On the other hand, the *lugal* would have been, first and foremost, the man in charge of military operations in a dispute with another power structure: this role was at first presumably restricted to a particular occasion but would then have been established as an independent and permanent function. This conception is reflected in normal translation, in which *en* is rendered as "priest-ruler" and *lugal* as "king." This general definition seems to be in accord with the observation that only sometime after the appearance of monumental architecture buildings were encountered that cannot unequivocally be called temples, and to which then the term "palace" had been imposed upon. A further hint at a secondary appearance of a power distinct from the temple was seen in the fact that in Sumerian the term for palace was differentiated as *é-gal*—"great house"—from the general *é,* meaning "house" and "temple."

This hypothesis has two weaknesses, however, one of them being that in the field of architecture the chronological succession can in no way be proved, because we do not have the relevant criteria for differentiation and our material for the early period is far too fragmentary. We can underscore our helplessness in the face of such terms with the random references to the large buildings in the central area of Uruk in the Late Uruk period as "temples" and "palaces" (see pp. 96–98).

As far as both terms for the holders of the highest offices are concerned, it is perfectly possible that the difference was regional, without the two functions having been greatly differentiated from each other. In addition, the entire concept rests solely on a few texts from the Early Dynastic III period in Girsu (see the detailed discussion on pp. 47–49), and was applied uncritically to other parts of the country and, above all, to the earlier stages in development. Though there are no complete and relevant texts from these earlier phases, we do have evidence in a very few cases that would suggest that conditions then were completely different from those in the following phases. Examples of this have already been provided in chapter 4, so that here we need only note that in an economic text from the Jamdet Nasr period, *en* and *lugal* appear together in a nonconspicuous position, and that, second, it is highly probable that the title of the actual highest representative of a political entity is the first entry in the list of names of professions and public offices (fig. 31) that has nothing to do with either *en* or *lugal*. Both titles in the Jamdet Nasr period clearly had different meanings from those they acquired later. These terms probably acquired their later significance only very gradually by functional and/or regional differentiation.

The evidence pointing to a contrast between "king" and "high priest" can thus no longer be sustained. In spite of this, we do find other references in the later Early Dynastic period directly suggesting that there must have been different forms of political leadership, of which at least one can be designated as "theocratic," whereas the other cannot be characterized so unambiguously. However, in order to elaborate on these contrasts, and possibly even to be in a position to define their origins, we must go somewhat further back in time.

I have already spoken of the manifold effects on agriculture, the structure of settlements, and politics caused by the changeover from a land on a broad plain interlaced with countless watercourses to a situation in which canal systems, branching off from one or two rivers, irrigated the land that had previously been watered naturally. One further consequence was that now the borderlines between canal-irrigated and unirrigated land, between land suitable for agriculture and land that could not be cultivated, became increasingly fixed.

This arable land was certainly not all to be found in regular strips on both sides of the main watercourses. It is rather more likely that at places where canal systems branched off, the limits of arable land were far removed from the main watercourse, whilst in between these limits came closer to it. If we now assume that the density and size of such canal systems was especially great near important settlements, we get a picture of irrigation oases threaded like pearls along the main watercourses. In the center of these was found the largest settlement of each respective area.

Of course, it was in the interest of every center to control and consolidate the prosperity and the integrity of its irrigation area—that is, of its own surrounding land. Thus, the survival interests of each

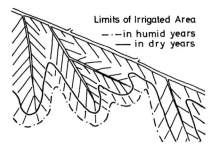

Figure 55. Scheme of a dendritic irrigation network. Author's original.

center were first and foremost related to these immediate surroundings, and not, for example, to the whole irrigation area or to Babylonia as a whole. In this we catch a glimpse of the main reason for the pronounced particularism of the Babylonian cities, which we shall frequently encounter in the remainder of this work.

A system in which the idea of a city god—that is, a deity who most emphatically represented the local characteristics of a city, and with them the idea of a demarcation vis-à-vis other entities of the same sort—was quite clearly established had no trouble in adjusting to the conditions that had arisen during the course of an ever-increasing recession of the waters. It was this situation, bringing with it the ever-growing need for some sort of demarcation from other units of power and the need to define boundaries between the settled peoples (living in irrigated areas) and the nonsettled peoples (who lived outside these areas), that may have led to a consolidation of the principle of the city god.

Apart from the primary necessity of having to take care of one's own environment, there were obviously other interests to be considered. We have already discussed the question of whether the expansion of trade necessary for survival because of Babylonia's lack of raw materials was directed by the individual cities or by some sort of higher authority, whatever form that may have taken. In that discussion, it was suggested that the so-called "city seals"—especially those we know from Ur, but also those from other cities—might be the distinguishing marks of trade associations made up of the cities named individually on the seals (see p. 79 and fig. 29c above). In addition, we may suppose that the increasing dependence of all the local irrigation systems on the one river system of the Euphrates made agreements between, and also perhaps associations of, all the inhabitants involved increasingly necessary.

As the clearest example of an attempt at creating at least a temporary higher institution, we have a report of a procedure in which the ruler Mesalim, although domiciled in the north of Babylonia, functioned as an arbitrator in the abovementioned conflict between the cities of Umma and Girsu. The conflicts built into the political system from the Early Dynastic II period on could only be resolved by the establishment of a higher authority—in effect, the creation of a new ruling center. During the following period, this led to what were at first faint-hearted, and then more and more lasting, attempts to create political unions in a land that, however, had to struggle for centuries with particularist interests. These were so strong that for a very long period any larger political alliance in Babylonia collapsed after only a short while into individual local units.

The important role played in this development by the city gods, or rather by their priests, demonstrates very clearly their partiality in these conflicts. For reasons that are not known to us at the moment, but that must surely be looked for in the political environment, hierarchies were fixed among the individual city gods in the form of a construct of family relationships, whereby presumably the position of a god within the family of gods corresponded to the importance of his home city. Lists with such groupings appear for the first time among the texts from Shuruppak, from the end of the Early Dynastic II period. Subsequently, the chief god of this so-called pantheon occasionally appears as the representative of the interests of the gods as a whole. We shall hear of examples in which the chief god of the Babylonian pantheon, Enlil, the city god of Nippur, attempted, in the abovementioned function, to mobilize the individual cities, but also groups coming from outside them, against the current ruler of a centralized state, and often enough was successful in this.

Inasmuch as the conflict between particularism and the central state was directly connected with changes in the settlement and irrigation systems during the first part of the Early Dynastic period, it should come as no surprise that the first obvious effects appear in the shape of increasing attempts to bring about supraregional political alliances toward the end of that period, when brought about primarily by changes in the course of the river over a considerable time.

The first known attempt of this kind was made by Eannatum of Lagash, who was gradually able to draw all the cities of Babylonia, even Mari on the middle Euphrates outside Babylonia, into his sphere of influence, at least for a short time. Although very little is known about the details, we do find from inscriptions that toward the end of Eannatum's reign his sphere of influence had shrunk back to its original

143

size. We know nothing about the background of, and motivation for, Eannatum's actions, but on the whole they conform to the reasons for centralization outlined above. In one case, however, we do find more direct reference to Eannatum, where, at the time of his conquests in northern Babylonia, he is called the "king of Kish." Kish was one of the great, ancient sites in northern Babylonia, and was thus not a place Eannatum could have ruled jointly from his own territory. In fact, Eannatum was not the only ruler of a southern Babylonian city who held this title. The matter becomes even more puzzling when we consider that we occasionally hear of rulers from the same period who actually ruled over Kish, and others who merely had the same title as Eannatum. In what follows we shall see that there is a complicated problem lurking behind these inconsistencies.

One thing that all those who held this title in addition to their own titles had in common was that they were important rulers and were more powerful than their respective neighbors. This has been interpreted to mean that a title whose prestige went back to the importance of an earlier role played by the city of Kish, perhaps even to the existence of an earlier kingdom of Kish, can be seen in this term. A world fragmented into many individual spheres of influence might have longed for the advantages of an earlier centralized government and have expressed this by using the name of the old capital city. Thus, "king of Kish" may be a title that had acquired an independent existence and may merely have been a symbol of the extent of the power of each respective ruler, which was true of the following Akkad Dynasty period as well. Quite apart from the fact that the process of development in settlement and irrigation conditions in Babylonia allows no room for such an early empire of Kish, its importance should in any case probably be looked for in another direction. For this purpose, we shall first take a short look at Babylonia's geographical situation.

Although Babylonia counts as part of Mesopotamia, the land created by the Tigris and Euphrates, the area that is inhabitable and arable is, with very few exceptions, identical with the area irrigated by the Euphrates. The reason for this is that the water level in the Euphrates, at least from the point at which it flows into the Babylonian plain, lies only slightly below the surface of the surrounding land, whereas the Tigris cuts deeply into the land. Hence, water for irrigation could be obtained from the Tigris only with great effort, and then only in small quantities, whereas it was no problem to divert water from the Euphrates.

The area irrigated by the Euphrates takes on changing forms in

Babylonia, and we can distinguish two major parts. These parts, northern Babylonia and southern Babylonia, differ in that in northern Babylonia the river flows through a relatively narrow plain where changes in the river bed that would be normal for a slowly flowing river with almost no gradient had little latitude to develop—with one exception, discussed below. In contrast to this, southern Babylonia is a very broad plain, which was always crisscrossed by several parallel arms of the Euphrates (see fig. 73). As we have seen already, shifts in the course of the river were capable of changing the settlement and irrigation systems of a whole countryside. At times when all the watercourses were carrying an abundance of water, shifts in the course of the river naturally had only a limited impact. On the other hand, where canal systems were laid out—and settlements and population were concentrated in the immediate vicinity of the canals—they were connected for better or for worse with the few rivers that bore water. In this case it was a vital necessity for the individual settlements to prevent changes in the course of the river, so as to avoid the waters being carried into areas that were less settled or not settled at all.

Although these shifts in the course of the river affected the Babylonian south more than any other region, the actual source of the shifts lay not in the south, but in the north. The danger was not only that the river might find another bed, but that, on top of this, the water would flow off uselessly into the depression to the southwest, near the present-day city of Nejef, where there had been a marshy area on the edge of the desert for ages.

This was, as noted, not so much a danger to the cities of northern Babylonia as a threat to the cities of the south, which depended on the Euphrates flowing in its normal bed for survival. Because the river was especially low-lying in northern Babylonia, the possibility existed that the annual floods might lead to a change of this sort in the river's course, if, after the floodwaters had receded, the water found a different course. Thus, from the time of the consolidation of the irrigation system on, it was of decisive importance for the south of the country for the river to be kept under control at this danger point. Kish, the former capital of northern Babylonia, occupied a key position in this.

The fact that, when there was any doubt, the Euphrates could only be controlled there was certainly not the least of the reasons why southern Babylonian rulers made repeated attempts to advance into the north. The title "king of Kish" would in this case have been the well-earned distinction of the southern Babylonian ruler who carried out this function, so important to the survival of the south. In this

145

case, too, the title would have been one of prestige, but the reason for the prestige would have been rather different from what we have assumed it to be up until now.

We know considerably less about a whole series of other rulers who bore this title, though it in no way seems to have been connected only with the short-term possession of the whole country. However, we do know that Eannatum also found successors in his attempt to bring larger

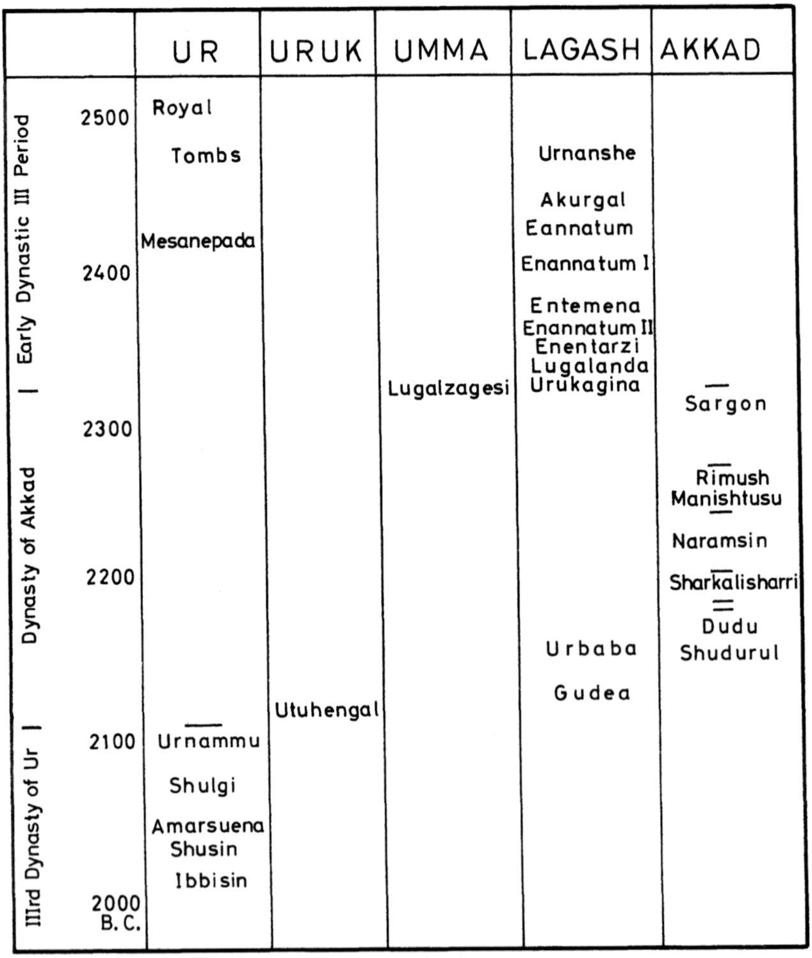

		UR	URUK	UMMA	LAGASH	AKKAD
Early Dynastic III Period	2500	Royal Tombs			Urnanshe	
					Akurgal	
		Mesanepada			Eannatum	
	2400				Enannatum I	
					Entemena	
					Enannatum II	
					Enentarzi	
					Lugalanda	
				Lugalzagesi	Urukagina	— Sargon
	2300					
Dynasty of Akkad						— Rimush
						Manishtusu
						Naramsin
	2200					Sharkalisharri
						= Dudu
					Urbaba	Shudurul
					Gudea	
			Utuhengal			
IIIrd Dynasty of Ur	2100	— Urnammu				
		Shulgi				
		Amarsuena				
		Shusin				
		Ibbisin				
	2000 B.C.					

Figure 56. Chronological chart containing the names of rulers and dynasties mentioned in the text. Author's original.

areas of the country under his rule. True, we do not learn more details about another attempt until the time of Lugalzaggesi, the last ruler of the south before the whole of Babylonia was conquered by Sargon of Akkad. But first we must talk of another development.

We have a whole series of texts from Girsu when it was capital of the city-state of Lagash, both "royal inscriptions," which tell us, for example, about the deeds of Eannatum, and a large number of economic texts that date mainly from the period of the last rulers of this city before its conquest by Lugalzaggesi. Many of these economic texts clearly stem from a complex of buildings used mainly during the reigns of the last three independent rulers of this place—Enentarzi, Lugalanda, and Urukagina. They deal, for the most part, with the administration of a building referred to as *é-mí*—"house of the woman," which was clearly under the direction of the ruler's wife. Many different economic transactions, administrative decisions, and so forth were, for example, carried out under the direction of Baranamtara, wife of Lugalanda. This complex of buildings, or parts of it, are expressly referred to as "the property of Baranamtara, the wife of Lugalanda." However, in the following reign, that of Urukagina, a remarkable change takes place in that the same complex of buildings now appears in the texts as *é-^{d}ba$_6$-ba$_6$* "economic unit of goddess Baba." This change of name must surely be connected with a formulation in this ruler's so-called "Reform texts," where it is stated that:

> In the house [household] of the ruler, in the fields of the ruler, he [the ruler] confirmed the god Ningirsu [city god of Girsu] as lord.
> In the house of the woman, in the fields of the woman he confirmed the goddess Baba [the wife of Ningirsu] as their lady.
> In the house of the prince, in the fields of the prince, he confirmed the god Shulshagana [the son of Ningirsu] as lord.

This passage is always interpreted as meaning that the economic units and fields in question had formerly belonged to the gods, were then usurped by the ruler and his family, and were now being returned to their original owners by this especially devout ruler, Urukagina, in an attempt to restore the old order.

On the other hand, let us remind ourselves that in the repeated attempts made during this period to create larger areas of control, centralistic aspirations took on a more concrete form as against the autonomy of the cities and the ideology of city gods that was so closely bound up with it. It would have been only natural if this development had set off another, opposing development emphasizing more strongly a phenomenon that already existed—particularism. In fact, this counterform is known to us in the type of state mentioned above. It is a kind of particularism, overemphasized for the sake of definition. We encounter it, in texts from Girsu dating from the last phase of Early Dynastic III. The central idea was that the city, together with its inhabitants and lands, was actually the property of the city god. Seen from this point of view, this form of state would be the result of one last attempt to unite all its forces against centralization and give them a structure. This interpretation would mean that we could determine precisely the historical place where this rigid form, the "temple city," was created, and that we could interpret it as the reaction to increasing attempts at centralization and thus also fix its chronological framework as being the last phase of the Early Dynastic III period. If Urukagina's "Reform texts" produce the impression that the restoration of an old order is being described, this probably conforms precisely to their original intention. In this case this text can be placed in the category of attempts to legitimize personal conceptions or new ideas by pointing to a fictitious "tradition."

The strict form of the temple city has often been seen as the prototype of the political and economic constitution of the whole country and for the whole of the early periods, an inadmissible generalization. It rather represents a counterpart to the concept of the centralized state that is very precisely fixed in time and possibly also in place. Further political development did not allow the "temple city" to survive for very long as a form of state, because developments toward the centralized state had already progressed too far. Thus, we cannot hope for any written evidence that would tell us whether the form would have been capable of surviving for a longer period. Only a few years after the "Reform texts," the area of Lagash, along with the rest of southern and central Babylonia, fell victim to the conquests of Lugalzaggesi, who himself came from the south—probably from Umma—and was able, after a short time, to unite quite large parts of Babylonia under his rule.

For this phase too, our information is, unfortunately, very sparse, but one piece of information about the way this ruler proceeded is striking. In a text from Girsu, there are moving lamentations by Urukagina about the way Lugalzaggesi destroyed the temples in the places he captured during his conquests. This sacrilege is reported in shocked tones, and the text ends with, "May Nidaba, the goddess of Lugalzaggesi, carry this sin on her head." This is a perfectly natural utterance for someone who himself stood by the concept that the ruler was only the instrument of the city god's will. But suppose Lugalzaggesi did not see himself fitting in with this concept at all, if the destruction of the temples, quite apart from the booty to be expected from it, occurred not as the result of hybris, but because of his insight into the fact that it was precisely these temples that were the centers of resistance to his plans?

What has been said makes it clear that it was, at the latest, during the time of the last rulers of the Early Dynastic period, that the contrasts between the various fundamental political tendencies manifested themselves. As already suggested, the extent to which the whole period covered in this chapter—Early Dynastic II and Early Dynastic III— must have been characterized by inner tensions is here once again clearly revealed. Even for the short segment of the late Early Dynastic period just dealt with, it can be seen that situations that seem possible to reconstruct from texts from the end of this phase should on no account be projected backwards even into periods that are only slightly earlier, of which we know little or nothing.

If we look for help from archaeological sources, the result is not much better. For several reasons, our information about this period comes mainly from excavations outside the actual Babylonian area. Practically no remains from this period were uncovered in Uruk and the excavations at Girsu were carried out too long ago, using methods that do not allow answers to our present-day questions. Excavations of Kish and Ur carried out research mainly on burial places of this period, and the results of the excavations in Nippur have not yet been completely published. Tell Asmar, Khafaji, and Tell Ajrab, three larger projects in the area that borders on the northeast, which is traversed by the Diyala River, have made a wealth of material available that seems to stand so directly in the line of Babylonian development that it has been used again and again to fill in gaps in our knowledge about Babylonia itself. However, more exact comparisons of smaller groups of finds from the Diyala area and Babylonia itself, such as, for example, cylinder seals, make it probable that there were fundamental local differences.

We do not, unfortunately, have the sort of complex of archaeological information for this period that Uruk provides for the one immediately preceding it, for which we had material from different contexts in the same region that could shed light on the multifaceted developments taking place under the same external conditions. For the Early Dynastic II and III periods we must therefore assemble a composite picture whose individual parts come from different regions and from different contexts and depend on the information provided by different

Figure 57. Cylinder seal and impression dating to the Early Dynastic II period. Height 2.8 cm. Collection of the Seminar für Vorderasiatische Altertumskunde, Freie Universität, Berlin. Photo M. Nissen. (Cf. U. Moortgat-Correns, "Die ehem. Rollsiegel-Sammlung E. Oppenländer," *Baghd. Mitt.* 4 [1968], no. 30.)

types of finds. Because such a procedure is only possible if we accept the fiction that there were neither regional, social, nor economic differences, it is, of course, not to be expected that we shall derive information about individual development from that sort of material. This is why we do not see the great social conflicts of this time reflected in works of art or in other archaeologically tangible evidence.

But there is yet another aspect that restricts our ability to evaluate archaeological data using a similar approach to the one employed for the earlier period. For it is, of course, also true for this period that the social conditions at a given time—with their ideas of value and their necessities—have influenced the form, appearance, and order of the things we can retrieve archaeologically, and thus that these conditions can to a certain extent be read from these objects. Thus, for example, it is now only possible in a few isolated cases clearly to trace changes in our archaeological material back to technical innovations or connect them with changes in society. It is not only that all the more important technical innovations took place in the previous period; so did the formulation of ways of using these new tools or technological aids. Thus, pottery now consisted almost exclusively of mass-produced wares. In the production of seals, "fast" mechanical tools such as the drill and the cutting wheel and "slow" tools such as the engraver were used in combination with such virtuosity that even complicated scenes could be cut into the stone cylinder relatively quickly (fig. 58). Any differentiation between "cheap" and "expensive" seals thus no longer plays a significant role in interpretation. Thus, from this period, we know only of such an infinitesimal number of abstracts—that is, scarcely individualized seals—that we may assume that they definitely no longer had the same significance as in the previous period.

In spite of this, study of the seals can nonetheless provide significant insights. From the latter part of the Early Dynastic II period, we find, among the cylinder seals and impressions from Fara, the first examples of seals with personal names inscribed on them. This, the highest form of individualization of a seal, makes it clear not only that people still felt a desire for individualization—or felt under pressure to achieve it—but also that they had reached the limits of the possibilities of individualization afforded by varying the decorations on seals. This is understandable for a time in which, because of an increasing population, progressive urbanization—which presumably increased the number of large economic undertakings in the country—and above all the close mutual ties both within Babylonia itself, but also with the outside world, the number of those who needed a seal in order to carry out their daily work must have increased. Increased trade, especially, must have demanded a more abstract means of identification tied to knowledge of a supraregional convention and not necessarily to knowledge of the small-scale conventions of the local community.

Relationships with the outside world are paraded before our eyes in an exemplary fashion in the finds from the so-called royal graves of Ur, which date from the beginning of the Early Dynastic III period.

Figure 58. Seals from the Early Dynastic II and III periods, from Babylonia. After (a) E. Heinrich, *Fara* (Berlin, 1931), pl. 42; (b) H. v. D. Osten, Collection B. Brett OIP 37 (Chicago, 1936), no. 21. Courtesy, Oriental Institute, University of Chicago; (c) C. L. Woolley, *The Royal Cemetery, Ur Excavations II* (London, 1934), pls. 194, 22; (d) ibid., pls. 197, 57; (e) A. Parrot, "Temple d'Ishtar," *Miss. Archaeol. de Mari* 1 (Paris, 1956), pls. 66, 545.

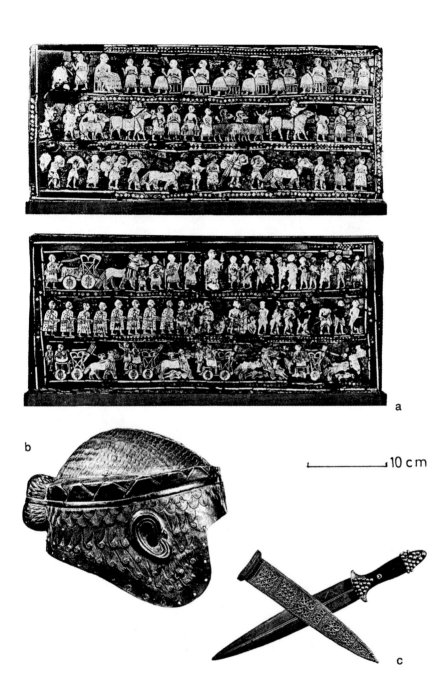

Figure 59. Finds from the Royal Cemetery at Ur (Iraq): (a) inlaid panels, (b) gold helmet of Meskalamdug, (c) gold dagger in sheath. From C. L. Woolley, *The Royal Cemetery, Ur Excavations II* (London, 1934), frontispiece, pls. 91, 92, 151.

The wealth of objects made of precious metals such as gold and silver, of copper and bronze weapons and jewelry, of vessels, tools, and jewelry made of semiprecious and precious stones and other colored stones is almost inexhaustible. Even if we cannot in every case say precisely where the raw materials came from, we do know that they must all have been brought from outside Babylonia. Where their origins can be established, they are found to come from the areas that are now Iran, Afghanistan, and Pakistan, or the areas around the Gulf. The origins of the metals in particular are still not clear. The same is also true for the large amounts of timber needed for the countless representative buildings, because the only timber locally available for building, the trunk of the date palm, is not suitable for the roofing of larger rooms; the trunks bend far too easily. It is only at the end of the Early Dynastic III period that we have some scant evidence about the provenance of wood for building from the "silver mountains," a name later used to refer to the mountains of Lebanon and western Syria.

Of course, trade with the neighboring regions had also been very lively in the period before this, as the examples from the era of early high civilization show. However, the rapid progress of urbanization, encouraging places that had formerly been quite small to grow to the size of centers, with the corresponding power structures that implies, must surely have made the scope of these exchanges considerably greater than it had formerly been. This trade was now definitely of the kind that had no need of a trading station, or of some sort of protection for trade routes, but was run along the lines of a mutual commercial enterprise.

This is, of course, quite natural for a period in which the trading partnership was no longer that between a highly civilized urban society on the one hand and societies with a considerably lower level of organizational structure on the other, but between two urban partners who differed from each other only in degree. The best example of one of these other partners has been known to us for only a short time—from the magnificent finds from Tell Mardikh, ancient Ebla, in northern Syria. However, we shall return to this later.

The finds from the so-called royal cemeteries of Ur and Kish allow us to cast a glance at an aspect we otherwise come across in isolated cases—the level of craftsmanship, primarily as shown in the sphere of the court, but also beyond it. We do not know which to admire most, the filigree techniques, the granulated dagger sheaths, the technique and craftsmanship of the inlaid work, or the artistry and taste involved in the execution of relief or sculpted objects made of materials of different colors and types.

Here, we see the result of a long tradition of craftsmanship. We would surely not be wrong if we were to regard these objects as evidence of a trend toward extreme specialization, whose main exponents were definitely in the direct employ of the ruling house.

The fact that these grave finds throw light on only a short part of a long tradition can clearly be seen in a sequence of finds, spectacular in a different way, made during excavations in the Diyala area. In several places in temple buildings that stretch in a long succession from the Jamdet Nasr period to the period of the Akkad Dynasty, excavators found repositories of statues that clearly belonged to the inventory of the respective temple up to a certain point in time, but then had to give way to new concepts or new statues and were interred in the temple area (fig. 60). The quantity alone prevents us from assuming that these could have been cult statues, just as, on the other hand, a comparison with the same type of statue from a later period makes it

Figure 60. Statues found at Tell Asmar (Iraq), dating to the Early Dynastic II period. From H. Frankfort, *Oriental Institute Discoveries in Iraq, 1933–34,* Oriental Inst. Communications 19 (Chicago, 1935), fig. 63. Courtesy, Oriental Institute, University of Chicago.

an attractive theory that we are here dealing with so-called "prayer statues." As we know from later inscriptions, these were put up in a temple by individuals in order to pray for the life of the benefactor in the sight of the god and in direct contact with him. Because such finds have not been made in the earlier levels there, we can assume that it is highly probable that the custom of setting up statues in temples with this intention began in the Early Dynastic period. This observation is of interest insofar as it certainly reflects a change in religious ideas. A notion of a god that makes it conceivable that the god can be influenced in this way differs fundamentally from one that sees in the god only what is spiritually elevated. It is a humanization of the divine image such as we have already seen as a precondition for the theological speculations about a pantheon in which the ranking order of the gods among themselves was expressed in the form of family relationships. The astonishing thing is that it was not merely members of the upper class in a particular place who donated statues, for the finds are from small shrines in normal residential areas, not the familiar large-scale buildings of a town's main places of worship. From this we can draw the conclusion that the custom of setting up "prayer statues"—and this obviously involved first having them made—must have been a very general one. That also means that this period quite clearly enjoyed a great demand for artists as well as for raw materials, an observation that can clearly be placed in the context of the steady growth in specialization.

We also see a change in the type of relief sculpture through its expansion into the area of historical relief. It is not pure chance that this occurs at the same time in which the first historical inscriptions are known to us. The best example—also, unfortunately, almost the only example—is the so-called "Vulture Stela" of Eannatum of Lagash (fig. 61). A long text tells us about the history and the details of the border conflict between the centers of Lagash and Umma, which is also known to us from other sources. This text is accompanied by the pictorial representation of some of the high points of this conflict. The departure of several army units under the leadership of the ruler (the largest fragment from the stela, which is illustrated here); the taking of prisoners among the enemy by Ningirsu, the god of Girsu; the burial of the dead of Lagash; and vultures carrying away the limbs of dead enemies—hence the title given to the stela—are all scenes from the parts of the stela that are preserved. Unfortunately, these only make up just a third of the original relief surfaces. The individual pictures, like the method of composition as a whole, set individual scenes side by side as if they were a picture-sheet, with hardly any relation to each other. Neither the figures in a scene, nor the attributes of individual persons, nor the parts of the bodies are in any way related to one another in the way they are presented. The extreme example of this can be seen in the presentation of the phalanx marching behind the ruler. The number of heads which are visible above the wall of shields corresponds neither to the number of arms protruding from this wall and holding spears nor to the number of feet.

Since the stela was not found in the place where it was originally set up, it is difficult to say anything about its function. Judging by the contents of the inscription, it is the documentation of a battle that was supposed to set the seal on the final victory of Lagash over Umma. The fact that this was an illusion is shown by an inscription by Eannatum's grandson, Entemena, who was also ruler of Lagash, which

Figure 61. One side of the largest fragment of Eannatums "Stela of the Vultures" from Tello, dating from the Early Dynastic III period. From E. Strommenger and M. Hirmer, *5 Jahrtausende Mesopotamien* (Munich, 1962), fig. 66. Courtesy, Hirmer Photoarchiv, Munich.

reports a resumption of the conflict. We may well assume that a period so full of internal political tensions that had a mode of expression like the historical relief surely made use of this medium to a greater extent than the surviving material lets us assume.

Interim results allow us to recognize the dilemma in which we find ourselves in dealing with a period from which the first completely historically evaluable written information is available, but that, as a whole, still lies in the realm of early writing. For the first time we think we can put a precise name to larger-scale relationships, only to be confronted immediately by tremendous restrictions because of our still inadequate material.

Naturally, in a case like this there is a great temptation to apply the statements made in such texts retroactively so as to fill in the gaps left by our lack of information. However, our knowledge is just sufficient to confirm that the vehemence of the changes in all areas was clearly so great, and the developments so varied and complex, that generalizations from texts that are only slightly more recent can only lead to errors of judgment.

If we now turn to the areas neighboring Babylonia, we encounter the same difficulties in an even more pronounced form because there the situation with regard to sources is even more inadequate. In most cases we can do no more than guess that these periods were as marked by violent changes and internal tensions as they were in Babylonia. One factor that makes the recovery of historical contexts even more impossible for the neighboring regions must be repeatedly considered. This is the practice of drawing conclusions from texts from one place or from finds in one excavation and applying them to a larger area or the whole region. Because of its collective dependence on the Euphrates as the source of its irrigation system, Babylonia was forced to move toward greater internal cooperation in spite of all its local differences. However, in contrast to this, centers in the flat areas of northern Mesopotamia and Syria, whose economies were based on extensive forms of agriculture, lay further apart and could thus unfold and develop far more independently of one another. Common factors thus only had to reach as far as was desired.

In other areas, such as Anatolia or Iran, topographical difficulties like those represented by the high, dividing mountain chains were an additional factor. At the end of chapter 4, we saw how it was precisely these geographical differences that brought about the separate developments that affected Babylonia and the neighboring regions. Pushed in more than one respect by the external conditions, Babylonia was able to build up new, more effective forms of organization, and the continuous stream of new challenges that it faced furthered development. The neighboring regions, which were not as intensively confronted with new problems, saw no reason, and also no opportunity, to follow in Babylonia's footsteps. The limited number of finds in these widely scattered areas might lead us to take the view that development stagnated in the neighboring areas and thus that the gap between Babylonia and these regions grew ever wider. However, this would quite definitely be a mistaken conclusion and a false interpretation of a gap in research. In any case, a few examples do show us that in the neighboring regions a further steady development did take place, visible to us first in the later part of the Early Dynastic period, that led to the flourishing of urban centers with characteristics that in every case allow us to point out a pronounced local development.

The most important development took place in the Syrian area, as is evident in the magnificent finds from ancient Ebla. Here, a community that, according to all our criteria, must be called an urban center had reached such a level of organization by the time of the Early Dynastic III period that both writing and parts of its higher literature were taken over from Babylonia. The Babylonian writing system was also adapted for use in reproducing the Semitic language of Ebla. Writing was used for literary compositions and, above all, for keeping a record of business. Just as in the beginning of the development of writing in Babylonia, the forms of economic organization in Ebla had clearly become so complex that it required some written record. However, in assessing these parallels, we must not underestimate the effects of the example of Babylonian civilization. Writing was patently an integral part of that civilization, and this alone cried out for it to be imitated.

In all of this, it must be noted first of all that what has been said about the high level of development in Ebla only holds good for the late phase of the Early Dynastic period because the written finds only stem from this period. The remains of earlier levels could only be excavated to a very limited extent, so that obviously nothing can be said about the degree of organization of the settlements in those periods, and it must inevitably appear to us as if the complexity of the phase that used writing was the consequence of a very rapid development. However, here we must once again refer back to what was said about the first appearance of writing in Babylonia. Writing first appears, or is first taken over, when a city's own development has progressed so far that the introduction of writing solves urgent and already existing problems. Thus, the level of development, mainly in the economic sphere, but also in other aspects of the period before the

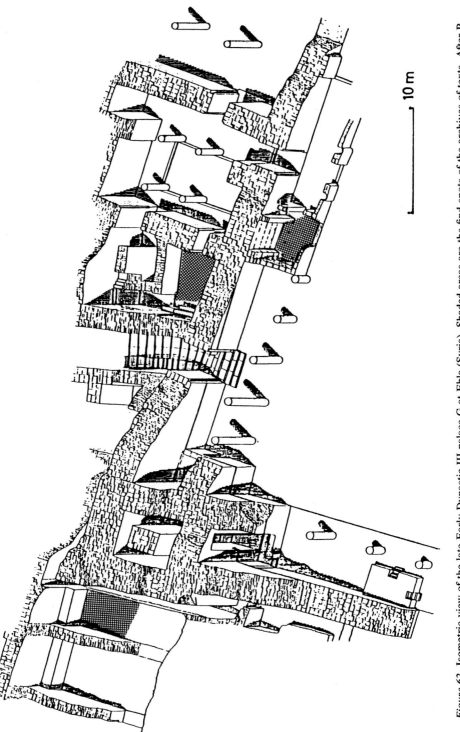

10 m

Figure 62. Isometric view of the late Early Dynastic III palace G at Ebla (Syria). Shaded areas are the find spots of the archives of texts. After P. Matthiae, *I tesori di Ebla* (Rome, 1984), pl. 6a, and G. Pettinato, *Ebla, un impero inciso nell' argilla* (Rome, 1979), fig. II.1.

introduction of writing, must have already been considerable. This means that we are completely justified in assuming that the Early Bronze II period at Ebla, which corresponds approximately to Early Dynastic II and III periods in Babylonia, and that is, as yet, hardly known to us from finds, was in no way as poorly developed as it may appear to have been at first glance.

How far this level of development can also be expected for other places in the Syrian area cannot yet be answered. The fact that no texts were found, for example, in the excavations at Hama and Tell Huera, which have revealed remains from the same period, cannot be used as a negative answer to this question. In Ebla it needed ten years of intensive work before the first written documents were found. Thus it is simply an exaggeration on the part of the excavators, albeit a legitimate one, when they take Ebla to be the center of Syria at that time.

Unfortunately, in this area, the problem is not only that very few excavations have been carried out, but also that the processing of what has been found is still in its infancy. Thus, the question of what belongs to the line of local development in Ebla or Tell Huera and what can be traced back to Babylonian influence cannot yet be answered with any degree of satisfaction, although this is necessary in order to fix some sort of chronological bracketing with Babylonia. Moreover, we could speak more precisely about the relations between these two regions only if we had a basic knowledge of this chronological framework. Fascinated by the fact that in so distant a place as northern Syria objects have been found that undoubtedly originated in, or were influenced by, Babylonia, scholars have until now discussed only these obvious relationships, while giving insufficient attention to the independent local development. The question of a counter influence exerted on Babylonia by the civilization of the centers in the west has seldom been discussed, and then only with caution. Quite apart from the fact that such a reciprocal influence must have taken place, this question can clearly be answered in the affirmative, at least in one sector, that of literary composition. Among the texts from the Babylonian sites of Shuruppak and Abu Salabikh from the beginning of the Early Dynastic III period, there are a few we now identify very clearly as copies of Eblaitic originals. Likewise, as was noted earlier, the transformation of writing into an instrument by which complicated texts with all the nuances of spoken language could be written at the beginning of the Early Dynastic III period could only be achieved with the assistance of non-Sumerian-speaking groups. Among these, in addition to the early Akkadians in Babylonia itself, groups such as the Semitic Eblaites must definitely have played a part, because of the necessity in each case of transforming the system of writing in order to reproduce their own language. A more significant reciprocal influence can hardly be imagined, since it is only after the transformation of Babylonian writing that the texts begin to be our main source of information about Babylonian civilization. The fact that, for the time being, we have not been able to perceive any traces of this reciprocal influence in other spheres, such as, for example, in archaeological remains, is thus clearly the consequence of considerable gaps in our knowledge.

According to evidence provided by pottery, the Anatolia of the Early Bronze period—as the period from the Early Dynastic I period through the period of the Third Dynasty of Ur is called in the terminology for Syria and Anatolia—had close commercial connections with the Syrian plains through a variety of pottery imports. However, the fact that we have hardly anything other than pottery for the Early Bronze II period—which corresponds approximately to the Early Dynastic II and III periods in Babylonia—already shows on what comparatively rough evidence any statements we make about this region must rest. The situation with regard to finds hardly allows us to draw any conclusions other than that on the whole we are clearly dealing with a continuous local development.

This also seems to be confirmed by an observation we can make based on material from the Early Bronze III period, which corresponds to the Akkad and Ur III phases. By examining a succession of strata on the same sites, we are able in this period to determine a change in the concentration of power that can be detected archaeologically and is exhibited in the development of mansions of a sort that had not previously existed in this sense. We shall deal with this in chapter 6.

The situation with regard to sources is equally inadequate for the western Iranian area, the Zagros region. Although remains from this period have been found in several places, in every case they were in such a limited area that only pottery is available for evaluation. From this evidence we may also reckon with a continuous local development in all fields. We do not find any visible signs for contacts with the western foreland plains in the data about the settlements, but we do know from other sources that such relationships must have existed. We have already mentioned that Tepe Yahya in southern central Iran was clearly at this time a center for the production of relief vessels made of chlorite. Their unique appearance made possible the identification—as Iranian—of a succession of such vessels, which have been found at Babylonian sites in levels from the Early Dynastic period.

The uncovering of cemeteries in Luristan, in the central Zagros area, has provided us with a second argument for close affiliations. The graves from the numerous cemeteries, which were often furnished with rich grave goods, probably define the areas in which copper was mined. Objects that stem from the chief area buying this raw material, Babylonia, are to be found here in large numbers and cover the whole period of Babylonian history from the Ubaid period onwards. A whole series of pieces imported from the Babylonia of the Early Dynastic II and III periods provide irrefutable evidence of the existence of very direct contacts.

The two remaining areas, Susiana and northern Mesopotamia, again show very much closer contacts with Babylonia, even if in a different way. The decline of settlement in Susiana, which had already begun in the Uruk period, had reached the point in the Early Dynastic II period where only very few places were actually inhabited apart from Susa, which, judging from the central terrace uncovered there, was clearly still an important center. However, we can see how distant Susa was from the development in Babylonia from the almost complete lack of written evidence, apart from a few "line inscriptions," which are not very productive for us, either in their numbers or in their content. At the end of the previous era—the Early Dynastic I period in Babylonian terms—the written tradition had ceased, and the tradition of painted pottery was revived. The latter had come to a complete standstill when the Babylonian unpainted pottery of the Late Uruk period had been taken over, but then a complete renunciation of Babylonian development becomes clearly visible. After this, in the late Early Dynastic period, the signs of direct Babylonian influence now begin to increase again.

This new development is especially tangible in that, in the cylinder seals that now again begin to appear more frequently, the same graphic content is used as in Babylonia. Above all, the pictures are subject to the same changes as in Babylonia. Toward the end of this phase, in the Early Dynastic III period, but above all in the period following that, the time of the Akkad Dynasty, writing was now once again taken over from Babylonia. In contrast to the first occasion, during the period of early high civilization, it was not merely the idea of writing and its technique that was drawn upon in order to write Elamite with the aid of their own writing system. Language and writing were now both taken over. Thus, the texts in Susa were now composed in Sumerian, and somewhat later in Akkadian. A few texts in Elamite do, however, show that the Elamites also knew how to transcribe their own language. When we hear, at the time of the Akkad Dynasty, that Elam, with its capital Susa, was numbered among their permanent foreign possessions and when the ruler in Susa refers to himself in his own writings as servant of the ruler of Akkad, this is not really a new development, but could also describe the situation in the later Early Dynastic period.

Conditions in northern Mesopotamia are different, and, for the time being, hardly accessible to us. In the foregoing period of early high civilization in Babylonia, local traditions and settlements influenced by southern Mesopotamia had coexisted. This component influenced by the south disappears, or is, at least after the Uruk period, no longer accessible to us, which may, however, be connected with the extremely poor situation as regards information. Local traditions such as, for example, the so-called Nineveh 5 pottery, with its characteristic style of painting, which was developed in the region, shape what is, on the whole, a rather vague image.

It is a remarkable fact that this also holds true for the settlement of Nineveh, which provides us with our best examples of southern influence during the Late Uruk period, in the shape of Uruk pottery, bevel-rimmed bowls, and cylinder seals. Contacts with the south were certainly not broken off, in spite of the prominence of the older, local tradition. Thus we should not regard the late Early Dynastic period finds from levels H and G of the temple dedicated to the goddess Ishtar in Assur, which are for the most part—and this is specially true of the statues found there—unambiguously in the Babylonian tradition, as being as isolated as they now appear, but rather as a sign of these continuing contacts. But unfortunately our material is once again inadequate for more precise assessment of the development of northern Mesopotamia. At the risk of reading too much into the material, we might on the whole already see a tendency at work here that can only be confirmed later on. Of all Babylonia's neighboring areas, only northern Mesopotamia—what was later Assyria—could perform and maintain the balancing act of continuing to participate in Babylonian development while at the same time maintaining some independence of its own. Whereas relations between Babylonia and other regions wavered between degrees of dependence and independence, relations between Babylonia and the north seem to have developed quietly and at a steady pace toward the state of distanced power-sharing that was later to govern the relationship between Babylonia and Assyria.

With this treatment of Babylonia's neighboring regions, our survey of the areas of the Near East is complete. Even if, unfortunately, it is also still filled with gaps that are all too large, we are at least left with the finding that there were considerable differences between the individual regions in cultural and economic development. Babylonia unambiguously represents the most highly developed form, so that, to our normally foreshortened way of viewing things, it might look as if Babylonia thus automatically also played the leading role politically. This is, however, erroneous. Although it may well be true that at times a direct imperial relationship existed for some of the regions immediately adjacent to Babylonia, such as northern Mesopotamia or Susiana, which always had a sort of love-hate relationship with Babylonia, the relationship between Babylonia and other regions of the Near East can hardly ever have been of that sort.

Although it is not yet evident and cannot be pinpointed until the next phase of development, it is in the growth, during the Early Dynastic period, of centers of power outside Babylonia, which gradually acquired supraregional significance, that the kernel of the gradual decline of Babylonia's position of preeminence is to be found. This may seem remarkable for a period in which Babylonia's great invasions of neighboring regions for the sake of gaining more political power had yet to take place, but it is in no way as paradoxical as may at first appear.

As will become clear in the following period with the conquests of the rulers of the Akkad and Ur Dynasties, it is precisely these invasions that demonstrate that it was now considered necessary to insist on a formerly unchallenged position of superiority. The attempts of these rulers to tie parts of the areas outside Babylonia politically with Babylonia itself did not thus mark the beginning of a phase in which Babylonia ruled the whole of the Near East. Rather, they signify the end of a period of preeminence for Babylonia. The neighboring areas became so fixed in their own forms of organization, linked, of course, with their own political ambitions, that in the final analysis Babylonia became only one center among many, some of which sometimes disposed of even greater power. Finally, Hammurapi's Babylon was only protected from the new powers, which were advancing ever closer, by the protective mantle of a few buffer states. Misjudging the situation, Hammurapi conquered these buffer states and thus destroyed the protective shield, with the resultant loss of Babylonia's position of preeminence. This spurred on the Hittite ruler Murshili to make war on Babylonia, thus ending the dynasty of Hammurapi. However, this was only the overt ending of a shift in power in the Near East that had already been long in the offing.

SIX

The Period of the First Territorial States
(ca. 2350–2000 B.C.)

We have thus far, in considering individual periods, been able to establish that in spite of all the differences and changes, which at times give the impression of an interruption of the tradition, there was on the whole an unbroken tradition in Babylonia. However, with the founding of the Akkad Dynasty, fundamental changes were apparent in more than one sphere, so that we may speak with some justification of a break with the past. In fact, the indications make it easy to regard all the differences from the foregoing Early Dynastic period as individual elements in one great change. It seems all too clear here that the contrast consists in the fact that, just as it seems justifiable to connect the civilization of the Early Dynastic period closely with the Sumerian ethnic group (hence the use of the term "Old Sumerian" for the Early Dynastic period), it seems accurate to associate the completely different style of the period of the Akkad Dynasty with the new holders of political power, the semitic Akkadians. It thus seems simple enough to reduce all the differences to the contrasts between Sumerians and Akkadians.

The difference was substantial. Instead of rulers with Sumerian names, we are suddenly confronted with rulers with Akkadian names. Instead of the use of the Sumerian language in literary and economic texts, we now find the almost exclusive use of Akkadian. Instead of a large number of city-states, there was now a territorial state with Akkad as its capital. Instead of trade relationships and trading partly connected with individual centers, efforts were now made to draw trade to the city of Akkad by means of an import monopoly. Instead of clumsy, ill-proportioned human figures in art, slim, well-proportioned forms are depicted that display anatomical details. In place of the inhibition about leaving even the smallest portion of the surface area of a picture empty, we now find the intentional inclusion of empty background as a part of the composition. In place of a paratactic ordering of the elements in larger compositions, an attempt was now made to represent the relationships between the characters pictorially.

If, in what follows, we mainly discuss the problem of the transition from the Early Dynastic to the Akkadian period and the further development of forms of political organization, and do not attempt a detailed account of social and political conditions, this is because we continually find ourselves in the dilemma that caused us problems in chapter 5. The archaeological finds scarcely permit us to make any statements except on art, because we have scarcely any excavation data. Nor can any technological innovations be shown to have taken place; if there were any, they must have occurred on a level not manifest in the archaeological evidence. The written sources are hardly ever detailed enough to reveal small-scale connections or short-term changes. If we wished to proceed merely from the material known to us, we would obtain a very fragmentary picture. Indeed, contradictions might even arise in the ordering of one or the other aspect of it, because the material in many instances does not permit us to lay the groundwork basis.

We have hardly any material from stratigraphic excavations. All too often, we must content ourselves with art-historical statements about isolated objects that are out of context. We have already put behind us the periods in which, with little effort, we were able to find archaeological material that proved to be the product of more or less rapid changes in production methods. Ideas about changes in technology and in the forms of organization of production acquired in this way often provided the starting point for statements about the economic and social background in earlier periods. There is no way of obtaining this sort of evidence for the period we are dealing with now, although this does not mean that no further changes took place in the fields of technology and organization. Presumably, these changes took place at a different level, so that, at best, direct effects on the appearance of the end product were very limited, or at least limited to the extent that we can no longer recognize them.

There is also very little to be reported about changes in the area of settlement systems, changes that provided us with important clues as to the overall process of development in the case of the earlier periods. It is true that we can make some assumptions here, such as, for example, that the concentration of political power in the north of Babylonia could have had the effect of increasing the amount of settlement activity in this part of the country. Opportunities for interpretation available to us through archaeological surface investigations are very limited for the period of the Akkad Dynasty, however, and it is only from this sort of investigation that we might expect to obtain the relevant information. During the period of the Akkad Dynasty, pottery, as the material we can mainly draw upon for the dating of settlement systems, became so mass-produced and differed so slightly from the mass-produced wares of the previous Early Dynastic III period and the following period of the Third Dynasty of Ur, that unequivocal classification of a site as belonging to one of the abovementioned periods solely on the grounds of the pottery found during surface investigations is hardly ever possible. Unfortunately, seals, clay tablets, and inscribed bricks, which would permit unequivocal dating, are not among the everyday finds in the course of an archaeological surface investigation. As far as we can tell, our evaluation of the surface finds shows that in one important point we can determine that there was no change with regard to the previous period—that is, in the distribution of settlement sizes. Babylonia remained an area almost exclusively of urban centers, with only a very few rural settlements. The assertion that the pattern of settlements during the period of the Akkad Dynasty can hardly have differed greatly from that of the earlier period is not contradicted by the texts either.

Thus, if we wished to proceed only on the basis of the primary sources available to us, we would have an extremely incomplete picture. Often enough, our material would not even be sufficient to allow us to establish some sort of basic outline. This is even more unfortunate since we are forced to assume that the creation in the towns of a centralized administration and communication system—that is, the establishment of a "civil service"—must have had its effects upon the social structuring of society. In every case, this "civil service" must have had stronger ties of loyalty to the central government than to the local powers. Unfortunately, the written evidence hardly helps us solve this problem. The few texts that allow us to make any relevant statements at all in each case only throw light on the smallest of details, which can in no way be merged into a larger picture. In addition, the geographically scattered origins of the texts make the danger of attempting to piece together tiles that never belonged in the same mosaic a very real one.

In spite of all these difficulties, the evidence handed down to us does allow us to draw a fairly coherent picture of the historical progression, which will be briefly sketched here to provide us with a framework. A member of the upper classes belonging to the Semitic speaking group, known later under the throne name of "Sharruken," "the true king," which was corrupted to Sargon, reached a high position in the administration of the city of Kish. Under conditions that are not clear to us, he was able to seize power for himself, but he did not choose the old city of Kish as his capital. Instead, he chose the town of Akkad, which was probably in the neighborhood, and thus it was Sargon who first gave it some importance. Unfortunately, to this day, we have still not been able to locate the city of Akkad.

Sargon was clearly able to expand the scope of his power very quickly, helped by the fact that in the meantime Lugalzaggesi of Umma had begun an attempt to unite larger areas of Babylonia under his rule, starting from the south. Victory over Lugalzaggesi thus provided Sargon with what was already a much greater portion of the country. After conquering the whole area, Sargon attempted to extent his sphere of influence beyond the borders of Babylonia. His own inscriptions mention Mari and Tuttul on the central Euphrates, in what is today Syria, as well as Ebla. Later writings also credit Sargon with expeditions to Cyprus and Anatolia, and these may be related to actual campaigns carried out by him. However, like Sargon's other campaigns, these in no way led to permanent possessions and were probably not even meant to. These efforts to extend his sphere of influence were also directed to the east and north.

With these campaigns Sargon went far beyond the scale of operations of the earlier period, so that in them we can also surely glimpse an element of the stabilization of his power. However, we have a more important clue for this in the statement that "sons of Akkad fulfill the role of the *ensi* in the country." Clearly, his own people had been installed as governors in the conquered areas. This process, the creation of direct links between parts of Babylonia and the capital city, is certainly an innovation in comparison with the earlier period. It is also a key to the answer to the question of why—in contrast to earlier attempts—Sargon's efforts to achieve centralization were successful. Further evidence, showing that administrative changes were carried out in order to secure the conquered areas, can be found in other, different parts of the writings. Thus, for example, the assertion that Sargon "made the ships from Meluhha, Magan, and Dilmun anchor at the quay of Akkad," must obviously be interpreted to mean that he secured the monopoly in what was most definitely a lucrative trade with the countries on the Gulf and the coasts of the Arabian Sea. The statement that he provided for 5,400 men every day could point to the existence of a standing army, or in any case to a large group of people who were charged with central duties.

We can only assume that in spite of all these precautions, which aimed at cutting off any possibility of internal revolt, the years of Sargon's reign did not pass without local uprisings. By the time of the reign of his son and successor Rimush, at the latest, efforts to win back independence had grown to massive proportions. Rimush had to fight

Figure 63. Fragment of a stela of Sargon of Akkad, showing prisoners being taken away in a "neck-stock." From W. Orthmann, *Propyläen Kunstgeschichte* 14 (Berlin, 1975), fig. 103. Copyright: State Organization of Antiquities and Heritage. Baghdad.

against what was clearly a broad coalition of cities under the leadership of a pretender from Ur. We hear about both this victory and a victory over Elam in the inscriptions of Rimush. The find of a votive inscription mentioning Rimush at Tell Brak on the Upper Habur river in present-day Syria, and the naming after Rimush of a place that must be looked for to the north of Nineveh, show that areas of northern Mesopotamia and Syria had also some ties to the Akkadian state under this ruler.

The little information we possess about the reign of Manishtushu, the elder son of Sargon, who followed after his brother, only allows us to draw the conclusion that he had to struggle with similar difficulties and managed to maintain his kingdom at about the same size. Special attention must be paid to the mention of a victory over Anshan, recently identified as the former name of Tell Malyan, not far from Persepolis. From a campaign against thirty-two cities "on the other side of the sea"—which probably means from the region to the east of the Gulf—he brought back the "black stone" used to make his statues. The aim of these long-distance undertakings—to secure the supply of raw materials—here becomes particularly clear.

Manishtushu's son Naram-Sin was his successor, and the exceptional power he possessed raises him, for his contemporaries and for later writers, to the same level as his grandfather Sargon. We are very well informed about his reign, even if at times this information comes from later inscriptions. A number of the inscriptions bear both his name and the determinative for a god, whereas there are others without this sign. Placed in front of particular names, the sign shows that they are the names of gods, so that Naram-Sin appears, at least in some of his inscriptions, to have been a deified ruler. The formality of deification probably means that we can assume, with some degree of certainty, that this title could not be used at will, but that, after this act, the name of the ruler could only be written in this way. We can therefore proceed on the assumption that the difference in the way the name was written corresponds to a chronological division. The inscriptions that bear the name of the ruler without the determinative are, therefore, probably to be placed at the beginning of his reign.

If we order the years of Naram-Sin's reign according to this division, campaigns and victories against cities that do not receive any further mention and against the eastern lands of Elam and Magan take place at the beginning, while struggles against the inhabitants of the mountain regions to the east and against Syria are concentrated in the later period. As before, there is a recognizable schema: first, uprisings in one's own country had to be put down before the consolidation of the outer regions could be considered. The clear necessity of fighting against inhabitants of the eastern mountains is of significance here, since the groups known as the Guti, who are in the text tradition made responsible for the collapse of the Akkadian empire, came from this area. We shall be discussing this further, just as we shall be discussing the significance of the abovementioned deification of rulers, which can here be proved for the first time in Babylonian history.

All that we maintain here is that the act of deification was probably directed against some principle of traditional political ideology. It is probably because of this that Naram-Sin acquired the reputation in the later religious literature—and even beyond that—of being an unpopular and unfortunate ruler, whereas in the original data there is nothing to indicate the disastrous end later writings speak of.

We also find a grouping of the inscriptions according to whether the name is written with or without the determinative for a god in the case of Naram-Sin's son, Sharkalisharri. Here, the sequence of events was probably the other way around, since Sharkalisharri probably found himself increasingly restricted to the narrow limits of his own city. This means that he must have assumed his father's tradition at the beginning, but have given it up soon after, presumably in partial response to a new constellation of power favoring the particularist principle as opposed to the central state that, almost like the swing of a pendulum, brought about the dissolution of larger alliances into smaller spheres of influence.

The sequence of rulers who can actually be proved to have belonged to one family comes to an end with Sharkalisharri. At the same time, the end of his reign signifies the end of the political entity that, for the first time, had managed for several generations to rule over the whole of Babylonia, from the city of Akkad. For this reason, we want to interrupt our presentation of external events and turn to other problems connected with the period of the Akkad Dynasty.

In chapter 5 the probability was suggested that two well-founded concepts of the political organization of Babylonia confronted each other from time to time and should be seen as the forces that determined Babylonia's political development. If these contrasts also played a decisive role under the Akkad Dynasty, then this theory can now be relatively easily tested. Since the political structure of this period can, without any doubt, be defined as a central state, we should expect this state to have defended itself vigorously against particularist tendencies emanating from the religious centers.

However, resistance by particularist interests reveals itself as the resistance of religious centers in only a handful of cases. Thus, not only the attempts of the different city states during the reign of the first ruler

Figure 64. Akkadian period stela from Tello. From W. Orthmann, *Propyläen Kunstgeschichte* 14 (Berlin, 1975), fig. 102. Courtesy, Musée du Louvre.

of the new dynasty to recover their independence, but also reports according to which individual cities or coalitions of cities from southern Babylonia attempted to free themselves from the central state must be excluded from the argument. It cannot be denied that in these cases the main idea behind the uprising was solely the attempt to win back independence. We cannot determine how far the steps Sargon took to have his daughter Enheduanna made a high priestess of the city god of Ur—with the possible intention of quelling local resistance—can be related to this. The fact that this was, in any case, regarded by the local body of priests as an affront—which I tend to see as a calculated one—was made very clear when Enheduanna was finally driven out of Ur.

Thus, the situation with regard to sources corresponds to the fact that in only one case do we have enough information about different aspects to enable us to bring them together in some sort larger association. This information is all related to the reign of Naram-Sin, the fourth ruler of the dynasty. However, in contrast to our usual way of proceeding, we shall in this case make use of information that comes from a somewhat later period as well. The great number of original inscriptions by Naram-Sin written down at a somewhat later date, as well as the numerous other reports about him, make it appear certain that at that time they still had very exact knowledge about Naram-Sin's period. Thus it is perfectly possible to place these later texts at the same level of dependability as the contemporary sources.

The only point that can be proved beyond a shadow of doubt in support of our argument in this connection is an apparent superficiality—the self-deification already mentioned, which was first observed under Naram-Sin. In one case, we have evidence for this from a pictorial representation of the ruler on his victory stela, where he is shown wearing a horned crown, the symbol of divinity (fig. 65). In addition, the determinative for a god is placed in front of the name of the ruler in numerous inscriptions, and finally, Naram-Sin is referred to, in numerous inscriptions of consecration and devotion made by his subjects, as "the god of Akkad."

It would hardly be the right approach to the problem to see this deification only as an act of hybris and the last step on the way to "oriental despotism," especially since the idea of deified human beings was not a particularly new one. Three hundred years earlier, in a list of gods from Shuruppak, other ancient rulers such as Lugalbanda and Gilgamesh are already listed among the gods. The claim to divinity alone would scarcely have caused as much uproar as the texts seem to suggest, unless this deification has to be looked at against a different background.

In fact, the stumbling block was probably not the deification itself. The title "god of Akkad," which appears in a few inscriptions, possibly suggests an interpretation different from that given above. This is quite clearly the title that actually belonged to the city god, or, in the case of Akkad, to the city goddess, Ishtar of Akkad. In order to grasp the importance of this, we should recall the more ancient view according to which, in a somewhat rigid form, the city god had a right to the possessions of the whole city. In this view, it was impossible to imagine a city god who did not possess land, and it was this concept that created the theoretical basis for the development of the special form of the "temple city" in the late Early Dynastic period.

The conclusion to be drawn about the designation of Naram-Sin as the "god of Akkad" is this: by the act of deification, he placed himself in the position of being able to enjoy all the rights of the city god, thus killing two birds with one stone. On the one hand, he would —at least in his capital city—by these means have resolved in his own person the conflict between particularist interests, supported by reli-

Figure 65. Victory stela of Naram-Sin of Akkad. From W. Orthmann, *Propyläen Kunstgeschichte* 14 (Berlin, 1975), fig. 104. Courtesy, Musée du Louvre.

gion, and the idea of the centralized state. On the other, the process must have meant that he claimed title to the land. Thus it is clear that this act must have been extraordinarily disturbing, not only for the local priests, but also for the holders of religious office throughout the whole country, since in both respects it was a central attack on the most important aspects of the power of local interests.

Contemporary evidence for this action may be missing, but a document from the period of the Third Dynasty of Ur first becomes understandable to us through this thesis. The composition in question is a quite long historical poem entitled "A Curse of Akkad" and describes things that happened during the reign of Naram-Sin. In it, Naram-Sin is accused of an unnamed sacrilege against Enlil, the city god of Nippur and highest god in the pantheon. Because of this sacrilege, he is supposed to have aroused the general wrath of the gods. However, only Enlil and the city goddess of Akkad, Ishtar of Akkad, are actually mentioned by name in this connection. By way of punishment, Enlil installs an opposing ruler in Nippur, but he is conquered by Naram-Sin. In this particular action, Naram-Sin destroyed Enlil's shrine in Nippur. As punishment, the gods called the Guti, a people from the mountains bordering Babylonia to the east, into the land to chastise Naram-Sin and his "house." The poem ends with the rejoicing of the city goddess of Akkad because Akkad, her own city, has been destroyed!

We have difficulties with the poem, because the statements made in it do not agree on several points with what we know about the situation. Thus in the course of the excavations of Enlil's temple in Nippur it was not possible to find any levels from the period of Naram-Sin that had actually been destroyed. On the contrary, bricks stamped with Naram-Sin's name show that he had clearly been as active as before in commissioning buildings there. In addition, the kingdom of Akkad and the city were not in any way destroyed during, or at the end of, Naram-Sin's reign. It may well be that the Guti began their raids at this time. However, quite apart from the fact that their role in history has certainly always been exaggerated because they are mentioned in the Sumerian King List, they first actually played a role here under Naram-Sin's successors. If we remove from the poem all the clear later accretions, what remains as the historical kernel is still the struggle between Naram-Sin and the gods, and especially the supreme god, Enlil.

If we assemble everything said up till now and accept the changes connected with the deification as the actual kernel of the conflict, then, apart from anything else, we now have a solution to the strange fact that the only co-plaintiff beside Enlil—who represents the interests of all the gods—is the city goddess of Akkad. If our interpretation is correct, the interests of Naram-Sin's city goddess would have been the first to have been affected by his actions. If we pursue this interpretation further, the deification would have been a clever move in Naram-Sin's game, letting us know simultaneously that the city gods or their priests were the actual opponents of the central government. This poem would thus not be, as has been suggested, a document about the conflicts between Sumerians, represented by Enlil, and Akkadians, represented by the rulers of the Akkad Dynasty, but would bear witness to the permanent conflict between local and central power, represented here by the most important of the local gods and the ruler of the centralized state. As to the supposition that the contrast between two different religious concepts is behind this, all that need be said at the moment is that we are not here speaking of the contrast between "Sumerian" and "Akkadian" gods—a theory often put forward—but rather of a difference in man's understanding of his own relationship to the gods. We shall have to return to this point.

However, first we must pursue another train of thought and try to establish the characteristics of the art of the Akkad period by contrasting it with the art of the late Early Dynastic period. This may perhaps contribute to the solution of the overall problem. We want, here, to restrict ourselves to two from among the many possibilities for comparison, because these two are the ones that provide us with the most information—reliefs and cylinder seals.

In the case of reliefs, we go back to the difference in interpretation that has long been observed between the so-called "Vulture Stele" of Eannatum of Lagash and the victory stele of Naram-Sin, most especially the completely different way in which the army is represented (figs. 61 and 65). Whereas on the older Vulture Stele the army is shown as a many-headed, many-armed, many-footed colossus made of shields, behind a ruler who is portrayed as being very much larger than they are, the soldiers on Naram-Sin's stele are represented as individuals. If we include one more fragment from another stele, probably originating from Tello (fig. 64), on which a battle between two opposing armies is broken up into a series of single combats, the difference in conception is completely clear. This treatment of the figures on the pieces from the period of the Akkad Dynasty, with its novel emphasis on the individual, can also be found in the same way on other objects in the field of plastic art and among the things represented on cylinder seals.

The fact that in Naram-Sin's stele human forms are depicted with remarkable freedom of movement, and the landscape is not merely incorporated in the scene via a series of symbols, has been emphasized often enough, and is rightly seen as a significant innovation. Here, however, the attention of the reader must be drawn to one further aspect in which Naram-Sin's stele reaches the limits of the representational potential of the ancient oriental artist as currently perceived. If we make a very rough comparison between the art of the ancient Orient and the works of Greek art, which came much later, all objects of ancient oriental art can easily be categorized as the juxtaposing of individual details to make a larger picture. The ideal typical representation of these details had, in consequence, hard lines between each individual detail. On the other side, there is the subordination of details to a total concept, and thus compositions containing details that are related to one another with natural transitions between them. The stele of Naram-Sin does not seem to fit into this clear antithesis. For, contrary to usual practice, where the individual figures, though they may have a substantive relationship to one another, are juxtaposed in an unconnected fashion, here the individual figures and parts of figures are related. This is evident in the row of fleeing forms lined up underneath each other on the right edge of the picture. They are turning round and holding out one or two beseeching hands to the ruler, who is shown in a victory pose. Whereas other works would have been satisfied with repeating the same figure of the enemy over and over again, here the way the enemies are standing is related to the way their position changes from the point of view of the ruler depending on where the figure is placed in the composition. Thus, according to the position of each enemy soldier, the face, and with it the line of sight, is turned increasingly upward. At the same time, the outstretched arm is held up in such a way that no matter what, the hand is always held out to the one they are appealing to so that it is in line with the mouth. In addition, the forces concentrated in the lines moving upward and downward in the work are so masterfully balanced that a completely harmonious picture was created. Only the figure of the ruler, because of its special position, still stands out, because it is hardly linked to the forces of the rest of the work. This clearly bears witness to a totally new independent concept of art. On the whole, we may say that this new way of seeing, this emergence of the individual, clearly reflects a change in consciousness, in which the independence and personal responsibility of the individual are for the first time given pictorial expression.

This individualization and naturalistic representation is also found on the cylinder seals. A comparison between pictures of animal fights from cylinder seals of the Early Dynastic period (fig. 58a, b, d) and the period of the Akkad Dynasty (fig. 66a, b) gives an especially good example of this. The fear of having an empty—that is, unworked—surface, which, in the Early Dynastic period brought about artistic patterns in which figures are connected and overlap each other, gives way to a striving for uninhibited individualization of each figure. However, the freedom of composition we saw on the stele of Naram-Sin could not work on cylinder seals, because the parameters were quite different: the band was strictly limited as to the upper and lower edges but was, ideally, of limitless length. In addition to the themes of animal fights that continued to predominate, the cylinder seals now show a confusing number of new themes. These may often have been taken from popular myths, but we hardly ever succeed in identifying them. Therefore, what at first seems to be the sort of material that opens up the spiritual ideas of this period to us is, unfortunately, a closed book.

Two themes should, however, be singled out. In both cases they are representations of gods, interpretation of which will perhaps make possible an important advance in our understanding. The two pictures

Figure 66. Seals of the Akkadian period. From R. M. Boehmer, *Die Entwicklung der Glyptik während der Akkad-Zeit* (Berlin, 1965), (a) fig. 53; (b) fig. 197; (c) fig. 611; (d) fig. 329; (e) fig. 399; (f) fig. 441.

in question are the so-called struggles of the gods (fig. 66d) and introduction or presentation scenes (fig. 66f).

In the first case we are dealing with representations of figures fighting with each other who, because of their horned crowns, can be clearly defined as gods. This theme, which is first attested in the Akkad period, clearly contrasts not only with the earlier practice, which was either not to represent gods at all or else only in noble poses, but also with the conception of the gods as we know it from texts of the earlier period. Depictions of this sort, as we now find them, seem inconceivable without a fundamental change in the conception of the gods. It is a new way of looking at the world of the gods: one that dissolves the earlier unity of the gods as all-embracing city gods—but who could also be given special characteristics—into gods with individual responsibilities, and into hierarchies.

This line of thought receives further support from an examination of a second group of seals, the "introduction scenes." During the period of the Akkad Dynasty a motif, very soon to become widespread, appeared characterizing the relationship between man and the gods in a particular way. In the "introduction scenes" a human supplicant is introduced to a higher divinity by another divinity who is interceding for him. From the way in which the figures of the gods are ordered, the rank of each god can be clearly seen. We do not only know of these ideas from a multiplicity of texts in which certain gods are portrayed as servants, messengers, or viziers of other gods, but, above all, from the idea that apparently personal tutelary gods were needed as well as the great gods. Clearly, the idea behind this was that a divine intercessor was needed if one was to be able to put one's problems before the god one was really praying to. However, this can only have meant that the higher gods were seen as more abstract and inaccessible, whereas the lower-ranking gods were seen as more accessible, but also as gods who did not have any power of their own. What appears here is a concept of gods that is no longer dependent on the idea of the god as a land and property owner. The fact that this would have called into question the theoretical basis of local power would have been more of a threat to the latter than political striving toward centralism. But at the same time, we see here the theoretical basis upon which an attack such as that made by Naram-Sin could even be thinkable.

In spite of all our attempts to explain and interpret individual phenomena, the question of why these innovations prevailed so forcefully at the beginning of the Akkad Dynasty remains unanswered. Any attempt to answer this question must include two premises. At the

Figure 67. Cylinder seal and impression dating to the Akkadian period. Height 2.6 cm. Collection of the Seminar für Vorderasiatische Altertumskunde, Freie Universität, Berlin. Photo M. Nissen. (Cf. Moortgat-Correns, "Die ehem. Rollsiegel-Sammlung E. Oppenländer," *Baghd. Mitt.* 4 [1968] no. 44.)

outset, it was proposed that even where there is apparent discontinuity, we should look for signs of continuity. In this sense, the thesis must be able to hold water that argues that just as the incorporeal, anonymous conception of man and the individualistic, naturalistic conception existed side by side as early as the Early Dynastic period, a concrete conception of the gods, largely related to a particular place, existed beside a more abstract one. It is also very difficult to imagine that the period of the Akkad Dynasty should not only have come forward with such completely new ideas, but was also able immediately to establish them so completely. The explanation for this could be that the period had merely given new priorities to older, already existing ideas.

The second premise also suggests a direction in which we might go to find a possible answer. For internal as well as external reasons, particulars of all kinds about the periods in question are known to us, in the main, only from, and about, the public sector of society. This is true for external reasons because there are hardly any areas apart from the public buildings in the settlements of that period that have been excavated. The internal reasons derive from the fact that we are dealing with written and artistic statements and with objects associated with the thin layer of upper-class citizens who were responsible for the form of government at any given moment, so that only the ideas of this class are reflected.

A series of antitheses has repeatedly been presented above that can in no way merely be defined by labels such as "old" versus "new" or even "progressive" versus "reactionary." Both have their own fair share of advantages and disadvantages, so that, in spite of their being absolute opposites, it is mostly a question of interchangeable options. From time to time we have observed connections between these pairs of opposites, not in the sense of causal dependences, but as conditions that converge in specific situations.

If, while making a comparison of antitheses—such as local power as opposed to central power, anonymity as against individuality, gods tied to a specific place against abstract notions of the gods—we assemble all the terms mentioned on both sides, we shall probably arrive at the best characterization of the overall antitheses. These are linked to each other just as much in the Early Dynastic III period as in the period of the Akkad Dynasty. The political system of the period determined which of the two complexes predominated at any given point. And it had become especially clear, precisely for the political systems, that the options were almost interchangeable. Thus, the relatively rapid and comprehensive change in forms of cultural expression, perhaps best seen in art, can be explained by the close, if in no way genetic, connection between cultural life and forms of political organization. The exclusiveness with which the two complexes of artistic ideals appear before us is not one of actual ideals, but merely a consequence of the close connection between forms of artistic expression and each particular ruling class's view of the world. Thus, for systematic reasons, we are bound to fail at any given time in our search for signs of the other complex.

We have taken up a good deal of space here, in working out this basic conflict in Babylonian society because here it has once again been possible to show very strikingly how much the creation of the first regional state in the Near East was the answer to problems that could only arise in this form and to this extent given the specific conditions in Babylonia.

The further we progress into the period from which thousands of texts allow us to draw up an ever more detailed picture of Babylonia, the more painful is our perception of the gaps in our information about many of the neighboring areas. While in the case of Babylonia we can already afford to argue about datings separated by only ten or twenty years, for most of the other areas we are still dependent on the use of terminology that bears witness to our total ignorance, such as "Early Bronze III period."

Happy to have any information at all about the relationships between different regions, we clutch at the statements by rulers about how they captured or conquered this or that city. Up to a short time ago, the silence of Babylonia's opponents forced us not only to take the statements of Babylonian rulers at face value, but also allowed us to imagine military campaigns directed against areas that were more or less powerless and in every case underdeveloped.

The texts from Ebla support a different view. Not only Ebla but a whole series of other places in the Syrian area prove to have been independent centers of political importance. However, there is absolutely no foundation for reading this to mean that Babylonia was even for a time subject to Ebla. Since during the excavations in Ebla unmistakable evidence was found that there had been two devastating

Figure 68. Aerial photograph of Norşun Tepe (Turkey) and plan of the Early Bronze "mansion." Courtesy, Dr. H. Hauptmann, Heidelberg University.

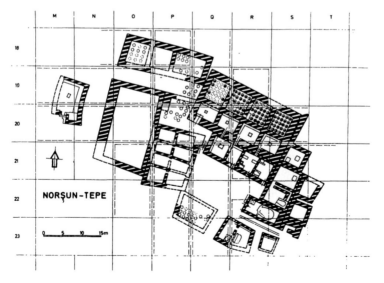

destructions there, it is rather more realistic to believe the claims made in the inscriptions of Naram-Sin that he destroyed the city of Ebla. Further research on the texts from Ebla, and the possible discovery of texts from other places in Syria will, it is to be hoped, soon allow us to draw a more detailed picture of conditions in this area. Although they were doubtless similar in complexity to those in Babylonia, the forms of organization there were probably constructed on other basic patterns.

In chapter 5 it was implied that we now, for the first time, find indications of greater changes in the Anatolian area bordering Mesopotamia to the north. Of course, we must start with the idea that here, too, changes had been in the offing for a long time before they become completely visible in the archaeological material. Finds from excavations at Norşun Tepe, near Elazig in the Keban Dam area in eastern Turkey, and the uncovering of contemporary remains in other places, provide us with the visible arguments here. Within the sequence of levels from the Early Bronze III period at Norşun Tepe, a remarkable change takes place in the complexes of buildings from the usual division into small single units, such as were typical of rural settlements during the early part of this period, to a well-planned central structure on the same spot that took up a very large area in the late phase. The excavator is right in seeing in this signs of the construction of a mansion, a process that can also be seen at other excavation sites in the same region, for example at Tepecik.

Thus it is probably no accident that we know of a whole sequence of burial sites in Anatolia from this period, such as the one at Alaca Hüyük, for example, whose individual graves were constructed at great expense and contained magnificent treasures either made out of precious metals or of high artistic merit as grave goods. These cemeteries undoubtedly contain the graves of members of a ruling class.

Unfortunately, however, we cannot go any further than to confirm that the establishment of a political ruling class was obviously consolidated at this time, because the equivalent research at other sites is still lacking. Thus, for example, we should expect that the obviously widespread changes in leadership structures also had some effect on the mode of settlement. The example of the plain on which Norşun Tepe and Tepecik are situated along with other places, where a concentration of settlement activity actually can be shown to have taken place around the new seats of power, cannot, for the time being, be carried over to the areas that have not yet been investigated.

We find a similarly divergent picture to that of the earlier period when we turn to northern Mesopotamia, because complexes clearly rooted in the Babylonian tradition seem to alternate with those in the local tradition and are found in some kind of spatial relationship to the latter, although the connection is unclear. On the one hand, a strong, local element is represented in the tradition of the so-called Nineveh 5 pottery, whose chronological distribution has not yet been adequately explained, although it definitely embraces the Early Dynastic period and the period of the Akkad Dynasty. In contrast to this local component, there are numerous individual finds that provide clear evidence for the continuation of contacts with southern Mesopotamia. This evidence consists, for one thing, of written finds, such as the ones known to us, for example, from Tell Brak in northern Syria. A large building, which, judging by its layout, must have been an administrative center, obviously indicates an outpost of Babylonia since Naram-Sin of Akkad is named as its builder. On the foundation inscription it is called *é-gal*, the normal term for a palace. A votive inscription to Rimush from the same place and a site, probably lying to the north of Nineveh, that was named after Rimush have already been mentioned.

One of the most beautiful examples of ancient Near Eastern sculp-

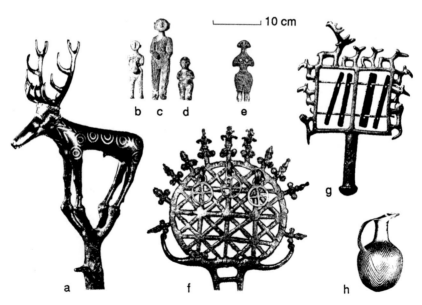

Figure 69. Finds from the tombs at Alaca Hüyük (Turkey): (a) staff ornament; (b) female figures made of bronze and (c) of silver; (d, e) "standards"; (h) gold jug. From E. Akurgal and M. Hirmer, *Die Kunst der Hethiter* (Munich, 1961), figs. 2, 8, 12, 21. Courtesy, Hirmer Photoarchiv. Munich.

Figure 70. Bronze head of the Akkadian period, from Nineveh (Iraq). From E. Strommenger and M. Hirmer, *5 Jahrtausende Mesopotamien* (Munich, 1962), pl. 22. Courtesy, Hirmer Photoarchiv, Munich.

ture, which by all criteria must be dated to the period of the Akkad Dynasty, comes from Nineveh itself. However, to try to identify this bronze head as the portrayal of a specific ruler would surely be stretching the resources we have for interpreting ancient Near Eastern art too far. Finally, just as there were for the previous period, there are important finds in both architecture and art from Assur that similarly prompt us to assume that there must have been very close relations with Babylonia.

The attempts made by Akkadian rulers to exert an influence in the neighboring regions and the creation of more direct and indirect relationships seem to have been restricted to the reigns from Sargon to Naram-Sin. At least there is no information to this effect from the following period, a situation that may be connected to the fact that we have hardly any texts either from the period of the last rulers of the Akkad Dynasty or, especially, from the years following the end of the dynasty. So far without historical context is an inscription by Shudurul, one of the later rulers of Akkad, which was found recently in southeast Anatolia. Unfortunately, our understanding of this phase is limited. This is very regrettable, because the small amount of information we have managed, with tremendous effort, to put together points to the fact that the territory of the central state of Akkad gradually disintegrated into ever smaller units toward the end, until finally a situation had been created that corresponded, at least externally, to that in the Early Dynastic III period: a fairly large number of independent political units assembled around some of the centers known from the earlier period. The end of the Akkad Dynasty was surely desired and brought about by many people for many and varied reasons. Considering the development just mentioned, it must definitely be assumed that the principle of particularism had forced its way into the foreground again.

Although we can only draw rough conclusions from the small amount of evidence available, it is clear that we can definitely rule out the official version, which both the so-called Sumerian King List and the poem "A Curse of Akkad" seek to convince us of: the claim that the Guti were solely responsible for the fall of the dynasty of Akkad.

Most of the information we have referred to about the last years of the dynasty of Akkad and the time that followed first comes from the beginning of the next phase, the period of the Third Dynasty of Ur, numbered according to the order of the dynasties in the Sumerian King List. Thus, at the end of what is mostly a "dark" age, we hear that in Ur, in the extreme south of the country, a "general" named Ur-Nammu, who had clearly only established himself there a short time before, was able to become independent and succeeded in bringing the whole of Babylonia under his control within a very short space of time.

The political situation in the country is illuminated by the facts that Ur-Nammu probably received his post in Ur from the local ruler, Utuhengal of Uruk; that according to his own reports, Ur-Nammu first had to conquer a ruler of Lagash before he could add that area to his territory; and that shortly before this Utuhengal, his former overlord, had fought and won a decisive victory over the last leader of a "dynasty" of the Guti. According to this, shortly before Ur-Nammu began his reign, there were at least three independent political units in Babylonia: the city-states of Uruk and Lagash and territory ruled by the Guti. The Akkadian central state had therefore clearly been broken up into smaller units, of which we can certainly name only the smallest. We can be almost certain that a further unit can be added to the three mentioned: the territory centering on the city of Akkad, which was in that period ruled over by two rulers called Dudu and Shudurul, who are in fact listed in the Sumerian King List as belonging to the Akkadian Dynasty, separated by a one-year interregnum from the earlier rulers of this dynasty, although they definitely no longer belonged to the same family.

Hardly anything is known about the reigns of Dudu and Shudurul. An inscription in southeastern Anatolia bearing the name of Shudurul should probably be taken less as a sign of the sort of actions Sargon and Naram-Sin engaged in in these distant regions than as a parallel to assertions made by Gudea of Lagash. In his temple-building hymns, Gudea shows off with reports of distant regions he brought the materials from to build a new main temple for the city god. The northern Syrian—southeastern Anatolian region played a very prominent role in this.

However, information about this period between the restriction of Akkad's power in the years under or after Sharkalisharri and the reinforcement of central political power under Ur-Nammu of Ur is not only limited in scope; it is also contradictory. On the one hand, we repeatedly hear what a great plague the Guti were. Obviously, this group originally came from the eastern border mountains. In the texts they are represented as barbarians who steal cattle and do not enjoy the best of reputations in other respects either. Thus it is also significant that in the poem "A Curse of Akkad," the task of carrying out the revenge of Enlil should fall to the Guti. They are described, in a not very flattering way, as people "who know no ties of affection and whose speech is like the barking of a dog." In Utuhengal's victory inscription, they are called "the snake, the scorpion of the mountains who does violence to the gods, who dragged the monarchy away from Sumer to far distant lands and allowed injustice and violence to set foot in the land." However, they were probably a far less stable political power than the Sumerian King List which places a Guti dynasty on the same level as the other dynasties, would have us believe. Their power probably rested more on the fear their widespread raids created. The main area they occupied seems to have lain in the vicinity of Adab. Situated as it was on the eastern fringe of the cultivated land, it probably served as a bridge into Babylonia from their easterly possessions.

Although, as noted earlier, this period is on the whole very poorly documented, there is one important exception. The reign of Gudea of Lagash must be included in the period after the end of the Akkad Dynasty. According to his numerous inscriptions, Gudea reigned, for the most part, independently; he was certainly not subject to any sort of overlordship. At the time of Gudea, the area of Lagash could clearly be counted among the small successors of the state of Akkad. However, in spite of the numerous inscriptions, opportunities for making a more exact evaluation of the area are limited. This is because, although Gudea's inscriptions report the erection of temples and the carrying out of every conceivable religious duty in great detail, they contain next to nothing that can be utilized for a political history. If we were to accept these inscriptions as representative, we would have a picture of a thoroughly peaceful period, notwithstanding the political fragmentation mentioned. This is supported by the fact that Gudea clearly exploited widespread trade relations in order to acquire building and furnishing materials for his cult buildings. Elam and the lands around the Gulf to the south of Babylonia, as well as the Lebanese forests in the west, are named as the countries of origin for these goods. The inscription referring to Shudurul of Akkad in what is nowadays the southeastern Anatolian area could also point to similar contacts. The "reign of terror" of the Guti thus hardly seems to have had the totally disruptive effect described in some sources. At the same time, this example can also serve as a warning against seeing the end of the phase of political centralization as a "collapse" and regarding the phase during which a once-unified area was split up into smaller parts as a politically troubled period.

Even if Gudea's inscriptions do not offer us much help in our reconstruction of political conditions, they do provide us with significant evidence from another point of view. There is hardly any other group of inscriptions by a ruler as saturated with the ideology of the "temple city" as Gudea's. Reports about his numerous temple buildings and continuing care for the different gods are not only to be found in his official inscriptions and on stelae and statues set up beside the temples, where the exclusive use of this theme would be quite comprehensible. They are also confirmed in the great number of building inscriptions, as well as in the fact that the sixteen year names handed down to us from his reign report exclusively on the building of temples, the appointment of specific priests, or the production of emblems of gods. As far as we can see, this was the first time that the custom which lasted for a very long time afterward of calling each year after the most important event of the previous year was put into operation. This year name was then used for dating all sorts of documents.

Gudea saw himself so much in the role of the representative of his city god, Ningirsu, that he never tired of stressing over and over again in his inscriptions that everything he had done was only by order of the different gods. There can hardly be a clearer illustration of what was seen as the idealized antithesis of the central rule of the recently defunct Akkad Dynasty.

The situation during Gudea's reign has in fact been explained as the reintroduction of the political and economic forms identified in the Lagash texts of the late Early Dynastic III period. The term "Sumerian Renaissance," which has been applied to the Third Dynasty of Ur, is—in the light of what we have already said—simultaneously right and wrong. It is wrong insofar as this term implies that the civilization of this period was a conscious reaction by Sumerians against Akkadian

Figure 71. Clay cylinders A and B containing temple hymns of Gudea of Lagash
from Tello (Iraq). Courtesy, Musée du Louvre, Paris.

tutelage. It is right insofar as here, just as in the Early Dynastic III
period, we can see the close affinity between particularism and the
principle of the city god. In a milder form, we can even observe how
this backward swing of the pendulum once again brought about changes
in artistic practice.

These changes are, however, considerably less noticeable than
during the transition from the Early Dynastic period to the period of
the Akkad Dynasty. It may well be that the ever more frequent appearance of the so-called introduction scenes on cylinder seals at least
partly mirrors the emphasis on the religious element. But the human
form is represented with the same thoroughness and individual detail
as it had previously been. Differences are, above all, perceptible in
works of plastic art, of which we possess a great number from the time
of Gudea. If we compare these numerous portrayals of Gudea seated
and standing with the statues from the period of the Akkad Dynasty,
we see that technical skill was used in the same way to convey anatomical details. These skills had been developed even further, so that
when it comes to the shaping of details such as, for example, the arm
muscles, the tradition of the previous period is directly continued. On

the whole, the statues of Gudea can, however, be clearly distinguished from works of the previous period on account of their greater bulkiness, lack of proportion, and, along with this, a certain monotony. Although this is not simply a reabsorption of the preindividualistic character as epitomized by the people of the Early Dynastic period, the more modest, more uniform style of representation seems to fit in very well with the humbler attitude of this ruler to the gods. This attitude emerges over and over again in his inscriptions and belongs to the theocratic model of organization once more being emphasized.

In other spheres, too, attitudes and forms that had grown up during the period of the Akkad Dynasty continued to exist, but were transformed. However, the often-quoted assertion that the civilization of the Gudea period was a combination of old "Sumerian" trains of thought and new "Akkadian" ideas is a very inadequate way of describing the new quality. The right way of evaluating it would probably be to say that the basic concepts of local rule and the Temple City of

a   b

Figure 72. Statues (a) of the Akkadian period and (b) of Gudea of Lagash. From W. Orthmann, *Propyläen Kunstgeschichte* 14 (Berlin, 1975), figs. 42, 54. Courtesy, Vorderasiatisches Museum, Berlin.

the city-states of the Early Dynastic III period, which during the centralizing period of the Akkad Dynasty had been forced into the background, were restored to first place, together with the new (old) form of government. They were, however, indirectly influenced by the fact that, in spite of all the parallelism, forms of organization obviously could not be exactly the same as they had been during the Early Dynastic period. And they were directly influenced by aspects that had evolved during the period of the centralized state and had proved to be generally valid.

Unfortunately we are in a situation parallel to the late Early Dynastic III period from another point of view as well, in the sense that almost all the information about the period between the end of the Akkad Dynasty and the beginning of the reign of the Third Dynasty of Ur, comes from the area of Lagash. This is why, for the time being, it is difficult to assess conditions during this post-Akkadian period. In the meantime, we remain in the dark above all about the events that finally led to what was clearly a very rapid political unification of the country under Ur-Nammu, who once again ushered in a very short period of central government for the whole of Babylonia with the foundation of the Third Dynasty of Ur. A total of five rulers from this dynasty ruled for a total of 109 years. Unfortunately, information about the 18 years of Urnammu's reign is once again very sparse. However, we do gain the impression, from various sources, that the new political entity must have achieved stability after a short time.

The most striking witness to the period of Ur-Nammu are the ziggurats, stepped towers with several stages that probably had temples on their highest levels. None of these temples are, however, extant. Even if these structures can be traced back to the different types of high terraces that had been a part of many central cult areas in Babylonian cities since the Ubaid period, the now-obligatory form, with its central stairs and two side flights of steps, seems to have been an innovation under the Third Dynasty of Ur, especially from the time of Ur-Nammu. It is possible that this form could date back to prototypes from the period of the Akkad Dynasty, but unfortunately we do not yet know anything about the architecture of that period. Incidentally, the ziggurat from the Babylon of the sixth century B.C., which we know as the "Tower of Babel," conformed exactly to this scheme of building.

A large number of the bricks used for these buildings bear stamped inscriptions. Apart from telling us the name of the builder, Ur-Nammu, they also tell us the name of the city in which the temple was erected, the name of the god who was worshipped there, and the name of the temple. The fact that such labor-intensive building works were erected

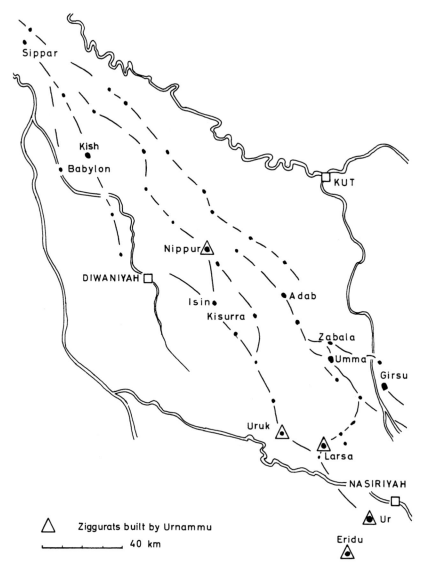

 Ziggurats built by Urnammu

|_____| 40 km

Figure 73. Babylonia in the time of the Third Dynasty of Ur. Sites of ziggurat construction by the first ruler of the Dynasty, Ur-Nammu, are marked by triangles. Author's original.

191

Figure 74. The ziggurat of Ur, partly restored. Author's photograph.

in many of the larger cities of southern Babylonia (fig. 73) allows us to conclude that there was obviously comprehensive control through a central body. In addition, in the light of the conflict between central government and local priesthood, the fact that the central ruler began with such an unusual building program in the former local centers soon after establishing his rule, thus making it clear that he was concerned with the local deities, seems extremely important. However, at the same time, Ur-Nammu made it unmistakably apparent where the actual power lay by central planning of building and organization, by his building inscriptions, and probably in other ways of which we know nothing. There are two further pieces of evidence for a high degree of central administration; on the one hand, we observe that the system of year names used in Ur was used almost without exception throughout the whole of Babylonia, and on the other hand, a lengthy text, something like a state land register, lists the administrative districts of Ur-Nammu's kingdom.

We are considerably better informed about the 48-year reign of Shulgi, Urnammu's son and successor. Even though we are not able to draw a complete picture of his period either, one innovation of this period is of decisive help in extending our knowledge. We know of only very few economic texts each year dating from the reign of Ur-Nammu and the first years of Shulgi's rule. But from the twenty-second year of Shulgi's reign on, this number suddenly leaps to thousands per annum. Because we also have other evidence as to changes on a large scale during these years of Shulgi's reign, we may assume that this sudden increase in texts is not the result of an imbalance in the finds—

although this can never be ruled out—but the result of an intentional change.

If we regard as one part of this change the fact that from this time on, proceedings in the public sector had to be recorded in writing to a much greater extent than previously, and as another aspect of it the reorganization of administrative practices in large households that is apparent in the annual formula for the twenty-first year of Shulgi's reign—"year, in which . . . , and Shulgi set to rights the field accounts in the temple of Enlil and Ninlil," i.e., the main temple in Nippur—then we can perhaps, in a very general way, call these changes, taken all in all, an administrative reform.

Figure 75. Brick with a stamped inscription by Ur-Nammu of Ur. Reproduced by courtesy of the trustees of the British Museum.

193

We cannot assess the scope of these administrative measures, but it does appear that here an important step had been taken in relating administrative procedures to politically desirable structures. In spite of all the gaps in our knowledge and all the parts that do not seem to fit in with the rest of the puzzle, the state of the Third Dynasty of Ur turns out to have been an extremely complicated entity, which created forms of organization that were more than just answers to the specific problems of Babylonia. This becomes clear when we consider things like the transferability of civil servants, for which we have evidence in several cases, as well as the beginnings of the creation of a *cursus honorum*—that is, a more or less fixed sequence of posts that candidates for the highest state offices had to have held. However, it would be a mistake to assume that Babylonia's fundamental problems had ceased to exist, since at least two observations to the contrary can be found.

If research into hydrological changes had not already pointed to the fact that in the period around 2000 B.C., that is, roughly in the period of the Third Dynasty of Ur, the water supply had reached its lowest point, we would have been able to draw this conclusion from the written evidence of this period. It is true that this is not direct evidence, but the numerous references to the building of canal systems in areas that were already settled provide us with very significant information. These canal systems were most probably not merely built in order to expand the existing area of settlement, but to ensure the supply of water to existing agricultural areas. However, it was not only new canals that served to improve exploitation of the available water supply. There was also a whole series of additional facilities, such as weirs, locks, and water-retaining basins, that were meant to ensure that water was available for a longer time. We can tell that these were innovations from the fact that the relevant technical terms for these additional facilities first appear in the texts of this period. At the same time, these texts allow us to see the great importance attached to the personnel responsible for the distribution and allocation of water. The irrigation system had now become so complicated, both from the organizational and from the technical point of view, that at this point in time at the latest there was an obvious need for central institutions for the building and maintenance of irrigation facilities.

We learn closely enough from the events that led to the end of the Third Dynasty of Ur that, in spite of the innumerable assurances given by the rulers that they would concern themselves with the well-being of the gods and their temples, in spite of the enormous amount of temple building undertaken not only by Ur-Nammu but also by his successors, in spite of the inclusion of the gods and their priesthoods in the coronation and confirmation rituals, the conflict between the central authority and the local priests had in no way been resolved. It is quite true that here again our sources give the impression that a single event brought about the end of the dynasty—an invasion by the Elamites, who conquered the capital city, Ur, and abducted the last ruler. However, if we take all our information into account, we see that a multiplicity of reasons must have been responsible, just as in the case of the end of the Akkad Dynasty.

For example, long before the end came, one local governor after another appointed by the last ruler of Ur changed sides and went over to a pretender to the throne who was advancing from northern Babylonia. A reciprocal sequence of letters between the central ruler and the local governors gives one reason for this changing of sides: the supreme god of the pantheon, Enlil of Nippur, had withdrawn his mercy from the central ruler. This can only mean that the highest god, who had to defend the interests of the gods and thus appeared as their spokesman, once more interfered decisively in a political disagreement against a representative of the idea of the central state.

We may assume that here, at the end of the period of the Third Dynasty of Ur, visible conflicts had already been in the offing, though we have very little evidence to support such an assumption. If we return again to earlier events, we might consider the fact that Shulgi was the first to demand the rank of a god again after Sharkalisharri, on the assumption that his reasons for doing so were similar to those that prompted the first introduction of self-deification under Naram-Sin of Akkad, a point already dealt with at length. Possibly the new order for the administration of the Enlil temple in Nippur mentioned in the year formula quoted for the twenty-first year of Shulgi's reign was imposed by the king in the interests of the central state. This must have been experienced as unnecessary interference in the affairs of the temple, a parallel with the procedure postulated above for the period of Naram-Sin of Akkad.

Thus the form taken by the state under the Third Dynasty of Ur is also still connected with the specific problems of Babylonia, with the basic conflict between centralism and particularism. However, it does seem, especially in the administrative sphere, as if a general applicability had been arrived at that went beyond this. We take this as our justification for concluding here with the reign of Shulgi after a short sketch of Babylonia's relations with its neighbors and detailed presentation of the sequence of events that should show the route taken by forms of political organization in attaining a certain degree of abstraction and general applicability. The final chapter will give a short view of further developments.

There is both much and very little that can be said about the relationships of the state of the Third Dynasty of Ur with neighboring countries. There is a lot to be said because, according to their inscriptions, the rulers of this period penetrated into the surrounding countries at least as far as the rulers of the Akkad Dynasty had done. There is little we can say because we have practically no evidence from these neighboring countries, and thus there are hardly any cases in which we can scrutinize the evidence obtained from Babylonian sources.

According to royal inscriptions, the rulers of the Third Dynasty of Ur for the most part followed the same routes, or used the same points of support, as the earlier rulers. This is, for example, the case with the great "palace" built by Naram-Sin at Tell Brak, in which an inscription of the time of the Third Dynasty of Ur was also found. A more calculated "foreign policy," directed toward more than ephemeral campaigns in the neighboring regions, can perhaps be seen in the fact that the areas that border Babylonia directly to the east, as well as the areas along the Tigris to the north, were clearly more strongly drawn toward the central government. For this reason, they achieved a special status compared with the other regions by being placed under the local rule of Irnanna, the second man in the state from the time of Shulgi's successors on. In this, we can probably recognize the intention of protecting the eastern flank of the state from the inhabitants of the mountain regions by means of a continuous strip of areas in close association with it. It is highly probable that the living memory of the Guti contributed to this measure.

For the first time, we also hear of a threat from the northwest, from groups characterized in a similar way to the previously mentioned inhabitants of the mountains. These new groups are described as not being settled and are subsumed under the name "Martu." This similarity of characterization is understandable. For the inhabitant of Babylonia, everyone who did not have precisely the same way of life as he did was a barbarian. But we must make a distinction here nonetheless. This is shown by the mere fact that all the rulers who took possession of the heritage of the Third Dynasty of Ur came from these groups, and they clearly had no difficulty in acquiring the skills of civilization and fitting in with the Babylonian lifestyle. Though definitely closer to the Babylonian inhabitants than the Guti, the "Martu" were politically no less dangerous. We take our evidence for this judgment from information about the structure supposed to prevent them from entering the land. The year name of the fourth year of the reign of Shusin, Shulgi's successor, reports on the erection of a "Martu wall": "Year in which Shusin, king of Ur, built the Martu wall [named] 'that which keeps the Tidnum away.,'" The Tidnum must have been a particular grouping among the Martu. This example also shows that walls were not in the long run impregnable, since, as already mentioned, only a short time later precisely the group that was supposed to have been excluded held the reins of political power in the whole country.

We have already mentioned the supposition that the expeditions the rulers of the Akkad and Ur III Dynasties sent to neighboring countries cannot be understood as only stemming from a position of strength. At the same time they must also be seen as a preventative measure against the irreversible decline in Babylonia's leading position among the lands of the Near East. Unfortunately, as already noted, there are practically no written sources of evidence from the neighboring countries for this period. This can, however, most definitely be traced back to gaps in research that—given the rapid progress being made in archaeological research, at least in the area of what is today Syria—will soon be closed up.

The form of cuneiform writing later used by the Hittites derives, both in its technical details and in the form of the written signs and syllables, from Babylonian script under the Third Dynasty of Ur and must have reached Anatolia by way of Syria at that period. This is a piece of indirect evidence for the existence in this area of strong cultural centers, which were also definitely important political centers. This history of Babylonia's relationship with its neighboring countries will, therefore, have to be completely rewritten and will definitely look completely different compared to what the sources available at present lead us to expect.

Prospects

How far can we speak of unity among, or of differentiation between, the regions of the ancient Near East? In chapter 1, we saw how what had originally been a cultural entity—that is, with all the regions at a similar level of cultural, technical, and economic development—gave way more and more to differentiation between the individual regions that was directly related to the degree to which specific solutions had to be found to the specific problems of individual areas.

Babylonia, the most specialized region in the Near East, whose few natural resources were even more restricted by the slow, but continuous, worsening of the climate, demanded solutions that had to be consistent in coping with these changes. They were challenges that could only be posed, and answers that could only be found, in this countryside. In the course of time, as a result of improvements and the substitution of more efficient processes for ones that had become impracticable, what had at first been formulated as answers to urgent problems produced forms of organization that were more and more divorced from their original character of specific solutions to specific problems. In chapter 6, especially in the period of the Third Dynasty of Ur, we saw how, according to the indications, such abstraction— the development of more generally valid political and administrative forms—increased.

The situation as a whole is considerably easier to grasp for the so-called Old Babylonian period that followed, especially since there is a good supply of written finds from the neighboring regions. The mere fact that cuneiform writing was used as a matter of course shows that the other areas were catching up. The way in which cuneiform was used also points to a preliminary phase of its usage that is not yet known to us. In addition, we see that far more must have been taken over than just the Babylonian way of writing.

The extent of this appropriation becomes much more evident in one specific example, the takeover and use of the so-called "forms." These had been developed in Babylonia to simplify the transaction of specific economic or legal processes that had to be continually repeated. Because of the fixed outline of these forms, only the facts relating to each specific procedure had to be filled in. Possibly this development has to be seen in connection with the considerable increase in the demand for scribes as a direct consequence of Shulgi's administrative reforms.

This is not the place to report on the extremely varied and well-documented relationships between Babylonia and the various political entities that constituted considerable power complexes in Elam and in the Syrian area. That will be the task of a more coherent presentation of the later history of Babylonia. The reason for this short, chronological overview is merely to draw attention to the turning point that can be connected with the Old Babylonian period at the latest, and that can briefly be referred to by the name of the famous Hammurapi of Babylon.

At one time Babylonia, which had only just become suitable for settlement and was thus far behind the neighboring lands in its development, had obtained its ideas and forms of organization from its neighbors—above all those to the east. Because Babylonia managed to use these ideas successfully in the solution of its own problems, it was able to develop them further, so that it soon left the original donor lands far behind in the speed of its development. Babylonia itself then became the victim of a similar development. In both cases, forms of organization had developed to such heights in the donor lands (in this case, Babylonia) precisely at that point in time when they could be, and were, exploited to their greatest extent by other regions to solve their own problems. In both cases, this led to a total reorganization of the political landscape of the Near East.

In the period we are now dealing with, the first half of the second millennium B.C., larger regional coalitions became possible on the broader plains of northern Mesopotamia and Syria thanks to the models of organization devised, but in no way brought to maturity, in Babylonia. It goes without saying that the much greater reserves in land, raw material, and people in states such as those of Hurri-Mitanni and Assyria, for example, which were consolidated during the following period, endowed them with such political weight that Babylonia could no longer hold its own as far as political power went. If Babylonia did in fact still have a role to play from this time on, it was because of its accumulated cultural goods and experience, which also ensured Babylonia a significant place among the concert of regions in the Near East during the following period. The role of political instigator was, however, withheld from Babylonia for a long time.

This attempt to present the different threads of development woven into the early period of the Near East must, of necessity, remain unsatisfactory. Too many questions remain unanswered. Gaps in our knowledge that are too large can often only be bridged in a makeshift way, and with the help of theses that are considered rather daring. In spite of this, it may be hoped that the fascination of the history of the early period of the Near East has become evident: the consistency built on divergent sources, the historical momentum checked by arrest, the variety in unity.

Bibliography

General

Adams, R. McC. *The Heartland of Cities*. Chicago, 1981.

Adams, R. McC., and H. J. Nissen. *The Uruk Countryside*. Chicago, 1972.

Akurgal, E. *Die Kunst der Hethiter*. Munich, 1961.

Amiet, P. *Elam*. Paris, 1966.

_____. *La glyptique Mesopotamienne archaique*. 2d ed. Paris, 1980.

Barrelet, M.-Th., ed. *L'archéologie de l'Iraq*. CNRS colloque no. 580. Paris, 1980.

Boserup, E. *The Conditions of Agricultural Growth*. Chicago, 1965.

Braidwood, R. J. *The Near East and the Foundations for Civilization*. Eugene, Ore., 1952.

_____. The First Great Change. In M. Liverani, A. Palmieri, R. Peroni, eds. *Studi di Paletnologia in onore di S. M. Puglisi*. Rome, 1985.

Butzer, K. W. *Environment and Archaeology: An Ecological Approach to Prehistory*. Chicago, 1971.

Carter, E., and M. W. Stolper. *Elam: Surveys of Political History and Archaeology*. Berkeley, Calif., 1984.

Cassin, E., J. Bottéro and J. Vercoutter, eds. *The Near East: The Early Civilizations*. Trans. R. F. Tannenbaum. New York, 1967.

Cohen, M. N. *The Food Crisis in Prehistory: Overpopulation and the Origin of Agriculture*. New Haven, 1977.

Coon, C. S. *The Seven Caves*. New York, 1956.

Damerow, P., and W. Lefèvre. *Rechenstein, Experiment, Sprache*. Stuttgart, 1981.

Diakonoff, I. M., ed. *Ancient Mesopotamia: A Socio-Economic History*. Moscow, 1969.

Ehrich, R. W., ed. *Chronologies in Old World Archaeology*. Chicago, 1965.

Falkenstein, A., and W. Frh. von Soden. *Sumerische und Akkadische Hymnen und Gebete*. Zurich, 1953.

Frankfort, H.: *The Art and Architecture of the Ancient Orient*. 4th ed. London, 1970.

Gibson, McG., and R. D. Biggs, eds. *Seals and Sealing in the Ancient Near East*. Bibliotheca Mesopotamica, vol. 6. Malibu, 1977.

Hallo, W. W., and W. Simpson: *The Ancient Near East: A History*. New York, 1971.

Heinrich, E. *Tempel und Heiligtümer im alten Mesopotamien*. Berlin, 1982.

_____. *Die Paläste im alten Mesopotamien*. Berlin, 1984.

Bibliography

Hole, F., ed. *The Archaeology of Western Iran*. Washington, D.C., 1987.

Hrouda, B. Vorderasien I: Mesopotamien, Iran und Anatolien. In *Handbuch der Archäologie*. Munich, 1971.

Jacobsen, Th. *The Sumerian Kinglist*. Assyriological Studies, no. 11. Chicago, 1939.

———. *Toward the Image of Tammuz*. Cambridge, 1970.

———. *Salinity and Irrigation Agriculture in Antiquity*. Bibliotheca Mesopotamica, vol. 14. Malibu, 1982.

Jacobsen, Th., and R. McC. Adams. Salt and Silt in Ancient Mesopotamian Agriculture. *Science* 128 (1958).

Johnson, G. A. Aspects of Regional Analysis in Archaeology. *Annual Reviews of Anthropology* 6 (1977)

Khalifa, Sheikha H. A., and M. Rice, eds. *Bahrain through the Ages: The Archaeology*. London, 1986.

Kramer, S. N. *History Begins at Sumer*. New York, 1959.

———. *The Sumerians*. Chicago, 1963.

Landsberger, B. *Three Essays on the Sumerians*. Trans. Maria deJ. Ellis. Monographs on the Ancient Near East, vol 1, no. 2 Malibu, 1974.

Larsen, C. E. The Mesopotamian Delta Region: A Reconsideration of Lees and Falcon. *Journal of the American Oriental Society* 95 (1978).

Lees, G. M., and N. L. Falcon. The Geographical History of the Mesopotamian Plains. *Geographical Journal* 118 (1952).

Levine, L., and T. C. Young, eds. *Mountains and Lowlands: Essays in the Archaeology of Greater Mesopotamia*. Bibliotheca Mesopotamica, vol. 7. Malibu, 1977.

Lieberman, S., ed. *Sumerological Studies in Honor of Thorkild Jacobsen*. Assyriological Studies, no. 20. Chicago, 1976.

Mellaart, J. *Earliest Civilizations of the Near East*. London, 1965.

———. *The Chalcolithic and Early Bronze Ages in the Near East and Anatolia*. Beirut, 1966.

———. *The Neolithic of the Near East*. London, 1975.

Mellink, M., ed. *Frühe Stufen der Kunst*. Propyläen Kunstgeschichte, vol. 13. Berlin, 1974.

Moortgat, A. *The Art of Ancient Mesopotamia*. London, 1969.

Muhly, J. D. *Copper and Tin*. New Haven, 1973.

Müller-Karpe, H. *Handbuch der Vorgeschichte*. Vols. 1–3. Munich, 1966–1974.

Nissen, H. J. Geographie. In S. Lieberman, ed. *Sumerological Studies in Honor of Th. Jacobsen*. Chicago, 1976.

Nissen, H. J., and J. Renger, eds. *Mesopotamien und seine Nachbarn*. Berliner Beiträge zum Vorderen Orient 1. Berlin, 1982.

Nützel, W. The Climatic Changes of Mesopotamia and Bordering Areas. *Sumer* 32 (1976).

Oppenheim, A. L. *Ancient Mesopotamia: Portrait of a Dead Civilization*. Chicago, 1964.

Orthmann, W., ed. *Der Alte Orient*. Propyläen Kunstgeschichte, vol. 14. Berlin, 1975.

Pfeiffer, J. E. *The Emergence of Society: A Prehistory of the Establishment*. New York, 1977.

Potts, D. T. Towards an Integrated History of Culture Change in the Arabian Gulf Area: Nothes on Dilmun, Makkan and the Economy of Ancient Sumer. *Journal of Oman Studies* 4 (1978).

_____, ed. *Dilmun*. Berliner Beiträge zum Vorderen Orient 2. Berlin, 1983.

Pritchard, J. B., ed. *The Ancient Near East: An Anthology of Texts and Pictures*. 6th ed. Princeton, N.J., 1975.

_____, ed. *The Ancient Near East: A New Anthology of Texts and Pictures*. Princeton, N.J., 1975.

Redman, C. L. *The Rise of Civilization*. San Francisco, 1978.

Renfrew, C., ed. *The Explanation of Culture Change: Models in Prehistory*. London, 1973.

Rowton, M. B. The Role of Watercourses in the Growth of Mesopotamian Civilization. In W. Röllig, ed. *Festschrift für W. Frh. von Soden*. Neukirchen-Vluyn, 1969.

_____. Autonomy and Nomadism in Western Asia. *Orientalia* 42 (1973).

_____. Dimorphic Structure and Topology. *Oriens Antiquus* 15 (1976).

Sollberger, E. Sur la chronologie des rois d'Ur et quelques problèmes connexes. *Archiv für Orientforschung* 17 (1954–56).

Sollberger, E., and J.-R. Kupper. *Inscriptions Royales Sumeriennes et Akkadiennes*. Paris, 1971.

Ucko, P. J., R. Tringham, and G. W. Dimbleby, eds. *Man, Settlement and Urbanism*. London, 1972.

Van Dijk, J. J. A. Sumerische Religion. *Handbuch der Religionsgeschichte*, vol. 1. Göttingen, 1971.

Westphal-Hellbusch, S. *Die Ma'dan*. Berlin, 1962.

Wirth, E. *Agrargeographie des Irak*. Hamburg, 1962.

_____. *Syrien: eine geographische Landeskunde*. Darmstadt, 1971.

Wittfogel, K. A. *Oriental Despotism: A Comparative Study of Total Power*. New Haven 1957.

Wright, H. T. Recent Research on the Origin of the State. *Annual Review of Anthropology* 6 (1977).

Young, T. C., P. E. L. Smith, and P. Mortensen, eds. *The Hilly Flanks and Beyond: Essays on the Prehistory of Southwestern Asia, Presented to R. J. Braidwood*. Studies in Ancient Oriental Civilization, no. 36. Chicago, 1984.

Chapter Two

Braidwood, R. J., et al. *Prehistoric Investigations in Iraqi Kurdistan*. Studies in Ancient Oriental Civilization, no. 31. Chicago, 1960.

Bibliography

_____. *Prehistoric Archaeology along the Zagros Flanks*. Oriental Institute Publication 105. Chicago, 1983.

Braidwood, R. J., H. Cambel, and W. Schirmer. Beginnings of Village-Farming Communities in Southeastern Turkey. *Journal of Field Archaeology 8* (1981).

Childe, V. G. *New Light on the Most Ancient Near East*. 4th ed. London, 1952.

Flannery, K. V. The Ecology of Early Food Production in Mesopotamia. *Science* 147 (1967).

_____. The Origins of the Village as a Settlement Type in Mesoamerica and the Near East. In P. Ucko et al., eds. *Man, Settlement and Urbanism*. London, 1972.

_____. The Origins of Agriculture. *Annual Review of Anthropology* 2 (1973).

Frey, W., and H. P. Uerpmann, eds. *Beiträge zur Umweltgeschichte des Vorderen Orients*. Beiheft zum Tübinger Atlas des Vorderen Orients, A8. Wiesbaden, 1981.

Gebel, H. G. *Das Akeramische Neolithikum Vorderasiens*. Beiheft zum Tübinger Atlas des Vorderen Orients, B52. Wiesbaden, 1984.

Harlan, J. R. A Wild Wheat Harvest in Turkey. *Archaeology* 20 (1967).

Harris, D. R. Settling Down: An Evolutionary Model for the Transformation of Mobile Bands into Sedentary Communities. In J. Friedman and M. Rowlands, eds. *The Evolution of Social Systems*. London, 1977.

Hole, F., K. V. Flannery, and J. A. Neely. *Prehistory and Ecology of the Deh Luran Plain*. Ann Arbor, 1969.

Kenyon, K. *Excavations at Jericho*. Vols. 1–5. London, 1960–83.

Kirkbride, D. Five Seasons at Beidha. *Palestine Exploration Quarterly* (1966).

_____. Umm Dabaghiyah: Preliminary reports. *Iraq* 35 (1973) and 37 (1975).

Mellaart, J. *Catal Hüyük: A Neolithic Town in Anatolia*. London, 1967.

Mortensen, P. Patterns of Interaction between Seasonal Settlements and Early Villages in Mesopotamia. In T. C. Young et al., eds. *The Hilly Flanks and Beyond*. Chicago, 1983.

Nissen, H. J., and A. Zagarell. Expedition to the Zagros Mountains 1975. *Proceedings of the Fourth Annual Symposium on Archaeology in Iran*. Teheran, 1976.

Oates, J. The Background and Development of Early Farming Communities in Mesopotamia and the Zagros. *Proceedings of the Prehistorical Society* (London) 39 (1973).

Perrot, J. *La préhistoire palestinienne*. Supplément au dictionaire de la Bible. Vol. 8. Paris, 1968.

Reed, C. A., ed. *Origins of Agriculture*. The Hague, 1977.

Solecki, R. S. *Shanidar: The First Flower People*. New York, 1971

Ucko, P. J., and G. W. Dimbleby, eds. *The Domestication and Exploitation of Plants and Animals*. London, 1969.

Uerpmann, H.-P. *Probleme der Neolithisierung des Mittelmeerraumes*. Beiheft zum Tübinger Atlas des Vorderen Orients, B28. Wiesbaden, 1979.

Vita-Finzi, C., and E. S. Higgs. Prehistoric Economy in the Mount Carmel Area of Palestine: Site Catchment Analysis. *Proceedings of the Prehistorical Society* (London) 36 (1970).

Voigt, M. M. *Hajji Firuz Tepe, Iran: The Neolithic Settlement*. Philadelphia, 1983.

Chapter Three

Adams, R. McC. *The Evolution of Urban Society*. Chicago, 1966.

Hall, H. R., and C. L. Woolley. *Al Ubaid: Ur Excavations*. Vol. 1. London, 1927.

Hijara, I., et al. Arpachiyah. *Iraq* 42 (1980).

Johnson, G. A. *Local Exchange and Early State Development in Southwestern Iran*. Ann Arbor, 1973.

———. Organizational Structure and Scalar Stress. In C. Renfrew et al., eds. *Theory and Explanation in Archaeology*. New York, 1982.

Lloyd, S., and F. Safar. Tell Uqair. *Journal of Near Eastern Studies* 2 (1943).

Mallowan, M. E. L. Excavations at Tall Arpachiyah. *Iraq* 2 (1935).

Nissen, H. J. Political Organization and Settled Zone. In T. C. Young, P. E. L. Smith, and P. Mortensen, eds. *The Hilly Flanks and Beyond*. Chicago, 1983.

Schmidt, H. *Tell Halaf I: Die prähistorischen Funde*. Berlin, 1943.

Vertesalji, P. P. *Babylonien zur Steinkupferzeit*. Beiheft zum Tübinger Atlas des Vorderen Orients, B35. Wiesbaden, 1984.

Weiss, H. Periodization, Population and Early State Formation in Khuzestan. In L. Levine and T. C. Young, eds. *Mountains and Lowlands*. Malibu, 1977.

Woolley, C. L. *The Early Periods: Ur Excavations*. Vol. 4. London, 1956.

Wright, H. T., and G. A. Johnson. Population, Exchange and Early State Formation in Southwestern Iran. *American Anthropology* 77 (1975).

Zagarell, A. *The Prehistory of the Northeast Bakhtiyari Mountains, Iran*. Beiheft zum Tübinger Atlas des Vorderen Orients, B42. Wiesbaden, 1982.

Chapter Four

Amiet, P. La glyptique de l'acropole. *Cahiers de la dél. archéol. franc. en Iran* 1 (1971).

Beale, T. W. Bevelled Rim Bowls and Their Implications for Change and Economic Organization in the Later Fourth Millennium B.C. *Journal of Near Eastern Studies* 37 (1978).

Brandes, M. A. *Siegelabrollungen aus den Archaischen Bauschichten in Uruk-Warka*. Freiburger Altorient. Stud. 3. Wiesbaden, 1979.

Bibliography

Delougaz, P. P., and H. J. Kantor. New Evidence for the Prehistoric and Protoliterate Culture Development in Khuzestan. *Proceedings of the Fifth Congress of Iranian Art and Archaeology.* Teheran, 1972.

Esin, U. Die kulturellen Beziehungen zwischen Ostanatolien und Mesopotamien und Syrien. In H. J. Nissen and J. Renger, eds. *Mesopotamien und seine Nachbarn.* Berlin, 1982.

Falkenstein A. *Archaische Texte aus Uruk.* Leipzig, 1936.

Finkbeiner, U., and W. Röllig, eds. *Jamdet Nasr: Period or Regional Style?* Beiheft zum Tübinger Atlas des Vorderen Orients, B62. Wiesbaden, 1986.

Gelb, I. J. The Ancient Mesopotamian Ration System. *Journal of Near Eastern Studies.* 24 (1965).

Green, M. W., and H. J. Nissen. *Zeichenliste der Archaischen Texte aus Uruk.* Archaische Texte aus Uruk 2. Berlin, 1987.

Heinrich, E. *Kleinfunde aus den Archaischen Tempelschichten aus Uruk.* Berlin, 1936.

Johnson, G. A. Early State Organization in Southwestern Iran. *Proceedings of the Fourth Annual Symposium on Archaeological Research in Iran.* Teheran, 1976.

Le Breton, L. The Early Periods at Susa: Mesopotamian Relations. *Iraq* 19 (1957).

Le Brun, A., and F. Vallat. L'origine de l'écriture a Suse. *Cahiers de la dél. archéol. franc. en Iran* 8 (1978).

Nissen, H. J. Grabung in den Quadraten K/L XII in Uruk-Warka. *Baghdader Mitteilungen* 5 (1970).

———. The City Wall of Uruk. In. P. Ucko et al., eds. *Man, Settlement and Urbanism.* London, 1972.

———. Zur Frage der Arbeitsorganisation in Babylonien während der Späturuk-Zeit. *Acta Antiqua Hung.* 22 (1974).

———. The Emergence of Writing in the Near East. *Interdisciplinary Science Review* 10 (1985).

———. The Archaic Texts from Uruk. *World Archaeology* 17 (1986).

———. *Mesopotamia before 5000 Years.* Sussidi Didattici, vol. 1. Rome, 1987.

Palmieri, A. Eastern Anatolia and Early Mesopotamian Urbanism: Remarks on Changing Relations. In M. Liverani, A. Palmieri, and R. Peroni, eds. *Studi di Paletnologia in onore di S. M. Puglisi.* Rome, 1985.

Schmandt-Besserat, D. *An Archaic Recording System and the origin of Writing.* Malibu, 1977.

Strommenger, E. The Chronological Division of the Archaic Levels of Uruk-Warka. *American Journal of Archaeology* 84 (1980): 479–87.

———. *Habuba Kabira: Eine Stadt vor 5000 Jahren.* Mainz, 1980.

Sürenhagen, D. *Untersuchungen zur Keramikproduktion innerhalb der späturuk-zeitlichen Siedlung Habuba Kabira.* Berlin, 1977.

Tobler, A. J. *Excavations at Tepe Gawra II.* Philadelphia, 1950.

Weiss, H., and T. C. Young. The Merchants of Susa. *Iran* 13 (1975).

Chapter Five

Bauer, J. *Altsumerische Wirtschaftstexte aus Lagasch*. Studia Pohl, vol. 9. Rome, 1972.

Biggs, R. D. *Inscriptions from Tell Abu Salabikh*. Oriental Institute Publication 99. Chicago, 1974.

Cagni, L., ed. *Il Bilinguismo a Ebla*. Napoli, 1984.

Cooper, J. S.: *Reconstructing History from Ancient Inscriptions: The Umma-Lagash Border Conflict*. Malibu, 1983.

Delougaz, P. P. *Plano-Convex Bricks and the Methods of their Employment*. Studies in Ancient Near Eastern Civilization, no. 7. Chicago, 1933.

Diakonoff, I. M. *Structure of Society and State in Early Dynastic Sumer*. Monographs on the Ancient Near East, vol. 1, no. 1. Malibu, 1974.

Falkenstein, A. *The Sumerian Temple City*. Monographs on the Ancient Near East, vol. 1, no. 3. Malibu, 1974.

Gelb, I. J. On the Alleged Temple and State Economies in Ancient Mesopotamia. *Studi in onore di E. Volterra*. Rome, 1969.

———. *Thoughts about Ibla*. Malibu, 1977.

Goetze, A. Early Kings of Kish. *Journal of Cuneiform Studies* 15 (1965).

Jacobsen, Th. Early Political Development in Mesopotamia. *Zeitschrift für Assyriologie* 52 (1957).

Jones, T. B., ed. *The Sumerian Problem*. New York, 1969.

Kohl, P. L. The Balance of Trade in Southwestern Asia in the Mid-Third Millennium. *Current Anthropology* 19 (1978).

Matthiae, P. *An Empire Rediscovered*. Trans. Christopher Holme. London, 1980.

———. *I tesori di Ebla*. Rome, 1985.

Nissen, H. J. *Zur Datierung des Königsfriedhofes von Ur*. Bonn, 1966.

Pettinato, G. *The Archives of Ebla: An Empire Inscribed in Clay*. Garden City, 1981.

Steible, H. *Die Altsumerischen Bau- und Weihinschriften*. Freiburger Altorient. Stud. 5. Wiesbaden, 1982.

Wolley, C. L. *The Royal Cemetery: Ur Excavations,* Vol. 2. London, 1939.

Chapter Six

Falkenstein, A. *Die Inschriften Gudeas von Lagasch I: Einleitung*. Rome, 1966.

Gelb, I. J. Makan and Meluhha in Early Mesopotamian Sources. *Révue d'Assyriologie* 64 (1970).

Hallo, W. W., and J. J. A. van Dijk. *The Exaltation of Inanna*. Yale Near Eastern Researches, vol. 3. New Haven, 1968.

Kraus, F. R. *Sumerer und Akkader: ein Problem der Altmesopotamischen Geschichte*. Amsterdam, 1970.

Wilcke, C. Drei Phasen des Niedergangs des Reiches von Ur III. *Zeitschrift für Assyriologie* 60 (1970).

Bibliography

Reports on the work in the two large sites, Uruk and Susa, appear in the following serials:

Susa: Mémoires de la Délégation Archéologique en Iran, Paris. Cahiers de la Délégation Archéologique Française en Iran, Paris.

Uruk: Vorläufige Berichte über die von dem Deutschen Archäologischen Institut aus Mitteln der Deutschen Forschungsgemeinschaft unternommenen Ausgrabungen in Uruk-Warka, Berlin.
Ausgrabungen der Deutschen Forschungsgemeinschaft in Uruk-Warka, Berlin.

Index

Ganj Dareh, 52
Gawra, Tepe, 117–119, fig. 48, fig. 49
Gilgamesh, 95, 172; epic, 95
Girsu, 131, 134–135, 143, 148–149; texts, 140
Godin Tepe, 113, 124–126, fig. 46
Gods, struggles of the, 178
Grinding wheel. *See* Cutting wheel
Gudea of Lagash, 186–189; inscriptions, fig. 71
Gulf area, 55–56, 126–127, 168–169, 187
Guran, Tepe, 32, 52, fig. 8
Guti, 170, 174, 185–187, 196

Habuba Kabira South, 48, 120–125, fig. 50, fig. 51
Hajji Firuz, 21, 33–35, fig. 5
Halaf Tell, 45; period, 45; pottery, 45–46, 57, fig. 12
Hama, 160
Hammurapi of Babylon, 164, 200
Hassuna, 115
Hiba, Tell al-, 135
Hierarchy of gods, 143, 178; of settlements, 8–11, 55, 66; social, 63, 79, 104–105
Huera, Tell, 127, 160

Inanna. *See* Innin
Innin, goddess of Uruk, 100, 105
Introduction scene, 178, 188
Iran, 157; central, 113–115, 161
Irnanna, 196
Irrigation, 43, 60, 69, 95, 118, 130, 144; area, 141, 145
Ishtar, goddess of Akkad, 174–175

Jaffarabad, Tepe, 52
Jarmo, Qalʾat, 27, 31, 52, 115, fig. 8
Jericho, 35–38, fig. 10
Jerusalem, 72, fig. 23

Kamarband cave, 19

Khafaji, 149
King of Kish (title), 144–146
Kish, city of, 106, 144–145, 149, 167; cemetery, 153
Kullaba, 100

Lagash, 106, 135, 147–148, 186, 190
List of officials and professions, 80, 94, fig. 31
Local center, definition, 11
lugal (title), 94, 140–141
Lugalanda of Lagash, 147
Lugalbanda, 172
Lugalzaggesi, 147–148, 168
Luristan, cemeteries of, 161–162

Magan, 168, 170
Malyan, Tepe, 114, 126, 169
Manishtusu of Akkad, 169
Mardikh, Tell (ancient Ebla), 153
Mari, 143, 168
Marshes, 67, 73
Martu, 196–197
Mass production. *See* Pottery
Mechanical tools, 150
Meluhha, 168
Masalim, 143
Mesopotamia, definition of, xii
Metal, 82, 89, 153
Mish, Chogha, 52, 124
Mixed economy, 25, 39–40
Monopoly, 165
Mount Carmel cave, 15
Mousterian period, 15
Murshili of Hatti, 164

Naram-Sin of Akkad, 169–170, 172, 174, 178, 182–184, 186,195–196; stela, 172, 175–177, fig. 65
Near East, definition of, 1
Nejef, 145
Neolithic, early pottery, 27; prepottery, 26–27
Nineveh, 119, 126, 163, 183–184,